LUTON SIXTH FORM COLLEGE

This book is due for return on or before the last date shown above.

3123

❧ The Prime Ministers ❧

By the same author

Fiction

Crisis in Zanat
The Robbers Passing By

General

The Twelve Days
The Crime of Mary Stuart
Vote of Censure
Sir Francis Drake
The North-West Passage
Warrior Prince
The First Churchill

The
Prime Ministers

From Robert Walpole
to
Margaret Thatcher

GEORGE MALCOLM THOMSON

SECKER & WARBURG
LONDON

First published in England 1980 by
Martin Secker & Warburg Limited
54 Poland Street, London W1V 3DF

Copyright © 1980 by George Malcolm Thomson

SBN: 436 52045 1

Filmset by Willmer Brothers Limited, Birkenhead, Merseyside
Printed and bound in Great Britain by
Morrison & Gibb Ltd. Edinburgh

❦ Contents ❧

List of Colour Plates

Between pages 104 and 105

❧ List of Illustrations ❧

❧ Prime Ministers in Chronological Order ❧

Sir Robert Walpole	1721–42	
Spencer Compton, Earl of Wilmington	1742–43	
Henry Pelham	1743–54	1745 Jacobite Rebellion
Thomas Pelham-Holles, Duke of Newcastle	1754–56	
William Cavendish, 4th Duke of Devonshire	1756–57	1756–63 Seven Years War
Thomas Pelham-Holles, Duke of Newcastle	1757–62	
John Stuart, 3rd Earl of Bute	1762–63	
George Grenville	1763–65	
Charles Wentworth, 2nd Marquis of Rockingham	1765–66	
William Pitt, Earl of Chatham	1766–68	
Augustus Fitzroy, 3rd Duke of Grafton	1768–70	
Frederick, Lord North	1770–82	1773 Boston Tea Party 1781 Surrender at Yorktown
Charles Wentworth, 2nd Marquis of Rockingham	1782	
William Fitzmaurice, 2nd Earl of Shelburne	1782–83	
William Cavendish-Bentinck, 3rd Duke of Portland	1783	
William Pitt, the younger	1783–1801	1789 French Revolution
Henry Addington	1801–04	
William Pitt, the younger	1804–06	1805 Battle of Trafalgar
William Wyndham, Lord Grenville	1806–07	

William Cavendish-Bentinck, 3rd Duke of Portland	1807–09	
Spencer Perceval	1809–12	
Robert Jenkinson, 2nd Earl of Liverpool	1812–27	1815 Battle of Waterloo
George Canning	1827	
Frederick Robinson, Viscount Goderich	1827–28	
Arthur Wellesley, Duke of Wellington	1828–30	1829 Catholic Emancipation
Charles, 2nd Earl Grey	1830–34	1831 Reform Bill
William Lamb, 2nd Viscount Melbourne	1834	
Sir Robert Peel, 2nd Baronet	1834–35	
William Lamb, 2nd Viscount Melbourne	1835–39	
William Lamb, 2nd Viscount Melbourne	1839–41	
Sir Robert Peel, 2nd Baronet	1841–46	1846 Repeal of Corn Laws
Lord John Russell	1846–52	
Edward Stanley, 14th Earl of Derby	1852	
George Gordon, 4th Earl of Aberdeen	1852–55	1854 Crimean War
Henry Temple, 3rd Viscount Palmerston	1855–58	
Edward Stanley, 14th Earl of Derby	1858–59	
Henry Temple, 3rd Viscount Palmerston	1859–65	
Earl Russell	1865–66	
Edward Stanley, 14th Earl of Derby	1866–68	1867 Second Reform Bill
Benjamin Disraeli	1868	
William Ewart Gladstone	1868–74	
Benjamin Disraeli, Earl of Beaconsfield	1874–80	1878–Berlin Congress "Peace with honour"
William Ewart Gladstone	1880–85	
Robert Gascoyne-Cecil, 3rd Marquis of Salisbury	1885	
William Ewart Gladstone	1886	
Robert Gascoyne-Cecil, 3rd Marquis of Salisbury	1886–92	
William Ewart Gladstone	1892–94	

Archibald Primrose, 5th Earl of Rosebery	1894–95	
Robert Gascoyne-Cecil, 3rd Marquis of Salisbury	1895–1902	1898 Boer War
Arthur James Balfour	1902–05	
Sir Henry Campbell-Bannerman	1905–08	
Herbert Henry Asquith	1908–16	1914 First World War
David Lloyd George	1916–22	1918 End of First World War
Andrew Bonar Law	1922–23	
Stanley Baldwin	1923–24	
James Ramsay MacDonald	1924	
Stanley Baldwin	1924–29	1926 General Strike
James Ramsay MacDonald	1929–35	
Stanley Baldwin	1935–37	
Arthur Neville Chamberlain	1937–40	1938 "Munich" 1939 Second World War
Winston Churchill	1940–45	1945 End of Second World War
Clement Attlee	1945–51	
Sir Winston Churchill	1951–55	
Sir Anthony Eden	1955–57	1956 "Suez"
Maurice Harold Macmillan	1957–63	
Sir Alec Douglas-Home	1963–64	
James Harold Wilson	1964–70	
Edward Heath	1970–74	
James Harold Wilson	1974–76	
Leonard James Callaghan	1976–79	
Margaret Thatcher	1979–	

🐉 Introduction 🦎

When there was a Lord Treasurer, that great officer was generally Prime Minister, but it was not until the time of Walpole that the First Lord of the Treasury was generally considered as the head of the executive government—Macaulay, *History*.

No political personage is more taken for granted than the Prime Minister, yet no office is harder to define than his. His powers and duties, the reality of which cannot be disputed, are hard to describe exactly; they have changed in the past; they are changing now. One Prime Minister in the eighteenth century* denied emphatically that he was anything of the kind; he was responsible only for his own department. His ministers were responsible for theirs. The King co-ordinated policy.

As a title, "Prime Minister" was given recognition in an official document for the first time at the Congress of Berlin (1878). He is usually styled Prime Minister and First Lord of the Treasury, although it is not absolutely necessary that he should be the latter. Chatham was Prime Minister and Lord Privy Seal. It has become essential that he is a member of the House of Commons.

It goes without saying that the prestige of the office varies with the strength of the holder's personality and with the personal political power which he may wield. It has also varied with the evolution of the British political system over the years.

It is customary to begin the list of Prime Ministers with Walpole, although the primacy of Godolphin and Harley in the reign of Anne can hardly be denied. But Anne dismissed first one and then the other, whereas Walpole resigned when he lost his majority in the House of Commons. He managed the Commons on the King's behalf and distributed the government's patronage, which he controlled as First Lord of the Treasury. When he could no longer count on control of the Commons, he gave up. Britain was a monarchy but George I and II were German princes, Electors of the Holy Roman Empire, who spent part of each year in Hanover. The British Prime Minister was their servant, and one on whose political knowledge and skill they were bound to rely. The trust and liking of the sovereign for his First Minister was, at that stage of political development, the essential element in the office.

A change in the system came as the King's position grew stronger, when he obtained a firmer grasp on British political realities so that he was able himself to manage the royal patronage and, through it, the House of Commons. He consulted individual ministers as he wished; he was the unifying element in policy.

The Prime Minister called the Cabinet meetings and, usually but not always,

---

* Lord North

presided over them; the individual ministers were responsible for the work of their departments, and the Prime Minister conducted the orchestra according to what he thought was the wish of the "Closet", i.e. the King. A brilliant politician with his own firm idea of what should be done, a Chatham, could be kept from power for years because he had the misfortune to incur the King's dislike.

In time, this factor became less important. The power of patronage declined and, with it, the power of the man who wielded it with the King's approval. Parties, which had been fluid political groupings based on common interests or on family relationships, began to be organized on the basis of shared opinions. The age of royal government was modified into one of Parliamentary government, although devotion and deference to the throne remained a reality in the minds of men like Wellington, Melbourne and, even, Canning, as it had been to Chatham, for whom, as Burke observed, "the least peep into the King's Closet intoxicates him". The Prime Minister came to occupy a position in which various forces converged, the Crown and the different strands of opinion in Lords and Commons, more or less organized and defined strictly or loosely.

When the Reform Act of 1834 was passed, Britain became a country governed by the House of Commons or, more exactly, by a Cabinet which could command a majority in the House on specific and important questions of policy. The Cabinet was "a hyphen which joins, a buckle which fastens the legislative part of the state to the executive part. In its origin it belongs to the one, in its functions it belongs to the other" (Bagehot).

The Prime Minister was its chairman, framing its agenda and appointing its members, although his power to do so was limited by the need to consult the opinions and preferences of other members of the Cabinet, and to take into account the feelings of any substantial bloc of MPs belonging to his party. Bagehot described the Prime Minister's role in the post-Reform Act period: "There is nearly always some one man plainly selected by the voice of the predominant party in the predominant house of legislature to head that party and consequently to rule the nation. *We have in England an elective first magistrate as truly as the Americans have an elective first magistrate.* The Queen is only at the head of the dignified part of the Constitution. The Prime Minister is at the head of the efficient part. The Treasury is the spring of business." Bagehot goes on to point to an important difference between the British Prime Minister and the American President. The Prime Minister is not elected directly by the people; he is chosen by the representatives of the people. (This, it may be observed, was originally the intention under the American Constitution.)

Since the time when Bagehot described what may be called the classical British Constitution, vast changes have occurred. Universal suffrage has enlarged the electorate. This has coincided with the emergence of mass party organizations with a committee in each constituency. The "caucus" became the typical institution of popular democracy; it could influence ministers who, if they were wise, would hear it with respect. The Crown withdrew from the party conflict into a position of neutrality, where its usefulness in the working of the Constitution remained unassailable.

At the same time two important developments have given the Prime Minister added prestige: government has become a more powerful and pervasive instrument—and the Prime Minister is head of the government! The Cabinet, of which he is chairman, is now served by a Secretariat so that, in effect, the Prime Minister has his own department of state at the very centre of the government machine. The meetings and findings of the Cabinet are formalized and recorded, which would have been unthinkable as late as Asquith's time. All this has put more authority into the hands of the Prime Minister.

A third factor, noted by R. H. S. Crossman in the analysis of the modern constitution which he set out in his introduction to a new edition of Bagehot's *The English Constitution* (1963), is the smoothing out of the difference between one department of state and another, so that we now have a unified bureaucracy. This centralization, Crossman thought, "brought an immense accretion of power to the Prime Minister. He is now the apex not only of a highly centralized political machine but also of an equally centralized and vastly more powerful administrative machine."

As Crossman saw it then, the Parliamentary government of the mid-Victorian age had evolved into a system of Cabinet government, and this is now turning into one of Prime Ministerial government: "a hyphen which joins, a buckle which fastens the legislative part of the state to the executive part" has become a single man, the Prime Minister. According to this view, the Cabinet has joined the other "dignified" parts of the Constitution, monarchy, Houses of Lords and Commons, not indeed in the dustbin of history, but among real, but reserve, powers, to be used only in emergency. And the Prime Minister has become more like the American President.

Crossman calls to the support of his argument the testimony of Lord Home*: "It is the Prime Minister's Cabinet, and he is the one person who is directly responsible to the Queen for what the Cabinet does. If the Cabinet discusses anything, it is the Prime Minister who decides what the collective view of the Cabinet is." In so far as ministers feel themselves to be agents of the Prime Minister, Crossman concluded, the British Cabinet has come to resemble the American cabinet.

It need not be said that Crossman's controversial view, in which there was more than a trace of propaganda because he was fascinated by power, has been strongly challenged by authorities of equal eminence, above all, by Lord Blake and Sir Ian Gilmour. The latter says: "The writers of the Prime Ministerial school make the same mistake as the Whig historians made about George III and the monarchy: they over-rate his power today and under-rate the power he had in the past."

Lord Blake criticizes Crossman's argument about the "super bureaucrats" who, by concentrating the power of the Civil Service, also increase the power of the Prime Minister. As Crossman himself agrees, these bureaucrats are not appointed by the Prime Minister but by the Head of the Civil Service: "So, if the Prime Minister has gained power as regards ministers, can it not be argued that he has, in some measure, lost it to the super-bureaucrats?" It can indeed, especially since the power of these latter formidable personages has been increased as an inevitable result of the enormous growth in scale and complexity and intricacy of the administrative machine which they command and which they understand better than anyone else.

On the wider issue of Prime Ministerial power, Blake is sceptical of Crossman's conclusions about a switch of power within the government: "The truth is that the

---

*Lord Home, the *Observer*, 16 September, 1962.

powers of the Prime Minister have varied with the personality of the Prime Minister, or with the particular political circumstances of his tenure. No one has come nearer to presidential government on the American model than Lloyd George. Yet none of the factors which Mr Crossman sees as causing this development in the second half of the twentieth century applied then." The stress which Blake lays on personality is highly relevant—the personality of the Prime Minister and the personalities of the members of his Cabinet. Would Asquith have been brought down in 1916 if there had not been in his Cabinet a man with the dynamic personality and adroitness of Lloyd George?

But the question of personality, which dictates what may be called the tactical incidents of political development, does not influence the underlying strategical issue. A tendency to move towards presidential and away from Parliamentary government is visible in many countries. Apart from the so-called Third World of under-developed and under-educated nations, in which there is a hankering after simple authoritarian forms, the example of France may be adduced. There, Parliamentary rule broke down and was replaced by a hybrid constitution in which responsibility was divided between an elected assembly and an elected president, the latter being the real centre of authority. This system, obviously tailored to fit de Gaulle, may not be found permanently workable.* But it came about because the Parliamentary system, in one of the most mature democracies in the world, had not been found up to the job. And if in France, why not in Britain?

One is, therefore, driven to conclude that the office of Prime Minister, which has evolved since the time of Walpole, will go on evolving and, in doing so, will take account of the growing intricacy and growing arrogance of government. But will it evolve into a presidential system? Two thoughts at once occur: (1) In a constitutional monarchy, the Crown performs some of the essential reserve functions of a president, besides carrying out some others which a president could not perform. (2) The trade unions have established themselves outside the law but, as it were, parallel to the law, as a power-structure which, while it does not pretend to supplant the Parliamentary system, claims a right of something resembling a veto over it. Already three Prime Ministers in succession have been brought down because they fell out with the trade unions.

This is an historical fact which may not be as sinister as at first appears. The vast majority of trade unionists would be horrified by the thought that, under the influence of furtive and malignant forces, manipulating and distorting an ostensibly democratic structure, they were weakening the Parliamentary system. But while the issue has still to be resolved, there can be no doubt that the emergence of trade unions—that is, of syndicalism—into an ill-defined rival and potential master of Parliament has the effect of weakening the Prime Minister's position in the state. Does this imply that his position must also be weakened in relation to other elements in the political system?

All this is only to say that the constitutional system in Britain, which has been developing ever since the Glorious Revolution and has passed through monarchical, aristocratic, oligarchic and Parliamentary phases, has produced at its apex an official

---

*De Gaulle himself did not expect it to outlive him.

known as the Prime Minister, that his powers have varied with changing circumstances and that this process is likely to go on.

The testimony of three recent incumbents as to the present constitutional position may be considered:

"A Prime Minister," says Anthony Eden, "is nominally *primus inter pares*, but in fact his authority is stronger than that. The right to choose his colleagues, to ask for a dissolution of Parliament and, if he is a Conservative, to appoint the chairman of the party organization, add up to a formidable total of power . . . I have sat in Cabinets or attended them under four Prime Ministers, MacDonald, Baldwin, Chamberlain and Churchill. I thought Baldwin's method of frequent consultation alone with each of his principal colleagues was good and I followed it."[*]

"A Prime Minister's sheet anchor," said Lord Home of the Hirsel, "is without question the Cabinet Secretariat, and, in particular, the Secretary to the Cabinet."[†]

Let the last word be with one who speaks with special authority:

"The power of a Prime Minister has steadily grown," writes Harold Macmillan. "Although he is only *primus inter pares*, the very complexity of affairs leads to the concentration of authority in his hands. The Cabinet is so burdened with business that the collective responsibility of ministers, although essential to our Constitution, tends to be reserved for the larger issues of national importance or political significance . . .

"As regards the Cabinet, I have read in some histories and text books accounts of decisions being taken by vote. This has not been my experience . . . If there was a clear difference of view between two or more sections of the Cabinet, it was my practice, after a kind of Second Reading debate, to postpone decision for another meeting . . . Agreement was invariably reached."[‡]

The picture which Mr Macmillan paints carries with it the danger that, as each minister's burden of departmental work grows with the growing complexity of government, so will the discussion in Cabinet of general matters of policy become more perfunctory. In that case, the doctrine of collective Cabinet responsibility would tend to be weakened. The minister without a department would, in those circumstances, alone have time, opportunity and responsibility to define and declare government policy. That person would be the Prime Minister, who would be in a position like that of George III during Lord North's administration, or like that of the President of the United States.

As was to be expected, the Prime Ministers of Britain have been a mixed bag, not conspicuously brilliant or imaginative, although displaying among them the occasional streak of something that can only be called genius. Think of Chatham, or Lloyd George, or Churchill. On the whole, though, a pedestrian gathering, a fact which should not be surprising. Did not Bagehot say, "A statesman combines the powers of a first-rate man and the creed of a second-rate man"? In other words, by the nature of his calling, he is liable to be pulled down to an average level of opinion.

---

[*] Anthony Eden. *Full Circle*, p. 269.

[†] Lord Home. *The Way the Wind Blows*, p. 195.

[‡] Harold Macmillan. *Pointing the Way 1959–61*, p. 34.

It is his task to manage a team of ambitious and temperamental individuals, some of whom will regard themselves as his rivals, if not his deadly enemies (e.g. Herbert Morrison in Attlee's government); to hold it together in times of stress and ensure that each member of the band contributes to a general harmony. "It does not matter so much what we say," said one of the ablest of them, "so long as we all say the same thing." Above all, he must avoid the temptation to play the instruments himself. The post demands a good deal of diplomacy and, even, a touch of mental dishonesty.

A democratic government is in a constant state of conflict with the Opposition. A Prime Minister should give the impression that he is the leader in a relentless fight, therefore he must seem belligerent whatever his private views may be. Failure in this respect cost A. J. Balfour the Tory leadership in 1911.* While he must avoid appearing to be all things to all men, he should remember that his government, like every other, is a coalition of opinions, stretching from the frigid Whigs, or their equivalent of today, across to the extreme Left.

The Prime Ministers were, for the most part, respectable family people, though there were startling exceptions; all married, but four; and more or less philoprogenitive. In this particular respect, the score is headed by the Duke of Grafton, who fathered seventeen children by his two marriages, which were separated by a spell of adultery. Earl Grey follows closely, with fifteen children, a total all the more creditable in that it was achieved with one wife. Spencer Perceval had become father of twelve children before he had the melancholy distinction of being murdered in the lobby of the House of Commons. The Earl of Bute was the father of eleven. This total—fifty-five children by four Prime Ministers—takes no account of the extra-marital activities of the list. One has only to think of the probable progeny of Lord Palmerston, who, it is said, was fertile until he was eighty.

Where were they educated? The story can be quickly told. Eton comes an easy first, with eighteen Prime Ministers; other public schools account for twenty. Among the universities, Oxford helped to mould twenty-four Prime Ministers, about half the total, and, of these, eleven were at Christ Church. The Eton-Christ Church label was so powerful an asset that it enabled a man like Canning, whose social background was dubious, to become Prime Minister at a time when the office was an aristocratic preserve. Fifteen Prime Ministers were Cambridge men, so that the two ancient English universities have nurtured three-quarters of the First Ministers of the Crown. Those who had no university education at all are an interesting group, which includes Wellington, Disraeli, Churchill, Bonar Law, Chamberlain and Callaghan.

Socially, the picture is one of unbroken aristocratic supremacy, with the exception of Addington (1801–04), a doctor's son, and Canning (1827), son of an actress, until, in 1834, the business community breaks through with Peel, after whom came Disraeli and Gladstone, representing in their different ways the higher bourgeoisie. The middle class, properly so called—defined by ethos rather than income—may be said to enter with Campbell-Bannerman (1905–08), since when it has been a dominant background, although not a monopoly. After all, Asquith, Lloyd George, Bonar Law, Baldwin, Chamberlain, Attlee, Macmillan, Wilson, Heath, Callaghan

---

* He was leader of the Opposition then, a role in which an aggressive spirit is even more advisable.

and Thatcher have to share the century with Balfour, Churchill, Eden and Douglas-Home, as aristocratic a quartet as the most snobbish could wish for. One class is represented by a single entrant: Ramsay MacDonald (1924; 1929–35) is the sole Prime Minister of working-class origin.* It may be confidently predicted that he will not be the last.

On religion a few words should be said, for the reason that a man's basic beliefs, however diluted and modified by time, supply a valuable guide to his probable attitude on moral and political questions. The first twenty-six Prime Ministers were Anglican, of greater or less fervour, although one of them, the Duke of Grafton, became a Unitarian. That carries the story down to the middle of the nineteenth century. The first Presbyterian Prime Minister, Lord Aberdeen, took office in 1852. After that, High Church Anglicanism was represented by Gladstone and Salisbury. Then there was a succession of Presbyterians: Rosebery ("While to the world he seemed like some polished eighteenth century grandee, at heart he was the Calvinist of seventeenth century Scotland"—John Buchan), Balfour, Campbell-Bannerman, Bonar Law (who may have lapsed before the end); and Nonconformists: Asquith, Lloyd George, Wilson (Congregationalist), Callaghan (Baptist), and Thatcher (Methodist). Against these may be set staunch Anglicans like Baldwin, Attlee, Macmillan and Douglas-Home. Ramsay MacDonald is described as a Theist. Others who do not appear in the list may be assumed to be traditional Anglicans. No Roman Catholic or professing Jew has been Prime Minister, although there could be no obstacle to either taking the office.

Another and more remarkable feature of the roll should be mentioned. Although the "hereditary principle" has no part whatever in the choice of Prime Minister in Britain, yet a study of the list of forty-nine Prime Ministers since Walpole reveals one interesting fact: of these forty-nine statesmen, *fifteen have a common ancestor.* They are descended from a country gentleman named Sir George Villiers of Brooksby, who, in the reign of Queen Elizabeth I, was Sheriff of Leicester and became the father of a good-looking youth who caught the eye of the impressionable King James I. George Villiers, the son, had not many scruples and no lack of ambition. He became the first Duke of Buckingham, the beloved of James I, the trusted friend of Charles I. If there had been a Prime Minister in those days, Buckingham would certainly have been one. Nor, with his murder in 1628, had his father's seed made its last contribution to British life. By no means!

The political influence of this potent strain, coming to the surface time and again through the centuries, was first brought to my notice by Mr Paul Bloomfield, author of that fascinating study, *Uncommon People,*† in which the whole question of the Villiers connection is discussed. Egalitarians may resent, moralists may deplore, scientists may dispute, but the fact is that the following British Prime Ministers are descended from Sir George:

1. The Duke of Grafton

---

* Mr Callaghan's father was a senior petty officer in the navy.
† Published by Hamish Hamilton, 1955.

2. The Duke of Portland
3. The Earl of Chatham
4. William Pitt the Younger
5. The Duke of Devonshire
6. Lord Melbourne (on the reasonable assumption that his father was Lord Egremont)
7. Lord Grenville
8. Lord Aberdeen
9. Lord Derby
10. Lord John Russell
11. Lord Salisbury
12. A. J. Balfour
13. Sir Winston Churchill
14. Sir Anthony Eden (Earl of Avon)
15. Sir Alec Douglas-Home (Lord Home of the Hirsel).

It may be admitted that the Villiers got off to a good start, providing a favourite for two kings, a mistress—Barbara, Duchess of Cleveland—for a third, and again a mistress for a fourth.* But this hardly explains why the latest—one should not say the last—Prime Minister of the connection left office as late at 1964. The quality of the brood is admittedly uneven; the Dukes of Grafton and Portland were hardly among the most brilliant of political leaders. Nevertheless, it would be possible to pick an administration from the fifteen (Chatham, Churchill, Pitt, Salisbury, Lord John Russell, Eden, for a start) which would hold its own in talent with one picked from the non-Villiers contingent, e.g. Gladstone, Disraeli, Lloyd George, Peel. Mercifully, in neither case were all these men contemporaries!

What specific talent did the Sheriff of Leicester transmit to his remote descendants? Force of character, determination, thrust, realism, or what? The question becomes all the harder to answer when the Villiers blood is traced outside the narrow field of politics and we find—to be exact, Paul Bloomfield finds—the following:

H. M. The Queen
The second Duke of Buckingham of the Cabal, Dryden's Zimri:
> Stiff in opinions, always in the wrong,
> Was everything by starts and nothing long,
> But in the course of one revolving moon
> Was chemist, fiddler, statesman and buffoon.

Bertrand Russell
Henry Fielding, author of *Tom Jones*
Lady Hester Stanhope
Lord Longford
Captain Fitzroy of the *Beagle*, etc.

---

* Elizabeth Villiers, later Lady Orkney, was the mistress of William III. She was more famous for her intelligence than for her looks. "She squints like a dragon" (Swift).

There are, at present, thought to be about 25,000 bearers of Villiers genes in Britain. All one can say is that they have a much better chance of climbing to the top of the political greasy pole than you or I. Their chances will be further improved if they have the foresight to be educated at Eton and Christ Church. But have not profound social changes altered the odds? Maybe, but it would be rash to assume so.

Here they are then, the Prime Ministers of Britain, a diverse and remarkable collection, from whom one could make some deductions about the character of the nation they led, or served—its acumen, its fickleness, its ingratitude, its self-confidence. But how tentative those deductions must be! For what a mixed crowd is this roll of worthies! It includes a scientist (amateur), a philosopher, racing men and rakes, a novelist, a historian, a great soldier, some dull men and a sprinkling of geniuses.* How brilliant the British have been to have spread their net so widely and brought in so glittering a haul! How successful has been the seemingly blind process of selection!

It may be so. But the roll of the rejected gives pause to any facile complacency. Consider: Charles James Fox, Edmund Burke, Castlereagh, Carteret, Cobden, Curzon, Bevin, Bevan, Gaitskell, Butler, etc. For one reason or another—health, rank, temperament, or mere misfortune—they failed to reach the top of the greasy pole. Yet they are not without gifts which rival those of the successful. They might fill another book like this one. It is only to say that the process of choice, whether carried out by lot, birth or election, involves a stern necessity to discard. Only one horse wins the Derby.

---

* Salisbury, Balfour, Rosebery, Palmerston, Disraeli, Churchill, Wellington.

❧ SIR ROBERT WALPOLE ❧

1721–42

Robert Walpole was an epitome of the kind of man the English like to see at the head of their affairs: gregarious, good-humoured, lacking in rancour (even his mortal enemy Bolingbroke was allowed to come back to England); able to take as well as to give hard knocks; no prude; content that an imperfect world should be managed by imperfect means and ready to take his own advantage from that fact. If he had not been Prime Minister, he said, he would have been Archbishop of Canterbury. If Robert Walpole had kept to his original purpose of entering the Church, which as the third son of a family of landowners he would normally have done, he would assuredly have been a "scheming political prelate" on a familiar pattern.* From this, England was saved by the death of his two elder brothers.

He was born on 26 August, 1671, at Houghton, Norfolk, third son of Robert Walpole, MP. The Walpoles had lived in Houghton for generations: solid, reasonably well-off country gentlemen, good farmers, highly philoprogenitive. Robert was one of a family of nineteen.

He went to Eton as a King's Scholar; later to King's College, Cambridge. He inherited the family property, comprising nine manors in Norfolk and one in Suffolk, with a total rent-roll of £2,169. To this he added as the years passed, until it was worth £8,000 a year.

In 1700 he married Catherine Shorter, daughter of a London timber-merchant, who brought him a dowry of £20,000, but all the money was spent, according to their son, Horace, on wedding and christening festivities. Walpole had three sons.

He went to the House of Commons in 1701 as a Whig member for the family borough, Castle Rising, and very soon attracted notice in Parliament, catching the eye of the Duchess of Marlborough and her Duke; in 1708 he became Secretary at War, and in 1710 Treasurer of the Navy, "by my interest alone", said the duchess.

He might have looked like a successful butcher and led the life of a young rake, but he had something that approached genius for the political hurly-burly. Having no more lavish a supply of scruples than any other politician of his time, there was an unusual degree of subtlety in his manoeuvring, based upon a cynical understanding of human nature, and a vast fund of common sense. "All men have their price" was a remark often, wrongly, attributed to him. What he said, speaking of a group of men whom he pointed to, was, "Those men have their price." It can be assumed that he knew the men and knew what their price was.

---

* One of the family had been a mediaeval prelate; another, a Jesuit martyr.

Very soon, while Marlborough was fighting in Flanders and Godolphin was caught in the machinations of Harley and Mrs Masham, young Robert Walpole became leader of the Whig party in the Commons. When Godolphin and Marlborough fell, Walpole fell with them. At this moment his brilliant Tory rival, Bolingbroke, set out to destroy him. Charged with corruptly awarding a contract, he was expelled from the House and committed to the Tower. His captivity was not, however, unduly severe. The case against him was too thin, and his friends were too powerful. He spent his time in prison writing a political pamphlet, and entertaining the Whig aristocracy.

As he was able to prove that he had kept none of the contract money, he was very soon released, breathing contempt for the accusation and swearing vengeance on his enemies. His pamphlet, *A Short History of the Parliament*, attacked the Tory ministry with such violence that no printer would touch it. Accordingly, Walpole had a printing press carried to his house, and there the pamphlet was run off. He was determined, above all, to be revenged on Bolingbroke. Few pledges have been so faithfully kept and few have been so politically significant. Thanks largely to Walpole's determination, Bolingbroke was kept out of the House of Lords all through the reign of the first George; in consequence, the Jacobite party, which he would have led, had no head during the years when the Hanoverian hold on the throne was still tenuous.

"When George in pudding time came o'er", a wide and smiling expanse of opportunity opened to Walpole, already a master of Parliamentary tactics, an impeccable Whig, able and popular, related to Townshend, the Secretary of State, who was married to Walpole's sister Dorothy. He became a Privy Councillor and Paymaster of the Forces, the richest of all political prizes. When Townshend fell to an intrigue, Walpole, his ally, insisted on going out with him, in spite of King George I's entreaties. As a private member, his power was now manifest, for no government bill could be passed if he disliked it.

This was the time of the South Sea Bubble, a financial scheme of which Walpole had not approved (but in which, it seems, he speculated, making a profit of 1,000 per cent). When the crash came in 1720, Walpole's financial ability was urgently required to save what could be saved. He became Paymaster-General and, on 2 April, 1721, First Lord of the Treasury and Chancellor of the Exchequer. He was from that moment master of the government.

But his authority did not rest simply on royal esteem (which he earned by protecting members of the royal set who had imprudently speculated in South Sea stock); there was, in addition, his command of the House of Commons. For that reason he is traditionally, and with good reason, regarded as the first of the long line of British Prime Ministers, an office which was evolving as the party system itself began to crystallize and the House of Commons more decisively became the political centre of gravity.

One important element in the situation was, of course, that the King was often in Hanover; his English was imperfect, while Walpole spoke neither French nor German, and the two conversed in dog-Latin. It was not possible, in these circumstances, for the King to build up a party of his friends.

This is something that Walpole did with the most assiduous care, finding a place for this man's son, a living for another man's nephew, inviting X to dine at Houghton (now becoming less like a country house and more like a palace), taking care that Lady Y at the proper time received a brace of pheasant, etc. No attention was too trifling for him to pay; and careful note was taken about how the attention was rewarded. For Walpole, politics was a wholetime business. Although he was unblushing in his use of bribery to influence Parliament, the Secret Service Fund, which was the main source of corruption, did not in his time amount to more than £79,000 a year, a sum smaller than it had been before the Revolution. There was also propaganda, in which, as Swift thought, he was less successful than he could have been: "he had none but beasts and blockheads for his penmen."

Walpole gloried in the political battle, debating with a ready tongue and a tactical suppleness which belied his appearance. But he had principles for which he was ready to fight and, if necessary, be beaten; above all he was determined that Britain should find her prosperity in peace. Not for nothing was he a country gentleman, one of those who had groaned under the Land Tax and, by their discontent, helped to bring down Marlborough. If Britain stayed at peace, he could win those powerful men from the Tory side to the Whig, as in large measure he duly did. So friendship with France and Spain must be sought. In short, Walpole, the arch-enemy of Bolingbroke, was wedded to the Tory foreign policy which Bolingbroke had pursued in Queen Anne's time.

He kept Britain at peace for close on twenty years. It was not an easy task, and finally it defeated him.

His relations with the House of Hanover were a vital element in his political system and were conducted with his customary finesse. When George I died in 1727, it seemed that Walpole's spell in the royal sunshine was over, for the new King had disliked his royal father and had regarded Walpole, his father's minister, as a rogue.

Walpole killed two horses driving to Richmond to bring the sad news to the new King, who told him to take his orders from Spencer Compton. But all was not lost. Compton turned out to be so incapable that Walpole had to be called in to draft the King's Speech. Tactfully, he took the opportunity to increase the Civil List by £100,000. After that, he was back in the royal sunlight once more.

The strength of Walpole's position, apart from his readiness in debate and the appeal of his personality, lay in his organization of patronage. There was, however, a power which, as a financial expert, he should have been able to assess: the City of London, the money power which Bolingbroke had denounced and which envisaged a successful European war as an enterprise which could lead to new markets for British goods and new sources of raw materials at the expense of colonial powers like Spain and France.

For a time it seemed that caution, a policy of neutrality and negotiation, would be enough to guard Britain's interests and those of her Protestant dynasty. One had only to count the ships loading or unloading in British ports to feel confidence in the country's prosperity. And the Land Tax, the crucial index of national well-being so far as the landowners were concerned, was kept down. However, there was no doubt that Britain's naval and military strength was sagging and that France's power to hurt her through the Jacobites was more serious than Walpole was prepared to acknowledge. The rebellion of 1745 eventually proved that.

His financial achievements were, however, real and considerable. He reduced the interest payable on the National Debt and invented the Sinking Fund, to pay off the debt which the War of the Spanish Succession had piled up. His annual budget was modest and he was able to borrow at three per cent.

The fiscal system he made more rational and more efficient, so that the vast evasion of customs duties (above all in Scotland) was reduced. The main tendency of his tax policy was to shift the burden from property to commodities, so that by 1731 the Land Tax was cut to a shilling in the pound, a reduction of three-quarters from its peak.

The general effect was to encourage Britain's exports and the import of raw materials used in making them. It was not entirely Walpole's responsibility that he presided over the most prosperous economy in Europe, but if he could not claim all the credit he must fairly be allowed some of it.

One fiscal measure he would not take: he would not tax America. "I have old England against me," he said in 1739, "do you think I'll have New England likewise!"

He was no constitutional innovator, no framer of large legislative programmes. Being a tireless administrator, he perfected the Parliamentary machine he found and employed it to maintain a smooth continuity of his power. As for the rest: "I am no saint, no reformer." It seemed to him unwise to disturb social waters which were calm. "*Quieta non movere*," he said. Let sleeping dogs lie.

That such a period of peace, foreign and domestic, could not last forever was a proposition which, if it had ever occurred to him, he would probably have admitted with a shrug and a grin.

Meanwhile he sat in the House, wary and imperturbable, his Garter ribbon and Star (given him in 1726) splendid on his coat, listening to the proceedings, every now and then intervening, without elegance but with point and pungency, and counting the men whose votes, for good reasons, he could count on, and those others who had to be wheedled or persuaded, dangerous men but men whom, in his heart, he understood.

During the season, he lived at Richmond; at every opportunity he went off to Norfolk to shoot or to ride to hounds. It was said that the first letter he opened when his mail arrived was the report from his gamekeeper. All his life he spoke with a Norfolk accent.

But to picture him as a hearty squire with no interests beyond his pack of hounds, his mistress, and a night of bawdy talk over the port would be to underestimate him. While he was managing Parliament, he was also amassing the finest private collection of pictures in England. It was believed to be worth £100,000, a likely figure when one considers that it included Titians, Raphaels, a Rubens, a Holbein, a Poussin or two.

His son came back from the Grand Tour loaded with treasures. In all, Walpole paid £30,000 for the collection, the balance being made up by gifts from ambassadors and place-hunters. After Walpole's death, his grandson's extravagances forced him to sell the bulk of the collection to Catherine the Great for £45,080. Horace was particularly annoyed because his nephew refused to apply any of the money to paying his father's debts. "It is stripping the temple of his glory and affection," he said. "A madman excited by rascals has burnt his Ephesus." Most of the pictures can be seen

1 A scene from Gay's *The Beggar's Opera*, by William Hogarth. Captain Macheath, here seen in irons, was intended to be a caricature of Sir Robert Walpole. "The most venomous allegorical libel against the government that has yet appeared is *The Beggar's Opera*," commented *The Craftsman*.

at the Hermitage, Leningrad. In addition, Walpole chose William Kent's finest suite of furniture for his house. He was a man of the most discerning taste.

It was, of course, only a question of time before opposition to his pacific policy sprang up and became powerful. The House he could dominate; the inner ring of ministers he controlled most of the time, more easily after the departure from office of his adventurous brother-in-law, Townshend, but the City was always restive, wanting a more aggressive foreign policy which might bring wider markets. And a generation of ambitious young politicians was growing up.

There were, too, his relations with the royal family, always an uncertain element. It was a risky game, which he played with zest. The King, who had fought bravely on foot at Dettingen, believed that he had a natural gift for war, and that he was denied a career of glory by the peaceful obsession of the Prime Minister, to whom he lectured on military matters by the hour. Queen Caroline was under Walpole's influence.

While success and security continued—as they did for years—Walpole's social life expanded with them. Every November there was a "Norfolk Congress" at Houghton, when a large and carefully chosen company assembled to deal with Walpole's choice cellar of claret and burgundy, and in one year 540 dozen empty bottles were sent back to one of his wine merchants.

"Our company," wrote one guest, "swelled into so numerous a party that we used to sit down to dinner a snug little party of about thirty odd, up to the chin in beef, venison, geese, turkeys etc; and generally over the chin in claret, strong beer and punch . . . In public we drank loyal healths, talked of the times and cultivated popularity: in private we drew plans . . ." Political plans; plans to ensure the stability of the government and the prosperity of the realm.

Houghton was not the only scene of Walpole's magnificence and extravagance. He arranged that his eldest son, Robert, should be made Ranger of Richmond Park and that he himself would be deputy. His residence in Old Lodge in the Park became a base for enjoyable hunting with his beagles when Parliament was sitting and there was no time to drive down to Houghton.

By the time of his greatness, his marriage had ended in estrangement. It is, in fact, doubted whether his youngest son, Horace, was his at all. He pursued women with ardour and eventually (1724) took a mistress, Maria (Molly) Skerret, a pretty Irish lady of good family, born in the City of London. It is said that Walpole paid £6,000 for the lady's virtue; what is certain is that she was soon installed in Old Lodge and that Walpole was very happy with her for the rest of her life.

When his wife died (1737), Walpole lost no time in marrying Maria, who brought him a fortune of £30,000. When she died, a few months later, his grief was profound.

By then the good time, the time of steady success for him, was coming to an end. When King George's consort, Queen Caroline, died in 1737, Walpole lost a staunch ally at Court, a woman whose friendship he had worked hard to obtain—whose wisdom had been very useful to him.

His colleagues in the Cabinet, men like Pelham and Spencer Compton, were not of the calibre of their predecessors. Politicians like Pulteney and Carteret were moving into opposition where, very soon, William Pitt would join them. By excluding able men from his government, Walpole allowed the balance of debating strength in the House of Commons to swing against him. Eventually he paid the price for this.

In 1734, there was a general election from which Walpole emerged, still in power, but weaker.

The King now favoured a policy of war in Europe, which Walpole looked on with intense dislike. In that year he had been able to keep Britain out of the War of the Polish Succession. "Madam," he had said to his ally, Queen Caroline, "there are fifty thousand men slain this year in Europe, and not one Englishman."

But the trend towards war, strongest of all among the City merchants, was, in the end, too strong for him. Reluctantly, he agreed to declare war on Spain in 1739, ostensibly over a merchant smuggler named Jenkins whose ear was torn off by Spanish custom-house officials, an incident which was used to whip up the war fever in Britain. Walpole said to his colleague, the Duke of Newcastle, that he wished him joy of his war.

According to modern practice, a Prime Minister who disagreed with his Cabinet on a major issue like war would resign. But at that time the doctrine was not firmly established. Accordingly, Walpole, the first Prime Minister, followed an earlier principle and chose to regard himself as the King's First Servant, in duty bound to stay in his place so long as he was able to do the King's business in Parliament.

When the war went badly, as Walpole had expected, he gained no advantage from

The text within the engraving reads:

walpole | The Great man easy sits in Borrow'd State, | The Injured Merchant calmly brings his Case, | While Monsieur makes a candid application —
The millions suffer by the Yoke of Fate. — | And craves Redress from him who is in Place. | And hopes they will accept his Mediation. — France sent am̄bas ᵈᵒ medᶜᵉᵗᶜ Sept 173⁹
Values not Widows Cries or Orphans Tears. | But to compleat his loss sustain'd before — | But Britons boldly shew Imperious Spain, |
... depredations or the loss of Ears. | So by a ... fool push'd out oth Door. | What tis to rouze the Masters of the Main. — Published & Inv'd by a Friend to ...
carit Jenkins ever cut off by Spaniards. | See Smollet D. ... VI. ... | | According to y late Act 1738. Price ...

2 *In Place.* **A satire on Walpole, 1739. Walpole is here seen rejecting the claim for compensation of Captain Jenkins.**

the new situation. The warlike Whigs, at whose head stood William Pitt, continued to assail him, and his majority in the House of Commons grew steadily smaller. In February, 1742, he was defeated on an unimportant issue. "It was a most shocking sight," wrote his son, Horace, "to see the sick and dead brought in from all sides [to vote], Sir William Gordon from his bed with a blister on his head." Walpole walked cheerfully out of the Chamber, resigned his office, and took an earldom. Now he was the Earl of Orford. He arranged that his illegitimate daughter by Molly Skerret had the rank of an earl's daughter.

It was the end of his long reign as First Minister, although it was not the end of his power in politics.

He was succeeded by Spencer Compton, who had by this time become Lord Wilmington. But the King still relied on Walpole's advice, and although various attempts were made to impeach him, they came to nothing and, when Wilmington died, the next Prime Minister was Henry Pelham, who depended on Walpole's guidance.

But by this time his health was failing fast and on 18 March, 1745 he died at his house in Arlington Street. He had given "Englishmen no conquests but he gave them peace and ease and freedom: the three per cents nearly at par: and wheat at six and twenty shillings a quarter" (Thackeray).

Prosaic trophies, no doubt, but no small achievements for a man who, lacking the fire that marks the great expansionist statesman or the high moral zeal of the great reformer, possessed, almost to the point of genius, common sense, force of character and a zest for hard work.

II

🌿 SPENCER COMPTON, Earl of Wilmington 🌿

1742–43

Spencer Compton looks at you out of Kneller's portrait, smooth, weak, pompous and petulant, wearing the ribbon and Star of the Garter on his velvet coat, not ill-pleased with himself as he surveys the world, and with good reason for his complacency—he was Prime Minister of Britain, although for a mercifully short time, a man of meagre ability and feeble character who, nevertheless, had reached the top of the political ladder. If Robert Walpole might be put forward as evidence that, under the British system, one of exceptional talent could not be prevented by intrigue or aristocratic influence from becoming the leader of the state, Spencer Compton might be adduced to demonstrate that the same system was capable of producing a near-cypher. He was called by spiteful critics "the favourite nonentity of George II". It was not undeserved.

Born in 1673, he was, therefore, only two years younger than Walpole; his father was the third Earl of Northampton. His forebears had fought for the King in the Civil War and had suffered in consequence. When the Revolution came, they were, however, firmly on the Whig side. One Compton, Bishop of London, helped Princess Anne, James II's daughter, to escape from London with her beloved friend, Sarah, later Duchess of Marlborough. Later he crowned William and Mary as King and Queen. The Comptons were well-off and well-connected, with big estates in Warwick and Northampton.

Spencer Compton was educated at St Paul's and at Trinity College, Oxford, where, as the son of a peer, he was automatically given a degree. After being called to the Bar at the Middle Temple, he went on the Continental tour which was almost obligatory on scions of the nobility and, while abroad, learned, in 1696, that he had been elected as MP for the Eye division of Suffolk. He was elected as a Tory but lost no time in changing his allegiance to the Whigs. In that direction the political fields were richer. Many of his Compton relatives were already grazing in those pastures.

In Parliament, the rich young bachelor was soon engrossed in the business of the House. He was chairman of the Committee of Privileges in 1705 and Treasurer to Prince George of Denmark (Queen Anne's husband) in 1707. Three years later, he lost his seat in a Tory landslide but in the meantime he had learnt the ins and outs of Parliamentary business; more important, he had become the friend of Walpole. When George I reached the throne and the Whig party was once more in the ascendancy, he was an MP again and was chosen as Speaker (1715), although he

3 Spencer Compton, Earl of Wilmington, by Sir Godfrey Kneller.

insisted to the King that "he had neither memory to retain, judgment to correct, nor skill to guide the debates". The Prince of Wales made him his Treasurer; Walpole made him Paymaster-General (1722). Thus he held three important offices at the same time. He was the sort of useful, trustworthy, harmless individual to whom secondary offices of state were given. And he was rising in esteem all the time. Then, in 1725, when he had been Speaker for ten years, he was knighted. When George I died, Walpole was told by the new King, "Go to Chiswick and take your directions from Sir Spencer Compton." In other words, Compton was to be the new Prime Minister.

Along with Walpole, he went to see the Duke of Devonshire, Lord President of the Council, a man who "had an uncommon portion of understanding . . . and was more able as a virtuoso than a statesman, and a much better jockey than a politician."* After a meeting of the Council, Compton confessed to Walpole that he needed help in drafting the King's Speech. The situation was one that appealed to Walpole's sardonic humour. He obliged at once, slipping in a phrase in which the former ministry, Walpole's, was warmly praised. When it came to the proposed figure for the Civil List in the new reign, Walpole named a sum greater than Compton's and the upshot was that Walpole kept his job as Prime Minister and Compton was consoled with a peerage. He became Lord Wilmington.

There were toadies at hand to tell him that he had been cheated by Walpole out of the highest office. And there were enemies of Walpole who saw in Wilmington "an instrument to bring Walpole down". In time, too, the chances became more favourable. Begging Wilmington to throw Walpole over, Bubb Dodington† said, "You and you only have all the talents that this critical time demands to save our country." The plea did not seem as fatuous to Wilmington as it does later to the historian. Walpole's long peace had bred its own boredom. His ally, Queen Caroline, died. And, in 1742, Walpole fell and Wilmington, already a Knight of the Garter (1732), who had acted as front man for the victorious clique which now came to power, was, at last, Prime Minister.

He did not live long enough to enjoy his triumph, earned by long and faithful service, if not deserved by any remarkable talent. Within a year his health had broken down and, very soon, he was unable to do any business. In any case he was little more than Prime Minister in name; the real power in his short-lived ministry lay with Lord Carteret, considered by many to be the ablest statesman of the time, although Lord Chesterfield thought he was better suited to be a minister in an absolute monarchy: "He would have been a great first minister in France, little inferior, perhaps, to Richelieu," but, "he degraded himself by the vice of drinking which, together with a great stock of Greek and Latin, he had brought from Oxford" (Chesterfield. *Miscellaneous Works*. Vol. IV, p. 29). The opinion that Wilmington's contemporaries had of his role in government is expressed in this quatrain, belonging to the time. It is supposed to be spoken by Carteret to the King:

---

* Lord Hervey. *Memoirs.*

† George Bubb (1691–1762) took the name of Dodington in 1720. He was a toady of Frederick, Prince of Wales, who made money out of him. He became Baron Melcombe in 1710.

The Countess of Wilmington, excellent nurse,
I'll trust with the Treasury, not with the purse,
For nothing by her I've resolved shall be done;
She shall sit at that board as you sit on the throne.*

Not a complete fool, nor a man of any consequence, this "dull important lord" filled the four highest offices in the state for nearly thirty years. The consideration that was given to a minister was something that he enjoyed; others could wield the power and do the work; it was enough that he looked like a minister:

Let Wilmington with grave contracted brow
Red tape and wisdom at the Council show,
Sleep in the senate, in the circle bow.*

He remained a bachelor, his life unspotted by amorous scandal, although Horace Walpole speaks of "private debauches, his only pleasure money and eating, his only knowledge forms and precedents; his only insinuations bows and smiles". For a few months, Wilmington was a stop-gap Prime Minister: no other achievement is remembered of his term of office. He died rich and left his money to his nephew, the fifth Earl of Northampton. The British constitutional process moved on, barely noticing the brief intervention of the phantom.

---

* Lord Hervey.

III

HENRY PELHAM

1743–54

The Pelhams were not giants in intellect, nor were they monsters of principle, but they fill a useful niche in the political history of the eighteenth century as showing that the old aristocratic system was capable of producing a set of tolerable rulers for the country.

Henry Pelham belonged to one of the great Whig families who, after the Revolution, had—not indeed a right—but a preference when political places had to be disposed of. The Pelhams had been rising for some generations by the time he came on the scene. By adroit marriages and a steadfast support of the winning side, they had climbed out of the ruck. Henry, born in 1696, was the second son of Thomas, Lord Pelham and his wife, Lady Grace Holles, and, which proved to be more important, the younger brother of Thomas Pelham-Holles, who acquired the dukedom of Newcastle, along with much of its revenue, from an uncle.

As the Duke of Newcastle was, by name and influence, one of the most eminent of Whig magnates, Henry, his brother and dependant, had a short route to the political heights. From his brother he derived his income and his seat in the House of Commons. This he took in 1717, after being educated at Westminister and Oxford (where he did not matriculate); his constituency was Seaford. He was twenty-one years of age and an impeccable Whig in politics, which he had proved two years before when he and his older brother, Thomas, raised a troop of cavalry with which Henry went off to fight the Jacobite rebels at Preston. It was as a reward for this display of loyalty that Thomas Pelham, already possessed of the bulk of the Newcastle revenues, was given the vacant dukedom.

Meanwhile, Henry Pelham departed on an educational tour of the Continent. When he returned, he appeared in the House of Commons and, as a loyal supporter of Walpole, with important family connections, was given a place on the Treasury Board. By 1722 he had advanced from being Member of Parliament for Seaford to that of the County of Sussex, which was, in fact, little more than a "pocket borough" at his brother's disposal. By 1725 he was Secretary at War, a splendid position for a young man of twenty-nine and, given his family associations, his way to the top seemed clear. However, there were difficulties; his brother, Newcastle, on whom he depended, was a temperamental man, anxious to increase his political power and inclined to quarrel with Walpole. Henry Pelham, loyal to his brother by necessity, was a close personal friend of Walpole's.

4 Henry Pelham, by William Hoare.

On one occasion, when Walpole was threatened outside the House by a "well-dressed mob" of his political enemies, Pelham drew his sword and called out, "Now, gentlemen, which of you will be the first to fall?" He was quite a combative politician, as was shown when he exchanged high words with Pulteney in the House. The Speaker intervened to forbid a duel.

When Walpole was, at last, defeated, Pelham and he remained on good terms and, when the nonentity Wilmington became Prime Minister, Walpole advised Pelham to take the Chancellorship of the Exchequer. But Pelham preferred to stay on as Paymaster-General (1730) and Leader of the House. "If you had taken the advice of a fool," wrote Walpole, "and been made Chancellor under Lord Wilmington, the whole had dropped into your mouth. Lost opportunities are not easily retrieved." However, Pelham was given a second chance not long afterwards, when Wilmington died.

Pelham, with his brother, Newcastle, supporting him, became Prime Minister. Gibbon described the situation with characteristic irony: "Some courtiers lost their places, some patriots lost their characters, Lord Orford's [Walpole's] offences vanished with his power; and, after a short vibration, the Pelham government was fixed on the old basis of Whig aristocracy." In short, Walpole's system continued; only the name over the shop-front was altered.

It was a surprise to many that the name was Pelham, for an abler and more conspicuous figure on the political scene at that time was John, Lord Carteret. Carteret (who now became Earl of Granville) was one of those brilliant figures who somehow fail to reach the top. He was unpopular with the House of Commons; he refused to dine with his own followers at The Feathers: "He never dined in taverns." He thought that it was sufficient to have the personal favour of the King: "Give a man the Crown on his side and he can defy everything." But, to be fair, he was equally haughty in his dealing with foreign powers. "He treated princes like little boys," said Frederick the Great. "When he died," said Lord Chesterfield, "the ablest head in England dies too." His achievements as a diplomat were remarkable: he persuaded Sweden to make peace with her enemies, and Maria Theresa to surrender Silesia to Frederick of Prussia. It was thought, then, that, when Walpole fell, Carteret, whom George II admired, would take his place. Carteret was then Secretary of State for the Northern Department. Things turned out differently. Carteret had not been willing to concede to Pelham any increase of power: "He was only a chief clerk to Sir Robert Walpole and why he should expect to be more under me, I can't imagine." Indeed, as second man to Walpole, to his brother, Newcastle, and to Carteret, Pelham seemed fated to be in a subaltern status all through his career. But it was a mistake to underrate him. He managed George II with skill and patience. Walpole had described the problem of dealing with the King and, at the same time, he had outlined the methods by which it should be approached:

"Address and management are the weapons you must fight and defend with: plain truths will not be relished at first in opposition to prejudices, conceived and infused in favour of his own partialities: and you must dress up all you offer, with the appearance of no other view or tendency, but to promote his service in his own way, to the utmost of your power."

Pelham followed the old master's advice—equally useful in managing a Parliament as a monarch—with such success that, before long, the King was declaring that Pelham was a sounder financier than Walpole, who "did not indeed give money abroad but gave it away liberally at home . . . with regard to money matters [Pelham] understands that much better".

With a Cabinet composed of dukes, himself the only commoner in it, Pelham was plunged into a war with France, during which he needed all the support he could muster in the Commons and was denied, by the King's intense dislike of the man, the help in government of his most powerful opponent, William Pitt. Worse still, the British army was defeated at Fontenoy and the Jacobites rose in 1745. Pelham was thought to have shown weakness in dealing with the crisis. To force the issue, Pelham resigned; Granville (Carteret) found that he could not form a ministry. Pelham and his brother, the Duke of Newcastle, thus compelled the King to choose between themselves and Carteret, and the King had found that he must choose Pelham.

George II was annoyed by the turn in events, especially by Granville's failure. "He is a man of the greatest abilities this country ever had," he complained to another minister. "You have forced him from me and I am weary of you all." But the City would not continue to finance the war: "No Pelham, no money."

In these conditions, Pelham came back and made Pitt Paymaster-General. Granville, after his failure, had lost his authority; the King was compelled to agree that he would not consult him. In 1748 came peace with France; three years later, Bolingbroke, that busy promoter of discontent, died. So likewise did Frederick, Prince of Wales, whose opposition to his father's Prime Minister had been a constant anxiety. Pelham had said: "The House of Commons is a great upwieldy body which requires great Art and some Cordials to keep it loyal; the Opposition is headed by the Prince who has as much to give in the present as we have and more in Reversion." That is to say, the Prince would, in the normal course of things, be King one day and able to reward his friends. "This makes my task a hard one." The Prince's death removed that particular burden. Pelham was now able to concentrate on the financial problems in which he excelled.

The man who was Prime Minister for eleven years in those trying conditions was a useful, rather than an eloquent, speaker, a careful political manager, who was as often the victim as the beneficiary of the family rivalries that rent, and, in the end, destroyed the old Whig party, a prudent guardian of the nation's money. He was leader of the government during the tense years which saw war with France and the Jacobite Rising, when David Hume was shocked to see that "the English turn everything into politics and are fast relapsing into the deepest Stupidity, Christianity and Ignorance". But 1744, when that was written, was not the best moment for a Scots philosopher to judge England.

Pelham was popular in the House, a man whose word was trusted. He had married, in 1725, Lady Katherine Manners, a daughter of the Duke of Rutland and, therefore, of the purest Whig blood. By her, he had two sons, who died in boyhood, to his grief, and six daughters. Apart from politics, his chief diversion was gardening; Kent beautified the grounds of his house, Esher Place, in Surrey, near his brother, Newcastle's, great house, Claremont. He was often seen at the gaming tables at White's. He quarrelled frequently, and sometimes bitterly, with his powerful and difficult brother, although disputes between the two never impinged on the deep basic affection between them, and, in fact, Newcastle had his dukedom recreated so that it could be inherited by Pelham's son-in-law.

Pelham worked hard at the House of Commons, ate too much and took too little exercise. When his health began to fail, he wanted to retire, but the King would not allow it. Walking in St James's Park one cold day, early in 1754, he caught a chill and died soon after. The King said: "Now I shall have no more peace."

Horace Walpole remarked of Pelham, "He lived without abusing his power and died poor." It was an unusual epitaph for an eighteenth-century statesman, especially for one who had for years been Paymaster-General. That is not to say that Pelham, himself honest, refrained from ruling the House of Commons by the normal methods of corruption. But it was said that he "would never have wet his finger with corruption if Sir Robert Walpole had not dipped in it up to the elbow".

IV

❧ THOMAS PELHAM-HOLLES, Duke of Newcastle ❧

1754–56; 1757–62

In his only recorded *bon mot*, the Earl of Wilmington said of the Duke of Newcastle, "He always lost half-an-hour in the morning, which he was running after for the rest of the day without being able to overtake it." This admirably sums up the fussy, nervous, ineffectual character of the Duke. Yet he was Prime Minister twice during eight years.

Why?

First, he was very rich, with a rent-roll of £25,000,* which, invested in obedient boroughs, gave him vast political influence. Sixty or seventy MPs owed their seats to his influence, although it seems that he was actually the proprietor of no more than a dozen constituencies, and this after a life in which he had spent a great part of his fortune and time on the grubby business of electioneering. Second, he was well-connected; for example, his brother-in-law, Charles Townshend, was married to Walpole's sister, Dorothy.

In the middle years of the eighteenth century, the high noon of the Whig ascendancy, these were sufficient reasons for a man, above all for a duke, to become a candidate for the highest political office in the land. It is true that Newcastle's intellectual powers were a matter of some dispute: George II thought they fitted him to be the chamberlain of some minor German principality. Nor were his effusive and affected manners to everybody's taste. When the Duke of Grafton lay ill covered in bandages, Newcastle burst into the bedroom, kissing and hugging him. Grafton shouted, indignantly, "Get away, get away," whereupon Newcastle spread the news that Grafton, delirious, had not known him.

Horace Walpole said of him, "He was a Secretary of State without intelligence, a duke without money"—but this was after Newcastle had squandered his fortune on buying political power which he could not use—"and a minister hated and despised by his master." Lord Waldegrave had a more balanced view: "Ambition, fear and jealousy are his prevailing passions." Yet, "if we consider how many years he has continued in the highest employments; that when his friends have been routed, he has still maintained his ground; that he has incurred his Majesty's displeasure on various occasions but has always carried his point, it cannot be denied that he possesses some qualities of an able minister."

---

* A rough idea of its value today (1980) would be about £300,000.

5 Thomas Pelham-Holles, Duke of Newcastle, by William Hoare.

6 An Election Entertainment, by William Hogarth. A satirical picture of the corruption of politics in the mid-eighteenth century.

In private conversation, says Waldegrave, he was confused and rambling; in Parliamentary debate his manner was ungraceful and his language barbarous; he was neither a reliable friend nor a bitter enemy. His hospitality was fabulous, his anxiety about his health inordinate. Once, when he called on Chatham, he found him in bed ill. The room was cold and there was a second bed in it. Into this Newcastle leapt, and the two statesmen continued their discussion from the two beds. It must be added, however, that Waldegrave and Walpole were among Newcastle's most bitter political enemies and that a man could not hold high political office for almost half a century without talents of some kind. They were, however, second-rate talents and Newcastle's greed for place led him to seek the highest position, for which he did not possess the qualities of mind or character.

For Thomas Pelham, politics began when George I came to the throne and he paid a crowd in the City to cheer for the new King. He was then aged twenty-one (born 21 July, 1692), the elder son of the first Lord Pelham and a nephew of the Duke of Newcastle, the bulk of whose vast estates he had inherited. He was educated at Westminster and Cambridge (Clare). When the House of Hanover came in, he was made, first, Earl of Clare, and then, Duke of Newcastle (1715). After that, he married Lady Henrietta Godolphin, whose grandfather was the Duke of Marlborough. He had a splendid house at Claremont in Surrey, entertained magnificently and wooed the favour of the royal family. Thus, every year, he sent pineapples from his hothouses to Hanover by courier. When, as a minister, he went with the King to Hanover, he took the family plate with him. "People came from every side," said Lady Bolingbroke, who was French, "to see his plate as, with us, to see the Treasure of St Denis."

For thirty years, until 1754, he served as Secretary of State in the ministries of Walpole and Henry Pelham, his brother. Apart from occasional outbursts of fretfulness, aimed at Henry, he seemed fairly contented. He had a splendid-sounding position; he had no grave anxieties about policy to disturb him. He had a political power which even Walpole had to respect. It was—or it should have been—enough. All this changed when Henry Pelham died.

Newcastle's jealousy boiled up, his feeling that he, the elder, richer brother, was worthy of the first political post. He sorrowed for his brother ("I have the greatest loss that man can have and now have no view but . . . particularly to do everything that can best comfort his poor family") but, within a few days, he was busy arranging to fill Henry's place. He was sixty years of age.

Although he had a natural gift for intrigue, the succession was not at all a simple job to arrange. He was a peer, at a time when the House of Commons was beginning to expect the head of a government to sit in the lower chamber. He had no remarkable ability. He had powerful rivals, above all, the most brilliant commoner, William Pitt. Pitt was loathed by George II because he spoke contemptuously of Hanover. After a few days of manoeuvring, the King took Newcastle as his First Minister in 1754, while Pitt, sulkily, stayed as Paymaster-General. Pitt was convinced that Newcastle had not done all he could to break down the King's antipathy to him, and that the new government was not likely to last long. His contempt for Newcastle was unconcealed. "Fewer words, my lord," he said, "for your words have long lost all weight with me." The government's weakness was made more apparent when Britain drifted into war with France and the war went badly. Pitt resigned and subjected Newcastle to so pitiless a bombardment in the House of Commons that, in the autumn of 1756, when Minorca was lost to the French and the City of London was alarmed, the Prime Minister resigned and the Duke of Devonshire became, for a few months, nominal head of the administration, with Pitt as Secretary of State. Pitt, however, could not command enough support among independent MPs and in June 1757 Newcastle was back as Prime Minister, although Pitt continued to direct Britain's strategy. Thus, Newcastle had what he wanted, the place, the patronage, the outward show of the great office. He managed Parliament and finance and appointed the bishops. Meanwhile Pitt got on with the problems of his world-wide strategy. It was an arrangement which suited both men admirably. Newcastle, in government with Pitt, was as much a cypher as he had been under Walpole.

All went well enough during those critical years when Pitt's genius was laying the military foundations of the British Empire. Then, in 1760, came the accession of George III, who hated the remnants of the Whig ascendancy, of which Newcastle was the symbol, and found Pitt too overbearing for his liking. He took the patronage from the Prime Minister and gave it to his favourite, Lord Bute, a Scotsman. Pitt resigned in October 1761 at a time when Newcastle, alarmed at the growing cost of the war, wanted to make peace. However, Newcastle hung on to office, through one humiliation after another, until, at last, he was forced to realize that he had no more power in what was nominally his ministry. He found that, to annoy him, the Court was ready to dismiss quite minor officials he had appointed. The last straw came when the bishops, his creatures, deserted him: "Even fathers in God sometimes forget their maker." On 25 May, 1762, Newcastle resigned. "His Majesty was barely civil," he complained, "after near fifty years spent in the service and in undoubted zeal for the royal family." Said the King's mother, the widowed Princess of Wales, "Now my son *is* King of England." Newcastle came back to office as Lord Privy Seal for a year in 1766, and died of a stroke in his house in Lincoln's Inn Fields on 17 November, 1768, aged seventy-five.

He had no children. His will showed that he was £300,000 poorer than when he started in public life. Not all the money had been spent on buying political power but a great deal had gone in that way, as a result of which Newcastle, that pompous, effusive, busy man, had enjoyed close on forty-five years of political office. Even for a duke, it was a considerable feat. One achievement of his—although it can hardly be called his creation—remains today, the garden at Claremont which was first laid out for him in 1715 by Vanbrugh and Charles Bridgeman, who had helped to lay out the gardens at Blenheim. After Vanbrugh's death the Claremont garden was continued by William Kent. There it is, an impressive monument of English patrician grandeur—an amphitheatre, belvedere and lake—of which Newcastle must have the credit as the arbiter and paymaster.

His public career had been a proof, thought Horace Walpole, "that even in a free country great abilities are not necessary to govern it". "An amused posterity," writes the biographer of Lord Carteret, "has granted [the duke] a unique fame as the most curiously ridiculous being who ever took a leading part in public affairs." The portrait may be biased but it has, on the whole, been accepted by the historians.

7 **The garden of the Duke of Newcastle's house at Claremont in Surrey.**

V

WILLIAM CAVENDISH, 4th Duke of Devonshire

1756–57

Of all the Prime Ministers on the roll, none surely has been so unwilling to serve as William Cavendish, fourth Duke of Devonshire. The chances of his escaping were, admittedly, slight. He was the head of one of the great families that made the Glorious Revolution. He was a leading Whig in an age when Whigs were still supreme. If the King and the Party wished him to be Prime Minister, how could he refuse?

His personal qualifications for the post—apart from his heredity—were not remarkable. He was modest, well-behaved, inconspicuous, a model of private virtue, who, like his father, "had great credit with the Whigs, being a man of strict honour, true courage and unaffected affability". It might be objected that he was a shade colourless, but was that not only another good reason to appoint him?

Born in 1720, no one knows exactly when, he was apparently educated at home and during the normal Continental tour. He was thought to have inherited his father's good qualities, although it was noted that he seemed "less averse to business". At the age of twenty-one, Lord Hartington, as he was then called, was elected Whig MP for Derbyshire, and was loyal to Walpole during the crisis which brought the great man down. With Walpole gone, he transferred his loyalty to Henry Pelham, who thought him "our mainstay among the young ones, of themselves liable to wander". In 1748, he married Lady Charlotte Boyle, who brought him a large increase of his property in England and Ireland. "I do not know any man," said Lady Mary Montague, "so fitted to make a wife happy." In fact, the marriage, although brief, was happy and fruitful—four children. In 1751, he took his seat in the House of Lords for one of his father's baronies, became a Privy Councillor and Master of the Horse. When Pelham was succeeded as Prime Minister by his brother, the Duke of Newcastle, Lord Hartington was appointed Lord-Lieutenant of Ireland. By this time he was a widower; in a few months he had succeeded to the dukedom.

He did so at a moment when the Newcastle ministry was crumbling. When Charles James Fox resigned as Secretary of State in October 1756, Pitt recommended to the King that Devonshire should be made Prime Minister on the grounds of his favour at Court and his popularity among the Whigs. Pitt himself proposed to be Secretary of State and the dominant personality in the Cabinet. So, after five days of pleading by the King, this amiable nobleman surrendered, although he warned George II that he would feel free to resign if he found that he "disliked the

8 William Cavendish, 4th Duke of Devonshire, by Thomas Hudson.

employment". It was early in November, 1756. The Seven Years War was going badly in India and America; it looked as if the government could neither wage war nor make peace. At that time nobody could foresee the transformation which Pitt's dynamic genius could bring.

But before Pitt's strategic plans could bear fruit, a deplorable incident had driven him out of the government (April, 1757)—the death sentence on Admiral Byng, which Pitt bitterly opposed. Devonshire, who had consented to the admiral's execution, served on, knowing very well that without Pitt his administration was doomed. He resigned in July, 1757. So ended, nine months after it had begun, the Duke's term of office as Prime Minister. His administration had not been a success mainly because the King disliked Pitt and because Newcastle, who had vastly more political influence than Devonshire, was determined to get back into office. There was another factor—Devonshire did not want the job. "The Duke of Devonshire," said the King, "has acted by me in the handsomest manner and is in a very disagreeable situation entirely on my account." Accordingly, Newcastle came back and Devonshire was consoled with the Garter and the post of Lord Chamberlain. "He lost no reputation," said a contemporary, Lord Waldegrave, "for great things had never been expected of him as a minister and in the ordinary business of his office he had shown great punctuality."

It was not, however, the end of the Duke's career in politics. When George III came to the throne, he and his minister, Lord Bute, had a particular dislike of Whig aristocrats like Devonshire. "The Duke of Devonshire was especially singled out as a victim by whose fate the magnates of England were to take warning" (Macaulay). They were altogether too arrogant and must be taught a lesson. In 1763, George III asked him to attend a Privy Council to discuss the terms of peace with Spain. Devonshire declined, saying that he did not know enough about the subject.

When the Duke went to Court to take leave before going to Chatsworth, the King refused to see him. The message reached Devonshire by way of a page. The Duke tore off the gold key, which was his badge of office as Chamberlain, and departed in a rage. With his own hand the King struck his name from the list of Privy Councillors. "The sword is drawn," he said. His favourite, Lord Bute, agreed. "The most factious combination of *soi-disant* great men against the lawful right and liberty of the King" had been driven from office. "A more severe political persecution never raged," reported Horace Walpole. So was the Prince of the Whigs* humiliated, although he was only one victim of the purge. It may be said, however, that the last word lay with Devonshire, for it was at a dinner party in his London house that the opposition to the government's Cider Tax was planned and this contributed towards Bute's resignation in 1763.

By that time, Devonshire's health was declining and he died of dropsy at Spa, in October 1764, aged forty-four.

---

* The name given Devonshire by the King's mother.

VI

JOHN STUART, 3rd Earl of Bute

1762–63

At Egham Races in 1747, a sudden shower of rain drove Frederick, Prince of Wales, to shelter in a tent. A table, a pack of cards, but, alas, no fourth to make up a four for whist. And nobody in sight who was socially fitted to partner the Heir to the Throne. An equerry was sent to search the course for a suitable player and brought back John Stuart, third Earl of Bute, who was presented to the Prince and sat down at the table. So began a friendship which soon had political consequences.

The Prince might have no high opinion of Bute, "A fine showy man who would make an excellent ambassador in a court where there was no business," but the Prince's wife, when she met Bute at Leicester House, had a more favourable opinion; "the sagacity of the Princess," said Lord Waldegrave, "has discovered other accomplishments of which her husband may not perhaps have been the most competent judge." For instance, Bute had a "fine leg", an attribute much admired at that time.

In other words, he was popularly believed to be her lover. When the Princess, rebuking a maid of honour for her behaviour, asked, *les raisons de cette conduite?*, "*Ah, madame,*" retorted the impudent girl, "*chacun à son but.*"

When Frederick, Prince of Wales, died and his son, George, became Heir, Bute was Groom of the Stole to the boy and his "dearest friend". It had been a vertiginous ascent for one against whom there were several counts: he was a Scot, a Tory, a dilettante and, as time was to show, a doctrinaire. None of these qualities was likely to help a man on the way upwards at that juncture in English public life. After all, on that day at Egham Races, the Jacobite Rebellion was hardly over and the name of Stuart was not a password to popularity.

Bute was born at Parliament Square, Edinburgh, on 25 May, 1713. He was educated at Eton and succeeded to the title on 28 January, 1723. His marriage to Mary Montague increased his property considerably. In 1737 he was elected a Scottish representative peer and in the following year was made a Knight of the Thistle. By that time, however, the more serious side of political life was beginning to catch up with him and, soon after the outbreak of the Jacobite Rising of 1745, he removed to London. Thus, he was on the brink of a wider life when chance brought him into contact with the Prince of Wales. He had a passion for performing in amateur theatricals, especially if he could be seen in becoming costumes. He was thought to be particularly successful in the part of Lothario.

THE WANTON WIDOW.

The widow is buxsome, & jolly I trow,
The widow has many good things to bestow,
And all to supply her tickling below,
With a bonny brave Laddie call'd Sawney.

With pleasure he sees her both early and late,
To kiss her & clap her no scruple does make,
And at her desire he can her well s——,
So stout and so able is Sawney.

The widow is neither so young nor so old,
But still loves a Scotchman, that's active & bold,
For all other men are but lifeless & cold,
Compar'd to the vigorous Sawney.

What could he wish better his fortune to crown
Than a widow y wantonest dame in y Town,
His greatest delight is w. her to sit down
And sport w. the widow brave Sawney.

He busses & smacks her by night & by day,
So well he does please her, she never says nay,
In return for his kindness she does him well pay,
So dearly she loves her own Sawney.

But Sawney be wise, Lad, before 'tis too late,
For Fortune proves fickle & changes her state,
Then what must the widow do, for her dear mate,
Alas: the poor widow and Sawney.

1762

9 The Wanton Widow of this satire (1762) is the widowed Princess of Wales, who was popularly believed to be the mistress of the Earl of Bute, here represented in tartan.

And so he was a notable figure in a "little, idle, frivolous and dissipated Court", admired by the Princess of Wales and despised by King George II, who would not even give Bute his gold key as Groom of the Stole. Instead, an official was deputed to slip it into the favourite's pocket. His most important task during those years was to form the mind of the young Prince, who, in 1760, became King George III. Bute filled him with the dangerous, intoxicating ideas expounded by Bolingbroke in *The Patriot King:* "the King, it was given out, would not be dictated to by his ministers."* At first, little of these ideas was apparent when the Prince came to the throne. When the Duke of Newcastle called at the Palace with a draft of the King's Speech, he was told by the new monarch to take it to My Lord Bute, who "will tell you my thoughts". In fact, Bute's sole intervention in the proposed text was a minor outbreak of Scottish nationalism, the substitution of the word "Briton" for "Englishman".

But the Privy Council and the Garter soon followed, and the Secretaryship of State of the Northern Department. By May, 1762, Newcastle was dismissed and the royal favourite became Prime Minister. His had been an ascent of extraordinary speed, although no more than Bute felt was his due. "He panted for the Treasury," said a rival, the Earl of Shelburne, "having a notion that he and the King understood it. He likewise had a confused notion of rivalling the Duc de Sully†—all of which notions gradually vanished."

His ideas at that time were simple and ambitious enough: to make peace with France, to cut Britain away from her entanglements with German politics, to destroy the political power of the great Whig families, and to assert the King's supremacy over Parliament. Bute was sure of the rightness of his cause but underestimated the unpopularity which the programme would bring him. He was mobbed on the way to the Guildhall Banquet; a jackboot and petticoat, hinting broadly at his friendship with the King's mother, were publicly burnt not far from his London house, and Buckingham Palace was publicly known as "Holyrood House". Above all, he was attacked in a weekly, *The North Briton,* by John Wilkes, son of a Buckingham distiller, a man who had, said Horace Walpole, "married a woman of fortune, used her ill to extort from her the provision he had made for her separate maintenance; he had debauched a maiden of family by an informal promise of marriage . . . Yet the man was commonly not ill-natured or acrimonious. Wantonness rather than ambition guided his hand."

"Pray, Mr Wilkes," asked Madame de Pompadour one day in Paris, "how far does the liberty of the press extend in England?"

"That, Madame, is what I am determined to find out."

Wilkes led the war against Bute and the Scots. For a time, however, Bute went on his way undeterred, dismissing the Whigs and their dependants and—which was more important—continuing his negotiations for a treaty with France.

This was finally got through Parliament. Bute spoke well, if theatrically, in the debate. He would be content, he said, that his tomb should have the inscription, "Here lies the Earl of Bute, who, in concert with the King's ministers, made the Peace!" The peace was, of course, a denial of all that Pitt, the great war minister, stood for, being in Pitt's opinion far too lenient to France. One reason why George III wanted peace was that while the war went on he dared not get rid of Pitt, whom he hated.

By this time Bute's unpopularity had become more than he could bear. He went about the streets attended by a gang of bruisers, "the scoundrels and ruffians that

---

* Horace Walpole. *Memoirs of the Reign of George III.* Vol. I, p. 200.
† Chief Minister of Henri IV.

attend the Bear Gardens". He resigned and, such was the hatred and suspicion that surrounded him, he was forbidden the Court. When he visited his friend, the Princess, it was necessary for him to leave by the back stairs. The King was not to set eyes on the man he had once admired. At last, he went to Italy, travelling incognito as Sir John Stuart.

Bute's last years were spent partly in his villa on a cliff by the sea at Christchurch in Hampshire, and partly in his castle on the Isle of Bute. As a political enemy wrote, "He had a gloomy sort of madness which made him affect living alone, particularly in Scotland, where he resided with as much pomp and as much uncomfortableness in his little domestic circle as if he had been King of the Island, Lady Bute, a forlorn Queen and his children, slaves of a despotic tyrant. He read a great deal but it was chiefly out of the way books of Science and pompous Poetry." He was accused of political cowardice and, in particular, of deserting any friend who seemed to be in trouble. What is more certain is that he lacked the toughness of fibre which was necessary to a politician at any time, but was particularly necessary to one who was challenging the Establishment at its strongest.

Against the Whig grandees, who regarded power as theirs by right, he could set his friendship with Augusta, Princess of Wales, and George III. But the first was, at best, an asset of doubtful value and the young King's affection turned sour. The royal influence was not a broad enough power-base for one who went out of his way to insult many men who were accustomed to be treated with respect, and he had not the oratorical accomplishment to impress the House of Lords. The matter was sometimes good, the delivery was halting and solemn, "like minute guns," said one listening peer. He had not the stamina for political warfare in that savage era, when a London mob or a hired and scurrilous pamphleteer were the regular tools of the politician's trade. Few public men have been attacked with the ferocity that Bute suffered; few were so sensitive to the attack.

When he retired, sickened of it all, it was to spend thirty years of unhappiness and boredom and to die at last on 10 March, 1792 at his house in South Audley Street, a forgotten man. By that time, the political aims of Bute, his friends and his enemies, were collecting dust on the shelves of history. The world had moved on to new interests and new excitements. The Americans had split the first British Empire; the French Revolution had shaken the whole political fabric in which Whigs and Tories had quarrelled and ruled.

Bute had one substantial achievement to his credit. He had by devious diplomacy made the Peace of Paris, which brought the Seven Years War to an end, and had driven it through Parliament in the face of intense opposition. Yet this feat was in itself a betrayal of the principles on which he had set out. For to obtain the crucial vote in the House, Bute had been forced to practise bribery on a scale and of a shamelessness from which Walpole himself would have shrunk, and which Walpole would never have found necessary. Ill at ease in the great world of affairs, in which he had arrived belatedly and by such an unorthodox route, and equally unhappy in his long exile from it, Bute was probably most comfortable in the company of men of letters. His pension of £300 a year to Dr Johnson was an official act which can be praised without qualification. Johnson's opinion of Bute was uninfluenced by the payment: "a man who meant well, a theoretical statesman, a book minister".

VII

❧ GEORGE GRENVILLE ❧

1763–65

The Grenvilles were one of the families of the English gentry for whose advancement and comfort, it seemed, the English political system was specially contrived. They were well-to-do landowners in Buckinghamshire; better still, they were well-connected—Temples, Pitts, Lytteltons and Grenvilles made a well-known cousinhood, each member of which could be relied on to look after the interests of the others. "All articles are now to be had at low prices," Lord Holland remarked, early in the nineteenth century, observing the success of the Grenvilles in obtaining office for themselves. A Duke of Buckingham fought a duel in Kensington Gardens with a Duke of Bedford, who had said that the Grenvilles were a family of cormorants. It was a rule with the Pitts that their relations, "the Grenvilles, must be taken care of ".* "The Brotherhood," said George III, "must always either govern despotically or oppose government violently!" They were like a clan or, more exactly, a Whig Mafia, working ceaselessly together, in good times and not so good, to promote the fortunes of the group.

George Grenville was typical of them, duller than some and more successful than most, tactless and long-winded, a singularly charmless person but with his full share of the family's tenacity. He was one of the "Boy Patriots", who, under Lord Cobham, fought to bring Robert Walpole down. For this reason he was pursued venomously by Horace Walpole, who said of him, "Scarce any man ever wore in his face such outward and visible marks of the hollow, cruel and rotten heart within." He was born on 14 October, 1712, eldest son of Richard Grenville of Wotton, Buckinghamshire, and went to Eton and Christ Church, Oxford, after which he practised at the Bar until Lord Cobham, his uncle, called him to duty in Parliament as member for Buckingham, one of the family pocket boroughs. This seat he held for the next thirty years. At thirty-six he married one of the Tory Wyndhams and settled down to a happy family life at Wotton, which his elder brother, Richard, lent him.

Though his wife's looks were marred by smallpox, she was an excellent partner for an ambitious politician and was, before long, the mother of nine little Grenvilles. The family was, just then, expanding its alliances: George Grenville's brother was Lord Egremont; more important, his sister, Hester, married William Pitt.

Grenville had a frugal side which he applied to the nation's business: "he preferred

---

* Clive Bigham. *Prime Ministers of Great Britain*, p. 99.

a national saving of two inches of candle" to all the victories of Pitt. When he began to earn an official salary, he used all of it to increase his capital, spending only his private income. Characteristically, his sole form of amusement was public business; an Act of Parliament was his favourite reading. When George III came to the throne, Grenville, by that time Treasurer of the Navy, thanks to family influence, formed an alliance with Lord Bute, the King's favourite, and became Secretary of State when Bute was promoted to the premiership. As already stated, eventually the unpopularity of Bute became so powerful that the King had to get rid of him and, in leaving office, Bute recommended Grenville as his successor.

But this, for several reasons, was not a success. The King was continuing to take Bute's advice; and, to the King, Grenville was a prosy and arrogant bore: "When Mr Grenville has wearied me for two hours, he looks at his watch to see if he may not tire me for an hour more." George III, among other defects, was "no listener". Between the two there were, however, not only differences due to temperament: Grenville found it intolerable that Bute should be the King's secret adviser and forced George to agree that he would have "no secret influence whatever". Immediately afterwards, with the King momentarily cowed, Grenville sailed into the great political crisis over John Wilkes. From that he emerged with his prestige in Parliament undiminished. But his position with the King was destroyed. "I would rather see the devil in my closet," said George, "than Mr Grenville." Grenville had, with his usual clumsiness, allowed the King to see that he thought him untrustworthy. More than that, in framing the Regency Bill, he had refused to include the King's mother, who was popularly supposed to be Bute's mistress. So Grenville was dismissed and an inexperienced young nobleman named the Marquis of Rockingham took over. Grenville took the blow with composure. He spoke occasionally in the House of Commons with the tedium and solemnity of the elder statesman. His thoughts were hardly profound; thus he thought the "seditious spirit of the [American] colonies owes its birth to factions in this House". It was an opinion to be expected from the author of the Stamp Act, which, by imposing taxation on America, gave "sedition" its opening. Grenville died in his house in Bolton Street, Piccadilly, on 13 November, 1770. He was in his fifty-ninth year.

The Right Honourable George Grenville
FIRST LORD COMMISSIONER of the ADMIRALTY,
And One of His MAJESTY's Most Honourable Privy Council.
Printed for Ja:. Brooke at the Black Horse in Cornhill London.

10 George Grenville, by James Watson, after William Hoare.

VIII

⚶ CHARLES WATSON WENTWORTH ⚶
2nd Marquis of Rockingham

1765–66; 1782

In the keen competition for the post of the most futile Prime Minister of the eighteenth century, the Marquis of Rockingham would hold a leading, if not a commanding, position.

He started with a good hereditary advantage. His early life was, in its course, the conventional career of a young Whig nobleman. He was born on 13 May, 1730, the fifth and, as it turned out, the only surviving son of the first Marquis of Rockingham and Mary, his wife, daughter of the Earl of Nottingham. He was sent to Westminister School and to St John's College, Cambridge. By that time, the boy had given evidence of his political sympathies. He ran off from the family home at Wentworth in the winter of 1745–46 with a single servant and took part in the Forty-Five Rebellion—not, however, on what was later thought to be the romantic side; he joined the Duke of Cumberland's forces at Carlisle.

The next chapter in his life was less exciting and more conventional: at that time known as Lord Higham, he went to explore the wonders and dangers of life in Italy where, so it was said, "some imprudent gallantries damaged an already weak constitution". What these gallantries were can be surmised. What their effect was, we can only guess.

That the young nobleman returned to England chastened is not in doubt. For the rest of his life, he was "splenetic" about his health. He was interested in racing and gambling. At his Yorkshire home, the enclosure for horses took the place of everything else, as Horace Walpole reported. However, he shared the fashionable enthusiasm for art, paying, when he was twenty-five, the top price for a classical bust of Antinous.

When he returned to England he married Mary Liddell of Badsworth and, in 1760, was made a Knight of the Garter at his own request. He was rich, of high social rank and impeccable Whig loyalty. He and his associates called themselves "a knot of stainless friends". He was soon to show that he had some independence of judgment and that there was a trace in him of the old ruling anti-monarchical feeling. Thus he would have no truck with Lord Bute's activities in building up a group of "the King's Friends", and when Bute pushed through the Peace of Paris, Rockingham (as he had become by that time) showed his disapproval by resigning from his place in the Bedchamber. King George III responded by dismissing him from his Lord

11 Charles Wentworth, 2nd Marquis of Rockingham. Studio of Reynolds.

Lieutenancies and his office as Vice-Admiral of Yorkshire. He was now in open opposition to the King.

However, the King's position was weak; he needed the support of the Whigs in Parliament and the Whigs, to his astonishment, chose Rockingham as their leader: "I thought I had not two men in my Bedchamber of less parts than he." So Rockingham became Prime Minister in 1765, and was as inept in government as the King had expected: "A weak, childish, ignorant man, by no means fit for the head of administration" (Horace Walpole). It was, unfortunately, not a time when incompetence in an administration was likely to go unnoticed. The quarrel with the American colonists, in which Rockingham's Whig predilections ran contrary to the King's wishes, was growing more serious.

The Stamp Act was repealed, in the hope of placating American opinion; it had the effect of irritating the King. On another issue, Rockingham and the Crown were at variance, the prosecution of John Wilkes: Rockingham was faithful to the old Whig policy of suspecting anything that might strengthen the royal authority. His attitude was manifest to the Palace, which he deliberately neglected, so that there was no surprise when he was dismissed and Pitt, although even more obnoxious to the King, came to power.

Rockingham's government had, as the powerful, mysterious pamphleteer Junius put it, "dissolved in its own weakness". He had been Prime Minister for a year, during most of which time the real power had rested with the Duke of Cumberland, under whom he had served as a soldier against the Jacobites.

Rockingham left office with no regrets: his main object was to win back his political freedom, so that he could oppose the King on the great question of the American colonies. He was a poor speaker, who suffered agonies every time he addressed Parliament. However, he had the help of Edmund Burke, so that his letters have more vigour.

He spent sixteen years in Opposition, during which the national cause went from bad to worse. When he was called back to office as Prime Minister in March, 1782, his health was declining fast. His second administration was as ineffectual as his first, and even briefer. After four months, he retired to Roehampton, where he died, aged fifty-two. "No man ever attained twice the great object of his wishes and enjoyed it both times for so short a session," said Horace Walpole.

IX

❧ WILLIAM PITT, Earl of Chatham ❧

1766–68

"England has been a long time in labour," said Frederick the Great, "but she has, at last, brought forth a man." Physically, the man was no great shakes. Not very tall, very slight, with a grim expression—one who served with him said that he "had the eye of a hawk, a little head and a long acquisitive nose".

His manners belonged to a bygone age of etiquette and formality—at the court of George III it was said that, when he bowed, the tip of his nose was visible between his legs. But, if his behaviour seemed to belong to the stately past, his gestures and his talk had a tincture of pride, a suspicion of violence, and a hint of fierceness, indicating one who thought daringly and would preside over a time of far-reaching change.

This man, William Pitt, later called Pitt the Elder, and Earl of Chatham, was essentially a leader, intolerant of cautious men and groping counsels, a "bad colleague", an imperious master. Not at all the sort of man one would have expected to dominate the Cabinets and the Parliaments of Georgian Britain? Maybe not. But his imagination was so contagious, his vision so compelling that assemblies, small and large, were swept along by the power of his intoxicating rhetoric. And the nation's need of an audacious lead against an ever growing danger created the atmosphere for Pitt's genius. Genius is not too strong a term.

Without some help from events, Pitt's extraordinary talents would hardly have achieved their triumph. His character was hardly one that appealed to the dominant political class of the time. He was ostentatious, showy, difficult, by no means the gregarious, easy-going man likely to be popular in Parliament or the clubs. He was conspicuously honest, no key to popularity in a corrupt age. But one virtue he possessed which won him the hearts of the public and the reluctant respect of politicians—a savage, devouring pride in his country.

The basic quality of Parliamentary success is not oratory but debate, which is different. Pitt's speeches were vibrant with power; they penetrated deeply into the minds and hearts of those who heard or read them. They had the quality of great State Papers. He did not simply think on his feet. It was on his feet, as he said, that he gave expression to his full range of feeling and personality.

The man who made those speeches was born in London on 15 November, 1708, son of Robert Pitt, grandson of a plundering East India merchant known as "Diamond Pitt" from his ownership of a fabulous stone, the size of a pigeon's egg, which he had acquired for £25,000 at Golconda and which, at length, he sold to the Regent of France, the Duc d'Orléans, for £135,000.

However, not much of the nabob's wealth came to the boy who was his favourite grandson, although there was enough to send him to Eton (which he hated) and to Oxford. His health was bad and grew worse, although he was fit enough to serve as a cornet in the 1st Dragoon Guards. Unusually for a young cavalry officer—but, then, he was an unusual officer—he read widely in military theory. But already his mind was turning to politics, in which his friends, the Temples, Grenvilles and Lytteltons, were involved as Whigs, bitter enemies of the Prime Minister, Walpole.

When he was twenty-seven, Pitt became a Member of Parliament for Old Sarum, a "rotten" borough belonging to his grandfather. It was, in fact, one of seven or eight boroughs owned by the Pitt family and consisted of seven "burgages" (houses or plots of land with a vote) and returned two members to the House of Commons. Pitt was the leading spirit in a group of politicians called the "Boy Patriots", who attacked Walpole without respite until the Prime Minister fell, in 1742. In a series of speeches, brilliant in irony ("the atrocious crime of being a young man which the honourable gentleman has, with such spirit and decency, charged upon me, I shall neither attempt to palliate or deny") and blistering in invective, Pitt set about the assault on the Walpole administration.

Walpole took away the commission of "this terrible Cornet of Horse" but the Prince of Wales, at odds with his father and in opposition to the Prime Minister, appointed him a Groom of the Bedchamber. But George III would not forgive Pitt for the violence with which he attacked the King's Hanoverian interests. Accordingly, it was four years before Pitt achieved a place in the government, and then only because the country was plainly unfit to defend itself. In 1744, a French fleet was at sea with an invasion force of 10,000 men aboard. At that time there were not more than 9,000 British troops in the country. The navy lacked discipline and fighting spirit. In the crisis, the House of Commons sat in permanent session. At White's Club, members sat up all night, betting on the quarter that the wind was in.

Pitt's hour had not yet come, however. At this time, he was afflicted with the first serious breakdown in his health. He spent the greater part of the year 1744 in Bath, suffering from gout and what seems to have been a manic-depressive condition— periods of frenzied exhilaration alternating with spells of black despair.

One stroke of good fortune came his way just then: that old dragon, Sarah, Duchess of Marlborough, died and left him £10,000 and an estate, as a reward for his "patriotism", i.e. his opposition to Walpole. Pitt, by nature extravagant, could now indulge his tastes. Numerous flunkeys wore the blue and silver Pitt livery. There was a strain of madness in the Pitt blood which came out in his sister, Elizabeth, whose behaviour was so outrageous that she became a social outcast. She was a constant trial to her brother. Some of his political colleagues, victims of his rages and his bullying, said flatly that Pitt himself was mad. It seems that his psychological affliction, which periodically induced total collapse, was in some way linked to his surges of passionate and effective energy.

He believed that the House of Bourbon, ruling despotically in France and Spain, must be curbed in power if Britain was to survive and that, for Britain, the security of her trade should be the purpose of war. "When trade is at stake, you must defend it or perish."

His policy was brutally simple: to destroy France as a great power, to lop off her overseas possessions, especially in the sugar islands of the Caribbean, to drive her out of India, to replace her in Canada. It was an enormous programme which only a man of genius—albeit unstable genius—could have contemplated, far less realized.

France might not have the military ascendancy which she had enjoyed before Blenheim, but her military superiority to Britain in Europe was manifest, and so too was Britain's need for a Continental ally. Pitt, who had spent much eloquence on denouncing the German entanglements of Britain's Hanoverian monarch, now, with no great mental discomfort, accepted the realism of an alliance with the Prussian King, Frederick the Great, who had, thought Pitt, the best army in Europe. Frederick confirmed this view by defeating the French at Rossbach.

But before he could direct Britain's policy, Pitt must climb what Disraeli called "the greasy pole" of British political power. It was eleven years after his first entry into the House of Commons before he became, in 1746, a minister, Paymaster-General, a post much sought after for its perquisites, which he rejected. He was then a man of thirty-eight, of undisputed ability, but still denied access to direct power over events. For that he had to wait another nine years, when a great international crisis swept away the objections of the King and the ministers. The opening years of the Seven Years War (1756) had gone disastrously for Britain. Minorca had been lost, Britain's main base in the Mediterranean; British forts on Lake Ontario—one of them held by Colonel George Washington—fell to the French. Diplomatically, France had scored a success—an alliance with Austria.

In the Commons Pitt, now out of the ministry, denounced the government in speech after speech. It seemed that the King, swallowing his pride, must accept Pitt, but Pitt set his terms high. He must be Prime Minister in fact, with the duty of concerting strategy. But that would involve seeing the King daily and this the King refused. Pitt lived at Bath, tortured by gout: "I am carried downstairs and packed like a bale of goods in my chaise to innure me to motion."

At last the King gave way. Called to office as Secretary of State in November 1756, Pitt's service lasted five months. The five months were not wasted. He raised new regiments, including two regiments of Highlanders—and this only eleven years after Culloden! His naval building plans were ambitious. In a coalition government, formed in 1757, the Duke of Newcastle was nominally the Prime Minister, making the less important appointments; Pitt picked all the men who mattered, the admirals, the generals, the ambassadors, and dictated the strategy of war. He said, "I am sure that I can save this country and that nobody else can."

A new pulse of energy and confidence, beating all through the war machine, justified the boast. He drove his subordinates hard. "You are asking impossibilities of us," complained one official. "Sir," Pitt retorted, brandishing the crutches he needed for his gout, "I walk upon impossibilities."

His ways were imperious, secretive, distrustful, and formal. He wore full dress in his office and would not allow his under-secretaries to sit in his presence. He wrote out the naval orders for the fleet with his own hand, and the First Lord of the Admiralty had to sign them with the writing covered.

One day he ordered the Master-General of the Ordnance to see that the battering-train from the Tower reached Portsmouth by seven o'clock next morning. "Impossible," said the Master-General. Pitt fixed him with his eagle's eye. "At your

12 William Pitt, Earl of Chatham. After R. Brompton.

peril, sir," he said, "let it be done. And let an express be sent to me from every stage until the train arrives." It arrived in Portsmouth on time.

In describing the part he played at that time, Pitt said later, "I used the Duke of Newcastle's majority to carry on the public business." That business went well.

While Frederick the Great, supported by British money, won battles in Europe, Pitt's ocean strategy laid the foundations of a vast mercantile empire, and Clive won Plassey in India. The great French stronghold of Louisbourg, at the entrance to the St Lawrence, was taken by joint naval and land attack. On the Ohio, Fort Duquesne (today Pittsburg) fell. Later, in 1759, Goree on the West African coast was taken.

Next year Guadeloupe fell. The French army was defeated at Minden; the Toulon fleet was shattered in Portuguese waters and, in September, Quebec fell to Wolfe's assault. This was a truly epoch-making event, the climax of the year of miracles. "Our bells are worn threadbare with ringing for victories," said Horace Walpole.

In a few months of hard fighting, the map of the world had been re-drawn, and fantastic opportunities had opened up for the future in America and Asia. And, more than anyone else, this was the work of a single man, crippled by gout, hovering at times on the verge of madness, unbearably dictatorial to his colleagues, and earning their hearty dislike. Montreal, Belle Isle and Martinique—these major prizes completed the galaxy of triumphs.

A free society has, however, its own methods of limiting the presumption of victorious statesmen. The taxpayers—the landed gentry—thought that the moment had come to reduce their burden. The City had doubts about the commercial consequences of the colonial war. The politicians began to quake at the fear of a great coalition being built against Britain in Europe. And in Britain, a new King came to the throne in 1760 with his own choice of a man to head the government—George III was resolved to make Lord Bute his Prime Minister.

In 1761 Pitt begged for a pre-emptive strike against the Spanish treasure fleet, then on its way from South America with the gold and silver to finance a new war on Britain. The Cabinet shrank from so daring a stroke. Pitt resigned. George made Lord Bute his Prime Minister. Bute and peace!

Pitt went to the House to denounce it. He was too weak to stand. His wasted features bore the signs of suffering. He was wrapped in flannel bandages and leaning on crutches. His case, developed in four hours of impassioned argument, was a powerful one: Prussia, a magnanimous ally, deserted; the Spanish treasure abandoned; France provided with the means to recover her prodigious losses. The House listened, applauded, and voted against him.

And within three months the war with Spain which he had predicted broke out.

In four years of office, he had turned disgrace and defeat into triumph, and had ensured that over vast stretches of the world a British—or Anglo-Saxon—civilization should rule. He had united Britain and, in doing so, destroyed Jacobitism. He could look back with pride on a fantastic achievement. He could look forward to retirement with a wife he adored.

Pitt, a bachelor, at forty had fallen passionately in love with Lady Hester Grenville and married her in 1754, after a brief, tempestuous courtship, amazed that she could love a man with "health shattered". In due course they had three sons (one of whom became Prime Minister) and two daughters.

From every point of view the marriage was a triumphant success. When the resounding military successes came, it was to his "adored angel" that he sent the first news of victory. When he fell ill, his beloved Hetty nursed him with devotion.

At last (1766), he returned to office and this time to power. "'Tis a great era, my dear sir, and a new birthday for England," Horace Walpole rejoiced. Pitt was what he had wanted to be, Prime Minister, although his disciple, the Duke of Grafton, became First Lord of the Treasury and he, Pitt, was Lord Privy Seal. This was the first time that anyone had been regarded as Prime Minister who was not First Lord of the Treasury. It showed that the office of Prime Minister was now established. At this point, Pitt took the decision to go to the House of Lords as Earl of Chatham, which annoyed Grafton, who had counted on the power which Pitt's oratory could exert in the Lower House.

The French Foreign Minister, Choiseul, was baffled by the move: "It seemed to us that all his force consisted in the continuation in that Chamber and he could well find himself like Samson after his hair was cut. What we have to fear is that this proud and ambitious man, having lost popular esteem, will try to compensate for his losses by war-like exploits."

All this might have mattered less, had the nation's business prospered. But this was not so. The building of a new alliance against the French defied his efforts.

At this juncture, Chatham's health gave way. He retreated to Bath. Gout tortured him and his mental illness returned in graver form.

The Prime Minister of Britain was, at times, mad, and, even in his periods of lucidity, would have nothing to do with his colleagues or with business. Grafton, a man of much smaller calibre, was overwhelmed by his task. At length, Chatham resigned in 1768, after which he recovered his strength to launch out in angry attacks on the government, which Grafton led until he handed over office to Lord North. In the violence of his onslaughts, Chatham did not even spare the King, George III, and the "corrupting power" of royal influence.

There was no lack of targets for his attacks; the East India merchants, "lofty Asiatic plunderers"; the expulsion of Wilkes from the House of Commons, "an axe laid to the tree of liberty"; the need for Parliamentary Reform, a cause which he did not find it easy to espouse, as one who had for years sat for one of the rottenest of all rotten boroughs.

The quarrel with the American colonies which became the capital issue before the nation was the subject of his last and, in some ways, his finest phase. He had an instinctive understanding of the American case, which might seem unreasonable since the British were only asking for the Americans to bear a share of the cost of their own defence, but was nevertheless founded on a principle which could hardly be questioned: "No taxation without representation." He had what the British government lacked, generosity and imagination in his approach to the issue. In a great speech, he said, "If I were an American, as I am an Englishman, while a foreign troop was landed in my country, I would never lay down my arms—never, never, never!"

Chatham was no more willing to concede American Independence than, as he said, he would believe in transubstantiation. But he thought that concession need never arise if only there was wisdom in London.

Meanwhile, he watched the French build up their naval strength for a new struggle with Britain, the struggle to which he had looked forward with foreboding ever since a ministry, under Bute's influence, had made peace with France and Spain on terms which he considered suicidally lenient.

At this time, Chatham was often in the depths of a pathological gloom. Living in a little upper-storey room at North End, Hampstead, in a house he had borrowed, he spent whole days alone, seeing nobody. The King offered to send him one of his physicians to treat his gout but Chatham insisted on being attended by a doctor named Addington, who dosed him with port and madeira, and discouraged him from taking exercise.

When Grafton was, at last, allowed to see him, he was appalled by Chatham's condition. He had sold Hayes Place, his house in Kent; now he insisted on buying it back again at a fancy price. When he roused himself to denounce the government, which was taking advantage of the "guilty tumult" at Boston to "crush the spirit of liberty among the Americans generally", his eloquence made little impression on Parliament, and none on George III. The American war went its disastrous way.

Meanwhile, in speech after speech, the old statesman urged peace: "You cannot, I venture to say it, you cannot conquer America." At last came the day when the Duke of Richmond, backed by the Whigs, begged the King to withdraw all his troops from the revolted colonies. Chatham went to the House of Lords to oppose this final, irrevocable step. "I am old and infirm, I have one foot, more than one foot, in the grave—I am risen from my bed to stand up in the cause of my country." As the speech went on, he became more incoherent, although with flashes of the old fire. "My Lords, any state is better than despair. If we must fall, let us fall like men." He sank back insensible.

Great actor as he always had been, he could not have contrived for himself a finer curtain.

A month later, on 11 May, 1778, he was dead. The House of Lords, after an emotional speech by Lord North, voted to attend his funeral as a body. "I am surprised," wrote George III, "at the vote of a public funeral and monument, an offensive measure to me personally." So, adored by the people, admired even by his political enemies, but saluted with unrelenting meanness by his sovereign, the Great Commoner passed into history.

X

❦ AUGUSTUS HENRY FITZROY, 3rd Duke of Grafton ❦

1768–70

When he succeeded his grandfather to become, against all odds, the third Duke of Grafton, Augustus Henry Fitzroy, aged twenty-one, had probably some inkling of the cares that lay ahead of him. But the office of Prime Minister? Hardly that, although it was a burden which dukes, willingly or reluctantly, might have to bear. *Noblesse oblige.* One thing was certain. He may not be the most illustrious Prime Minister in Britain's political history, but he is unique in one respect.

He is the only Prime Minister who is a member of the House of Stuart, albeit on the wrong side of the blanket, which was not an unusual misfortune for offshoots of that family. He was great-great-grandson of Charles II and his lewdest concubine, Barbara Cleveland. In youth, Grafton was said to resemble, in looks, his royal forebear; later on, it was apparent that he had some other of Charles's characteristics. Junius, the corrosive pamphleteer of the time, who detested Grafton, wrote of his forebears: "The character of the reputed ancestors of some men has made it possible for their descendants to be vicious in the extreme without being degenerate. Those of Your Grace, for instance, left no distressing examples of virtue, even to their legitimate posterity . . . Charles the First lived and died a hypocrite. Charles the Second was a hypocrite of another sort and should have died on the same scaffold. At the distance of a century, we see their different characters happily revived and blended in Your Grace."

Grafton was born 28 September, 1735, son of Lord Augustus Fitzroy. His education was conventional, i.e. Westminster; the Grand Tour, during which he met the best society in France; a degree at Cambridge (his right as a nobleman). He married Lord Ravensworth's daughter, Anne Liddell, after which he plunged into the life of politics (MP for Bury St Edmunds), and the Court (Lord of the Bedchamber to the Prince of Wales). Not long afterwards, he succeeded his grandfather in the dukedom (1757).

Let it be acknowledged that most of his energies were devoted to fox-hunting and racing. Not all of them, however.

As a Whig, he visited Wilkes in the Tower, "to hear from him his own story", but, as a cautious man, he refused to go bail for the popular hero. He formed an early and deep admiration for William Pitt and when, in 1765, at the age of thirty, he was made Secretary of State in Lord Rockingham's government, he did all he could to persuade Pitt to join the administration. But Pitt had an invincible objection to another member of the government, the Duke of Newcastle.

13 The City Chanters, by Collett, depicting the London mob rioting for "Wilkes and liberty", after Wilkes was expelled from the House of Commons.

A few months later (May, 1766), Grafton resigned, not, he later insisted, for "a love of ease and indulgence to his private amusements", as had been reported, but because the ministry lacked strength. The truth was that Grafton wished that Pitt should serve with him, having a shrewd idea that without him the government would fall. This it did.

A year later Pitt—Chatham—became Prime Minister and Grafton was given the Treasury. But to serve with the great man was almost as difficult as to face him in Opposition, especially as Pitt, in an hour of crisis, was liable to have a spell of madness. To Grafton's annoyance, one of these intervals now occurred and, as a consequence, Grafton became Prime Minister in March, 1768. Just then there was trouble over Wilkes and more serious trouble with the Americans. Wilkes was expelled from the House of Commons after being elected for Middlesex. Grafton, opposed to any arbitrary use of executive power, was overborne. What was worse, his Cabinet colleague, Townshend, proposed to make up a loss of revenue on the Land Tax by taxing the Americans. Grafton urged a repeal of the tea duties on the Americans but was defeated.

At this point he was exposed, as a weak and ineffectual Prime Minister, to a violent and sustained onslaught by the anonymous Junius. On his private life, where he was highly vulnerable, the attack was unsparing.

His first wife, Anne, was "secretly" with child by the Earl of Upper Ossary in 1763 and the deplorable fact was known to all fashionable London. Grafton divorced her. They had three sons and a daughter. He himself had taken up with Miss Nancy Parsons, the wayward daughter of a Bond Street tailor, who, among other

14 Sir Philip Francis, reputed author of the *Letters of Junius*, by J. Lonsdale.

adventures, had lived with one Horton, a West Indian "captive merchant" (i.e. slave trader), with whom she had spent some time in Jamaica. Very soon she was being spoken of as "The Duke of Grafton's Mrs Horton, the Duke of Dorset's Mrs

Horton, everybody's Mrs Horton". The description was exaggerated, but not altogether unjustified.

Said Junius, "The name of Miss Parsons would hardly have been known if the First Lord of the Treasury had not led her in triumph through the Opera House even in the presence of the Queen." The affair with Miss Parsons would not in itself have caused any remark in the England of that time, where the morals of dukes were regarded with a great deal of tolerance, but it was thought that the Prime Minister had gone too far.

However, Grafton did not devote all his time to Miss Parsons. In marked preference to his ministerial duties, he hunted at Wakefield where he had a house. "Pretty occupations for a man of quality," said the King, "to be spending all his time tormenting a poor fox that is generally a much better beast than any of those that pursue him." In addition, he raced at Newmarket, "thinking the world should be postponed to a whore and a horse race", as Horace Walpole acidly remarked. What made matters worse was that, just then, the nation's affairs were deteriorating: a war with the American colonies was impending and, more ominous, the price of bread was rising.

Grafton did not, however, change his business methods: "a Cabinet meeting was put off, first, for a match at Newmarket and, secondly, because the Duke of Grafton had company at his house." He felt, indeed, that he had been shabbily treated by fortune: he had a job he did not want and tried in vain to find someone to whom he could transfer it. Chatham, who could have enabled him to carry the day against the tea duty, refused even to see him. When he did, it was to tell Grafton that he was "unequal to the government of a great nation". Chatham's opinion of Grafton was widely shared: "The natural cloud of his understanding . . . made his meaning as unintelligible as his conversation was uninteresting."

By this time, Grafton had married again (1769) Elizabeth Wrottesley, a niece of the Duke of Bedford and, therefore, a lady nurtured in the bosom of the Whig aristocracy. She was "not handsome, but quiet and reasonable". Grafton lived with her happily for forty years. As for Miss Parsons, her career was by no means over. Six years after Grafton disowned her, she married Viscount Maynard and thus became a peeress.

In 1770, just after his second marriage, Grafton decided to resign, the King having persuaded Lord North to shoulder the burden, while remaining of the opinion that Grafton's departure was plain desertion. Grafton's term of office as Prime Minister had lasted two years and a half. In spite of the fact that he had remained a Whig, he was a semi-detached member of Lord North's Tory government until 1775, when he found the policy towards the American colonies more than he could stomach.

When William Pitt the younger formed a government in 1783, Grafton, who had, by this time, been Lord Privy Seal twice, refused a third term in that office. It was thought greatly to his credit that, although his family was by this time numerous, he would take no place or pension. The King gave him the Garter.

He retired to the country, collected many books, took up theology and became a Unitarian. He was a regular attender at the Unitarian Chapel in Essex Street. As the years passed, his appearance became more amiable and distinguished. His frolics with Miss Parsons by this time forgotten, he wrote about the need for the upper classes to amend their lives and was regarded as the beau idéal of a dignified English gentleman of the highest principles.

He died in 1811, aged seventy-seven, surrounded by a large and affectionate family (four children by his first wife; thirteen by the second). Basically a lazy man, without any marked ability, he had carried out without much enthusiasm the public duties which his rank and the times had thrust upon him.

15 Augustus Fitzroy, 3rd Duke of Grafton, by Pompeo Batoni.

XI

❧ FREDERICK, Lord North ❧

1770–82

"I found the American war when I became minister. I did not create it. It was the war of the country, the Parliament and the people." Such is the apologia of Lord North, who has been more blamed than any other man, with the possible exception of his master, George III, for the loss of the American colonies. It is, so far as it goes, a truthful statement. But it does not clear North from the guilt his accusers try to fix on him.

He was an amiable, genial man, not without brains, popular, honourable, but with a notable weakness of character. In fact, he was just the sort of minister a strong-minded monarch would choose to steer an unpopular policy through Parliament. This was the fate of Lord North.

Born on 13 April, 1732, he had the usual upbringing of a young aristocrat, the son of a peer, Lord Guildford—Eton, Oxford, the Grand Tour, from which he returned with some reputation as a linguist. After that, he became MP for Banbury, a borough his family owned. He married, aged twenty-four, a notably plain young woman named Anne Speke and lived with her happily ever after. They had four sons and three daughters.

Young North differed from his fellows in one respect: he was closer than they were to the royal family. His father and mother had been members of the household of the Prince of Wales, so that when North grew up, blond, plump and blue-eyed, it was thought that his father might, in fact, be the Prince and not Lord Guildford. It is a story for which there is no evidence at all, apart from North's "Hanoverian" looks. What is certain, and was soon important, was that North was the companion of the boy who became George III.

After an undistinguished climb up the political ladder, he became, in 1767, Chancellor of the Exchequer and Leader of the House at thirty-five. He had the qualities needed for both posts: business ability and personal popularity. Three years later, when it was clear to everybody that the Duke of Grafton, the Prime Minister, had neither the will nor the talent to stay in power, the King (1770) sent for his friend, Lord North. He had hardly any more taste for the job than Grafton but he could not resist the King's offer, which he regarded as an imperative call to duty. Although the American crisis was slowly coming to the boil, for a time all went smoothly.

He amused the House of Commons and, which was just as important, pleased the King, who gave him the Garter and paid his debts. These had become onerous to a man whose private income was only £2,500 a year. He had a tendency to fall asleep

16 Frederick, Lord North, by N. Dance.

during debates—or to appear to do so. A speaker who was attacking him violently stopped in indignation. "Even now, in the midst of these perils, the noble Lord is asleep!" North opened one eye. "I wish to God I was!" he said. By such remarks he endeared himself to Parliament and made it possible for him to do his master's business.

He would perhaps have been a satisfactory Prime Minister in quiet times, but in a storm as violent as the American crisis proved to be, his inadequacy was soon discovered. He could not cope with the political problems as they arose; he was even more baffled by the strategic questions that followed. It is fair to say that North was as aware as anyone that he did not measure up to events. Repeatedly, he implored the King to release him, but this the King would not do until, at last, he was absolutely compelled to. In due course, the issue was decided on the battlefield. The war went not badly—it went disastrously.

The issues were not at all as simple as they later seemed to be. The two sides were not so unequally divided: six million inhabitants of the United Kingdom on the one hand, two million colonists on the other; but an ocean intervened, across which the more powerful and richer side would have to deploy its strength. Morally, there was some right on both sides: should not the Americans have to pay towards their own defence, especially as it would be deployed against the French and the Indians? On the one hand, a few thousand pounds of revenue, on the other, the founding of a new nation established over countless square miles of territory between one ocean and another. It was soon apparent that the man whose task it was now to deal with this problem was as incapable of realizing the scale of it as Grafton had been.

Nevertheless, in this hour of growing difficulties, North took over the premiership. The situation seemed to demand someone of his equable temperament and ability to command the House of Commons and the trust of the King. However, as it soon turned out, these attributes were not enough.

By the spring of 1771, North hoped that tax concessions he had made to the colonists had averted an outbreak of war; his government seemed by that time to be firmly established in popular favour. A year later it was plain that these hopes were too optimistic. Then came the incident known as the Boston Tea Party. North thought that a small naval force would be able to settle the business. Soldiers would not be required. They were. In the autumn of 1777 came the first intimation of disaster: General Burgoyne surrendered at Saratoga.

From that moment onwards, North did not cease to assure the King of his utter incompetence in his post as a war-leader. "Let me not go to the grave with the guilt of having been the ruin of my King and country." His supplications, which lasted during three years, were rejected. The war went on, unpopular with the City and with a great section of the Nonconformists, who sympathized with the Calvinists of New England, but sustained by the bulk of the population, who regarded the Americans more or less as law-abiding citizens regard tax dodgers. Misfortunes came, military and diplomatic. All Europe became a coalition for the purpose of bringing Britain down. Yorktown came in 1781: the capitulation of the British army on American soil, a total disaster. And suddenly it was clear to everybody that the war could not be won.

By that time, France, Spain, Russia, Prussia, Holland and the Scandinavian countries were, by a diplomatic miracle that has never been repeated, united in opposition to Britain. But that, after all, was scarcely more notable than the triumphs achieved when the thirteen American colonies, hitherto adamant in their refusal to co-operate with one another, produced the Continental Congress and the Declaration of Independence. Nothing is so far-reaching in power as a misguided policy of taxation!

For these remarkable feats Lord North bears some share of the blame: he was the acquiescent minister of a stubborn king. He had not the strength of will to argue with George III; indeed, he seems to have thought that a minister's duty was to execute the monarch's orders, rather than contumaciously to devise a policy of his own. He had never visited America and probably thought of it, if he thought at all, as a country rather like Essex with a population unduly composed of Puritans. A handful of frigates would settle its hash and, if military intervention should be called for, that could be left to the generals! It could not. The military campaign was planned by Lord George Germain, who, in a masterpiece of ineptitude, contrived to bring a British army at Saratoga into a position where it could neither fight nor flee. It was only the first of the series of calamities which culminated in Yorktown.

But if North cannot reasonably be blamed for the strategy that lost the war, he is responsible for the failure to give the army adequate supplies. General Burgoyne, the victim of Saratoga, wrote home, "After a fatal procrastination, not only of vigorous measures but of preparations for such, we took a step as decisive as the passage of the Rubicon and now find ourselves plunged at once in a most serious war without a single requisition, gunpowder excepted, for carrying it on." The outbreak of full-scale war, in fact, coincided with a reduction in the strength of the navy! Nor was any attempt made to exploit the divisions within the colonies, which might have reduced their will to carry on the war. The truth was that North's real interest was in saving the nation's money. It was this, above all, that he was hoping to achieve as Prime Minister; it was in this direction that his policies and his genuine administrative talents were aimed. It was hardly the mood in which a man embarks on a war, especially a war of a novel kind with limitless and unpredictable ramifications.

It may be said that North conceived it his duty as Prime Minister to stay in office so long as the King wished him to, that the King was stubborn and that, in those days, the limits of the political power of the throne had still not been clearly defined. The rights that James II had asserted, and which George III, following Bolingbroke and Bute, had sought to win back, were real but indeterminate. They were at last brought under control as an outcome of George Washington's victories.

George III saw Britain's admission of defeat as "the downfall of the lustre of this empire". North saw the event in equally sombre colours—"Oh God," he exclaimed, "it's all over!"—in a mood of gloomy self-reproach. If that did not last long, it was partly no doubt due to the natural buoyancy of the man—"It is a paltry eulogium . . . yet the best that can be allotted to Lord North, that, though his country was ruined under his administration, he preserved his good humour." So said Horace Walpole, at his most waspish. But, as things turned out, the country was not ruined. Canada was saved for the Empire; India was saved; the command of the sea was restored by Rodney. The first British Empire had vanished, a second was emerging.

Time after time, North tried to persuade the King to release him. When things were desperate, he urged that Chatham, whom the King detested, be brought in. He told the King: "The current is too strong to be resisted . . . the Prince on the throne cannot oppose the deliberate resolution of the House of Commons." But Chatham died. When, at last, North was allowed to go, in 1782, "Remember," said the King, "it is you who desert me, not I you." This was after Cornwallis had surrendered at Yorktown and after the House of Commons had passed a resolution deploring the tendency of the King's influence to increase. "Nothing can save the country but the heads of six ministers on the table," said Gibbon one evening in Brooks's. But he agreed, "It is better to be humbled than ruined."

The American war was coming to an end.

North was retiring from an office which, in his opinion, had no constitutional existence: there was no place for that "animal called a Prime Minister". He was given a pension of £4,000 a year and lived ten years to enjoy it. The money was welcome for, unlike many politicians of the time, he had not feathered his own nest. Although he was out of office, he did not give up politics. By no means. With his old opponent, Fox, he carried on a ceaseless opposition to his successor, Lord Shelburne, a course of action which led the King to accuse him of the blackest treachery. It seems that the most likely explanation of this alliance, which puzzled both his friends and Fox's, was that he hoped to prevent an enquiry into the conduct of the American war which might have led to his impeachment and even—although this is unlikely—to his execution as a traitor.

In August 1790, on his father's death, he became the second Earl of Guildford. He lived on, cheerful and witty, although nearly blind, until in 1792 he died of dropsy in his house in Grosvenor Square. He was in his sixtieth year.

XII

⚔ WILLIAM PETTY FITZMAURICE ⚔
2nd Earl of Shelburne
1782–83

It was hard indeed for one who was outside the magic circle of political power in the eighteenth century to rise to the top. The Scotsman, Bute, did it for a little, bespattered by insult and brought down after a brief stay in the sunshine. And there was William Petty Fitzmaurice, "factious, a foreigner and a Jesuit": in other words, gifted with an independent mind, Irish and altogether too insinuating in manner to be trusted by the Whig aristocrats. True, he reached the top, as Bute had done, but, like Bute, he did not last long there.

He was born in Dublin in 1737, in the old Irish family of Fitzmaurice; in due course, he was rich, with a rent-roll of £22,000 and the ownership of vast stretches of land in Kerry; one of his ancestors had been Cromwell's Surveyor-General in Ireland, Sir William Petty. The boy lived for a time, wild, healthy and untaught, with his grandfather in Kerry, from which he was rescued when his father became Earl of Shelburne and the boy was sent to Christ Church, Oxford. At twenty he was an ensign in the Scots Guards, serving with conspicuous gallantry in the battle of Minden. When his father died in 1761, young Shelburne, aged twenty-five, took his seat in the House of Lords. Already he had attracted attention; he was a colonel, an aide-de-camp to the King. He was burly, florid, pleasant in manner and an object of envy to other young men for his quick promotion. They were more envious, two years later, when Shelburne achieved his first ministerial post as President of the Board of Trade (1763).

He did not last long in the job, having annoyed the Court by speaking against the government on proposals to expel John Wilkes from the House of Commons. During his retirement in his Wiltshire house at Bowood, where he brought in Capability Brown to beautify the estate, he collected a fine library and played host to intellectual figures of the age: men like David Hume, Dr Johnson and Bentham. He was unusual among politicians of that time in his liking for the company of first-class minds. When he returned to office (1766) it was as Secretary of State for the Southern Department, which was responsible for American and Indian business. It was one of the key appointments at that time, and Shelburne's handling of it was heavily attacked. His reputation as a shifty intriguer was established when he was employed by Bute in plots to put Grenville out and bring Pitt back into the government.

In 1768, when it was plain that the government meant to use force against the American colonies, Shelburne resigned, hated by the King, who called him "the

17 William Fitzmaurice, 2nd Earl of Shelburne. After Reynolds.

Jesuit of Berkeley Square", where his London house was situated. But all his efforts to build up an effective Opposition came to nothing: the British public, at that stage, were hostile to the Americans and their friends in Britain.

About this time, Shelburne fell foul of a Scottish MP, Lieutenant-Colonel William

Fullerton, who took exception to some remarks about him which Shelburne had made in the Lords and replied by accusing Shelburne of corresponding with the enemies of his country. Shelburne was not a man to overlook such a calumny. The two men fought a duel in Hyde Park and Shelburne was slightly wounded in the groin. He said, "I don't think Lady Shelburne will be any the worse for it." Shelburne had married Lady Sophia Carteret in 1765, by whom he had a son; and, after her death, Lady Louise Fitzpatrick, in 1779 (no children). In the Fullerton affair the public took Shelburne's side, believing that Fullerton had been put up to it by the government.

But Shelburne was well enough endowed, financially and intellectually, not to feel too deeply the unpopularity which had become his lot. He had his lavish table in Berkeley Square, his parks and his books at Bowood, the company of the circle of clever men who were his cronies. He had also his passion for acting as go-between in the political game. Sooner or later he was sure to be needed. And so, indeed, it proved.

When Lord North resigned, the King made Shelburne his intermediary in negotiations, the purpose of which was to bring in Rockingham as Prime Minister. Shelburne came in as Home Secretary in Rockingham's government, although he was at variance with Rockingham and his friends on important matters. For instance, Shelburne wished the American colonies to develop into a voluntary federal association with Britain and for that reason was unwilling to accept American independence, which Rockingham was ready to concede. Generally speaking, however, he was more "radical" than his associates. It was the extreme independence of his outlook as much as anything which made him distrusted. His contemporaries could not be sure where he would stand on any issue.

It was his duty, as Home Secretary, to negotiate with the Americans, while Charles James Fox, the Foreign Secretary, conducted peace talks with the European states. The two men were in sharp disagreement when Rockingham died on 1 July, 1782. Shelburne became Prime Minister; Fox resigned. Shelburne was, more than ever, suspected in Whig circles. Burke called him "a Borgia, a Catiline and a serpent with two heads". However, he was able to form an administration which survived until its terms for a peace treaty with the Americans were rejected by the House of Commons. Shelburne left the office he had held for less than eight months, defeated because the peace he had hurriedly put together was thought to be too humiliating. The British were not yet ready to admit how calamitous had been their defeat. They were glad to have someone like Shelburne to blame and he, for his part, put the blame for his downfall on the King, who had, as he thought, first tricked him into taking office, and then had encouraged dissensions in his government.

He was given the Garter and a marquisate (of Lansdowne); he was promised a dukedom if ever non-royal dukes were made again; but, although he lived another twenty-two years, his political career was ended. He had no party to support him in Parliament and only a coterie of personal friends outside it. He paid the price of the high-handedness which had estranged his colleagues, including his friend, the younger Pitt. Ever since his association with the detested Scotsman, Bute, he had been watched with suspicion by the radical thinkers who, in other circumstances, would have been his natural allies. He never threw off that suspicion. He had relied on the King to rescue him in 1783 when the political crisis blew up over his proposed peace with the Americans; the King had failed to do so. Disheartened, he left politics.

His economic ideas, picked up from his friend, Adam Smith, were radical and novel; so, too, were his ideas on Parliamentary Reform; it was left to other men in a later generation to apply them. It was no comfort to him that his peace terms, which Parliament rejected, were substantially the same as those his successors made. The French Revolution was now at hand, alarming many moderate men. Throughout the storm, Shelburne remained consistently on the liberal side, opposed to the increasingly repressive and reactionary policies of the younger Pitt and his friends. As time went on, he was more and more an isolated figure, with no part to play in the drama of events. It was a pity because, for all his arrogance and his deviousness, he could have made a great contribution to British political thinking in his time. What stood in the way? Not wealth—he was very rich. Not talent—he had plenty of it. The impression is left that he did not completely understand the English political system; that he remained somehow alien to it, an outsider.

He died on 7 May, 1805. This Irishman was the only Prime Minister of his time who was basically a frustrated man; as Disraeli says, "one of the suppressed characters of English history and the ablest and most accomplished statesman of the eighteenth century".

XIII

✣ WILLIAM CAVENDISH-BENTINCK ✣
3rd Duke of Portland

1783; 1807–9

To have been Prime Minister twice, with a quarter of a century separating the two terms of office; to have led the first time a Whig, the second time, a Tory ministry; such is the distinction of William Henry Cavendish-Bentinck, third Duke of Portland. He was born on 14 April, 1738, and grew up very rich; owner of great properties from both his father and his mother; an enthusiastic Whig on a traditional pattern, just the kind of austere young aristocrat whom King George III most disliked. It was, indeed, his loyalty to the Whig cause that helped to reduce him at one time to comparative poverty; he spent so much of his money on promoting the political fortunes of the party.

Once, when there was a crucial election in Carlisle, he carried £30,000 up with him in a coach to encourage the electors to vote the right way. The money went in no time at all. For one reason and another, then, the Duke was reported to live in comparative poverty and "ducal dudgeon behind the ramparts of Burlington House, with half-a-dozen toadies for company". But brighter times lay ahead. Portland married, in 1766, Lady Dorothy Cavendish, daughter of the fourth Duke of Devonshire, by whom he had four sons and a daughter. His mother died and left him £12,000 a year; he was now rich enough to buy the famous Portland Vase for £1,000. He could devote time and money to politics. But something more than time or money was needed with a monarch as strong-minded and anti-Whig as George III, especially when one was a duke as strong-minded and Whig as Portland.

In 1783, Portland became Prime Minister, with a Cabinet composed of ministers whom the King openly disliked and meant to be rid of at the first opportunity. But his colleagues, rent by mutual animosities, found him agreeable; besides, he was a duke, which, at that time, meant something. Portland's first brush with George III came over the amount of income he proposed to allow the Prince of Wales, twice the sum which the King had been given when he was Heir to the Throne. The King would have nothing to do with it. In his opinion, his son was a fool. There was a furious scene in the Closet (the King's private study) between monarch and minister. Eventually Portland persuaded the Prince to accept half the suggested income, plus the Duchy of Cornwall revenues and a vote from Parliament to meet his debts.

A few months later, before the year was out, came the dispute that ended the ministry. An India Bill which would have kept the Indian patronage funds in the

18 William Cavendish-Bentinck, 3rd Duke of Portland. After Reynolds.

hands of Fox and his associates was defeated when it became known that Pitt was about to use the King's disapproval of the bill to ensure that it was thrown out. Portland resigned and was succeeded by Pitt. He was out of office for eleven years. He gave himself up to collecting books and works of art; Welbeck Abbey, his house, became "a devastation", as Horace Walpole thought.

When he came back into government in 1794, it was as Home Secretary in a very different political climate. The French Revolution had frightened the aristocrats, Whig as well as Tory. Portland's London house, a quarter of a century earlier, had been the only mansion of any distinction to illuminate its windows for "Wilkes and Liberty". Now the Duke was responsible for law and order at a time when troubles threatened. He remained so for seven years. In 1807, he volunteered to be Prime Minister again, although he was doubtful if he had the strength of mind or body for the job. In this he was right. But he was a duke, a man of principle, respected by politicians if not much known by the public. He scarcely troubled to read official papers; when he did so, he often fell asleep in the middle of the task. His colleagues used to hold Cabinet meetings without bothering to invite him. The ministry was his in name only. When Canning and Castlereagh quarrelled, Portland let things fester until Castlereagh resigned in a rage and fought a duel with Canning. By that time, Portland's health was growing rapidly worse. In August, 1809, he suffered a stroke and died at Welbeck in October.

He was a man without conspicuous ability and certainly with no gift of oratory— "He possessed in an eminent degree the talent of total silence," an unusual aptitude for a politician. Without any driving ambition, he was sustained through a remarkable political career by something that proved to be more valuable, the conviction that in England there was always room for an honest duke.

XIV

❧ WILLIAM PITT, the Younger ❧

1783–1801; 1804–06

William Pitt, born on 28 May, 1759, was the son of the most famous British statesman of the eighteenth century, the Earl of Chatham. How hard it would be for him, should he aim at a career in politics, to avoid the charge that he was a mere shadow of his great father! Let it be said, then, that Pitt did aim at such a career, that he triumphantly survived that danger and that his ascendancy over the political scene was as great as Chatham's had been. He was the nation's leader in a struggle more dangerous than that of the Seven Years War.

In addition to his own talents, it may be acknowledged that he was lucky in one respect; his father specifically educated the boy for politics, the service of the state. Above all, he was trained in public speaking, the key art of the politician in a Parliamentary system of government.

Pitt's health was too bad to allow him to be sent to school: after private tutoring, he went to Cambridge (Pembroke College), and, after that, to the Bar (Lincoln's Inn). The family life he shared was lively and cheerful. At thirteen, he had written a tragedy which the Pitt children performed for their parents.

Pitt was present at his father's collapse in the House of Lords, an event as heroic as death on the battlefield. Thanks to Chatham's wildly extravagant ways, he found himself a poor man (income £300 a year) and practised law on the Western Circuit until Sir William Lowther gave him the Parliamentary seat of Appleby, in 1781. After hearing the young man's first speech in the House, Burke said, "It is not a chip off the old block. It is the old block itself."

When Lord Shelburne became Prime Minister in 1782, he made Pitt Chancellor of the Exchequer. The pace of change quickened: Shelburne fell; a coalition of North and Fox, with the Duke of Portland as its nominal head (1783), did not last long. How could it? North and Fox! The figure-head of George III's bad government and the man who had attacked it most strenuously! It was too cynical a combination for the public to stomach.

In December, 1783, Pitt was appointed Prime Minister, a promotion which was greeted with derisive laughter in the House. Few of his contemporaries would serve with him, so that his first Cabinet was composed entirely of peers. The City of London gave him its freedom, but his political enemies were active enough to arrange that his carriage was overturned outside Brooks's. However, things improved. Before a year was out, Gibbon wrote, "A youth of two and twenty, who

19 William Pitt, the Younger, by John Hoppner.

raises himself to the government of an Empire by the power of genius and the reputation of virtue, is a circumstance unparalleled in history and is no less glorious to the country than to himself."

There he was, a young man with a long neck, a sharp nose and an expression too solemn for his years; with no known interest in women—unusual in those days—and, already, a marked partiality for the port decanter—by no means unusual! To this weakness, indeed, he had been encouraged by his doctor, who recommended it as a specific for the disease he had inherited from his father: gout. With that exception, he appeared to be a cold, ascetic being. Coleridge described his character with more eloquence than charity: "He has patronized no science, he has raised no man of genius from obscurity; he counts no prime work of God among his friends. He has no attachment to female society, no fondness for children, no perceptions of beauty in natural scenery; but he is fond of convivial indulgences, of that stimulation which, keeping up the glow of self-importance and the sense of internal power, gives feelings without the mediation of ideas."

The portrait, or caricature, is vibrant with dislike, but it expresses something that the men of his time felt about Pitt—a glacial quality in his personality. He floats through the seas of his age, chilling and impressive as an iceberg. About his public presence there seems something calculated, something of the great actor, who is suppressing some of the complexities of his character because they are irrelevant to a grand effect he wishes to produce.

Thus, it is not true that he had no fondness for children; he had, but the public knew nothing of it. And his feelings for women, too, existed, but they were suppressed, partly by his poverty and partly by his absorption in the passionate

The GIANT-FACTOTUM amusing himself

20 **A caricature of William Pitt, by James Gillray, 1797.**

drama of affairs for which he had cast himself. He was, by instinct as well as upbringing, an actor on an ample stage. His main political concern was with administration, above all with the national finances which, at the time he arrived on the scene, were in great need of reform. To this task he applied himself with enthusiasm and—until external events overtook him—with success. But he was not, then, what he later seemed to become, an enemy of reform. Thus, he spoke magnificently for the abolition of the Slave Trade.

Before long, however, it became plain that mere concern for the nation's money was not going to be his main business; he was destined to lead the nation in a vast European convulsion. For this role, his aptitude was less apparent.

Meanwhile, he bought a property, Hollwood, at Bromley in Kent, and retired there when he could, with a few boon companions, to continue in leisure the work of undermining his health with port wine. His private affairs he neglected; his servants robbed him; his debts mounted; by 1798 he owed £30,000. When he became friendly with Lord Auckland's daughter, Eleanor Eden, he was quick to explain to her father that he was too poor to offer her marriage. His niece, Lady Hester Stanhope, looked after his house. In 1792, life became a little easier for him when the King made him

21 The House of Commons, 1793, by K. A. Hickel. Pitt is addressing the House, and Fox is seen on the Opposition front bench.

Warden of the Cinque Ports—a sinecure which carried with it a salary of £3,000 a year and Walmer Castle as a residence.

On the outbreak of the French Revolution, he was at first inclined to be optimistic. At a dinner party in Downing Street he told his guests that "things in England will go on as we are until the day of judgment". Burke, who was present, was not so sure. "Very likely," he said, "but it is the day of no judgment that I am afraid of."

Very soon, Pitt's outlook and policies underwent a change. Having been a moderate progressive, a Liberal, as we would say, the shock of the turmoil in Europe and the horrifying events in France drove him towards repression, especially as revolutionary propaganda began to have an effect in England and, more strongly, in Ireland. Until then, the only thing that had shaken his government had been when the King seemed to go mad—really went mad, as the doctors thought then, not having heard of a malady named porphyria—and a Regency Act had to be hurried on to the Statute Book. Charles James Fox, from the beginning Pitt's rival and a bosom friend of the Prince of Wales, argued that the Prince was automatically Regent.

Fox was one of the most brilliant and attractive figures of the age: a man of enormous talent and no judgment; a compulsive gambler, who had run up card-table debts of £140,000 which his doting father paid; a "man of pleasure", who had married a tart and lived with her in perfect bliss. As an orator, "he waved the wand of a magician" (Pitt), as a man—let Brougham speak—"A life of gambling and intrigue and factions left the nature of Charles Fox as little tainted with selfishness or falsehood and his heart as little hardened as if he had lived and died in a farmhouse."

22 **Charles James Fox,**
   by K. A. Hickel.

"We'll join hand in hand, all Party shall cease, } The UNION-CLUB. { "In the cause of Old-England we'll drink down the Sun
And Glass after Glass, shall our Union increase". } London, Pub^d Jan^{ry} 21st 1801, by H. Humphrey, St James's Street. } Then toast Little Ireland, & drink down the Moon!"

23 In 1801 Pitt proposed Parliamentary Union with Ireland. This came to nothing because of the opposition of George III. Gillray here satirises the proposed Union in a cartoon which figures Fox, the Prince of Wales (later George IV), Sheridan, Pitt and other political figures of the time.

He had the blood of the Stuarts and the Bourbons* in his veins and was the leading foe of George III in Parliament. Now, in the controversy over the Regency, he was on the Prince's side. Pitt insisted that while the Prince undoubtedly could be Regent, yet Parliament must retain the power to nominate him. It was not simply a procedural question. If the Prince were Regent, Fox would be made Prime Minister and Pitt's system would be dismantled. But the danger passed. The King recovered.

Pitt went on with his administration of the nation's finance with such success that the Three Per Cents, which were at 74 in 1783, stood at over 96 nine years later. Taxation was reduced, the navy cut. Then came one disaster after another: the French invaded Belgium and declared the Scheldt an open river, something that no British government could accept; Louis XVI was executed; France declared war.

The war, which Pitt expected to last only a short time, owing to France's weak financial position, dragged on, and, in spite of Nelson's victory at the Nile, did not go well. Pitt had not the talent for strategy of his father and the Continental coalition he built up against France collapsed. But his popularity did not wane; his speeches

---

*His father having eloped with Lady Caroline Lennox.

continued to impress, although Sydney Smith said, "At the close of every brilliant display, an expedition failed or a kingdom fell."

As long as the King approved of him, Pitt was safe, for George III had built up a control of Parliamentary votes such as the Whig landowners of a previous generation had enjoyed. In 1798 came an incident which for a time seemed to be sensational. Pitt accused an Opposition member named George Tierney of deliberately impeding public business. Tierney sent him a challenge. He was a rich man, born in Gibraltar, with an Irish father who, for reasons which were mysterious, did not live in England. He was a clever debater, but the fact that he belonged to what was called the "mercantile class" was against his success in politics. The duel, with pistols, was held on Putney Heath before a large crowd. Both men fired twice in the air, after which honour was held to be satisfied. Tierney continued to attack the government in the House.

The King was not likely to criticize Pitt for measures taken against the English sympathizers with revolution, especially after the Terror in Paris and the French invasion of neighbouring countries. The repression may have been severe; it may often have been misdirected. But the danger of a revolutionary outbreak was real enough and London, the London of the Gordon Riots of 1780, had a record of mob violence older than that of Paris. The break with the King came over another issue— Emancipation, which Pitt had promised to Catholics in return for the Parliamentary Union with Ireland, but which George III believed was forbidden by his Coronation oath. In consequence, Pitt resigned early in 1801 and Addington, the Speaker, took his place with his approval. Meanwhile, the state of Pitt's personal finances became worse. His debts mounted to £40,000. City merchants offered him a gift of £100,000 which he declined, although he accepted a loan of £11,200 from friends. At the same time he sold Hollwood.

When war with France was renewed in 1803, it was soon obvious that Addington was not the man to wage it. In alliance with his old enemy, Fox, Pitt brought the government down. But the King would not have Fox in the government, and in consequence Pitt (Prime Minister again in 1804) faced a powerful Opposition in Parliament. In April, 1804, he formed a ministry and organized an attack on the Spanish treasure fleet, an enterprise his father had wanted to carry out forty years before. Then came a dreadful setback: his crony, the Scotsman, Dundas, who had become Lord Melville, was charged with misuse of public money.

Pitt at this time was trying to build up a new European coalition against Napoleon. In this he was helped by Napoleon himself, who, by making himself King of Italy, upset both Austria and Russia. But the year 1805 ended in a cataract of disasters: Trafalgar was won but Nelson was dead. Austerlitz followed, making Napoleon, as it seemed, master of Europe. The disaster, it had been said, was more than Pitt could endure. He said, "Roll up that map [of Europe]; it will not be wanted for these ten years." Then he died, on 23 January, 1806.

Pitt was at Bath, in very poor health, the outcome of overwork, anxiety, the bottle. He was likely to die anyway. Also, he resembled his father in this respect: he knew a good exit when he saw it. He had shown at a Lord Mayor's banquet that he could supply the necessary words for the scene: "England has saved herself by her exertions; and will, as I trust, save Europe by her example." Since Chatham, in the

24 James Gillray, 1802. Fox (Citizen Volpone) is here shown making his bow to Napoleon.

midst of a great oration, fell speechless in the House of Lords, what exit line could be better?

He died in 1806 in an hour of defeat, but he had created, by his financial policy, the national wealth that saw Britain through a long and terrible war, building her fleets, paying her soldiers and sustaining her allies. More than that, his equable temper and unflinching courage had been contagious. When, at last, victory came, it was Pitt's spirit that had triumphed. But by then he had been dead nine years.

He was aged forty-five when he died, and had been Prime Minister for twenty years.

⚝ HENRY ADDINGTON ⚝

1801–04

Shed a tear for Henry Addington! There he is, poor man, a thin and not very succulent sliver of premiership between two thick slices of Pitt. Of him hardly a good word is spoken, except to say that he must have had some gift of mind or character in order to be chosen as successor to the younger Pitt, even when allowance is made for the fact that he was never meant to be more than a stopgap and that he was a close friend of Pitt, his junior by two years.

Addington's father was Anthony Addington, the doctor who attended Lord Chatham in his last years and acquired fame and popularity by his faith in port wine as a specific for gout. To Pitt, as a sufferer from the same complaint, he recommended the same remedy, with results which were not entirely satisfactory. The physician's son, Henry, born in London on 30 May, 1751, went to Winchester and to Brasenose, Oxford; after which he practised at the Bar in London, until Pitt, who was rising fast in Parliament, persuaded him to go into politics.

Addington became MP for Devizes in 1784, by which time his friend, Pitt, was Prime Minister. It seemed that Addington was just the trusted comrade that the new premier wanted. He might not be a distinguished orator; indeed, when Pitt put him forward to second the Address, Addington made a lamentable failure of the job. But he was a hard-working member of committees, busily seeking out new friends in the House, a student of Parliamentary procedure, and recognized for the good sense, if not the depth, of his opinions. In short, just the sort of sound man who would make a good Speaker of the House. And this he became, in 1789. Pitt chose him for the post because he did not seem to be a man who would make the Speaker's chair a stepping-stone to higher office.

The choice was popular, the new Speaker a success. His only defects were pomposity, prosiness and a total lack of humour. When he spoke on the corn shortage, he gave the Commons a lecture on the beneficial effects of bran and grew emotional about "the rarefying warmth, the solvent moisture and the grinding action of the stomach". No doubt he was surprised by the ill-suppressed merriment such thoughts produced. At such times, MPs were likely to remember Addington's origin—"a son of Lord Chatham's physician and, in fact, a sort of dependant of the family".

However, he was twelve years in the Chair, during which time he talked often in private with the Prime Minister and enjoyed his company and his port at the table.

25 Henry Addington, by George Richmond.

In 1801, Pitt resolved that, if the King would not accept Catholic Emancipation as part of the price for the Parliamentary Union with Ireland, he would have to find a new Prime Minister. The King begged Addington to open Pitt's eyes to "the danger of agitating this improper question". When Pitt would not budge, the King asked the Speaker to form a government.

Addington begged that somebody more suitable should be found. But George III had recently visited Addington in the country to inspect a yeomanry unit which the Speaker commanded and had decided that he was just the man to lead the country. Pitt was much of the same opinion: no other man would be acceptable. He pledged "diligent" support to Addington's government. "Addington, you have saved the country!" said the King. He gave the new Prime Minister a house in Richmond Park and sent him seven cows from his own herd.

Addington's first task was to make peace with France. This he did reasonably well, although his agreement to cede Malta was heavily criticized. (But, as it turned out, Britain did not quit Malta, thus giving Napoleon a just cause of complaint.)

However, Addington had to contend with several weaknesses. He was a wretched speaker, so that the House soon longed for Pitt's eloquence, which had wearied it only a year before. He was undeniably middle-class in a snobbish age and a Parliament dominated by the aristocracy. Finally, he could not depend on Pitt's followers to refrain from attacking him. Above all, George Canning, the most brilliant of Pitt's younger disciples, kept up a constant fire of criticism and derision against Addington, the doctor's son, whom he called "*Le médecin malgré lui*" and who lived, so he alleged, in the "Villa Medici".

Addington tried in vain to persuade Pitt to come back into the government. Pitt would only come as Prime Minister. Pitt's friend, Lord Melville, was sent by Addington to find what Pitt thought. He brought back the report: "There should be an avowed and real minister possessing the chief weight in council and the principal place in the confidence of the King. In that respect, there can be no rivalry or division of power. That power must rest in the person generally called the First Minister." Thus, in 1803, the necessity for a Prime Minister was stated by the man who could speak with the greatest authority on the subject, and his powers and duties were defined.

While the peace lasted, matters went tolerably well. In his Budget, Addington halved the "boldly tyrannical" income tax which Pitt had introduced; this was much to the satisfaction of the public. But peace, always precarious, was shattered when Napoleon invaded Switzerland. Soon it was plain that Addington, like Chamberlain in 1940, could not supply the inspiration and leadership that the country wanted. His speech on the day war was declared was more than usually feeble and, to his misfortune, Pitt spoke so brilliantly that Fox said, "If Demosthenes had been present, he must have admired." Increasingly, public confidence ebbed from the ministers, "the feeblest, lowest almost, of men, still more of ministers", as Creevey thought.

With Pitt and Fox combining their fire, the government could not last long. It fell on 10 May, 1804 and Pitt resumed his sway. Addington became Viscount Sidmouth, with thirty years of political life before him. He did not have long to nurse a grievance against Pitt, who, he thought, had left him with a burden too heavy to carry. For, by

January, 1806, Pitt had died. Addington served briefly as Lord Privy Seal in the Ministry of All the Talents; he was Lord President under Spencer Perceval and, finally, Home Secretary in Lord Liverpool's government for almost ten years. By the time George IV came to the throne, he had served in six administrations for almost thirty years. "He is like the smallpox," said Canning. "Everybody is obliged to have him once in their lives."

While he was at the Home Office, the melodramatic incident known as the Cato Street conspiracy occurred when the whole Cabinet was to be murdered as it sat at dinner. The conspirators were amateurish; the alarm they caused was natural.

As Home Secretary, Addington acquired fame of a new and disagreeable kind. These were days of unrest and unemployment, when the horrors of the French Revolution still lingered in men's memories, alarming all law-abiding people. Against the ferment of disaffection, the ministers reacted nervously and the Home Secretary, responsible for internal order, was identified with the measures against the Luddite mobs, Peterloo, the suspension of Habeas Corpus, censorship of the press and the machinery of repression known as the Six Acts. The result is that Addington won a place in Radical demonology alongside his colleague, Castlereagh:

> Two vultures sick for battle,
> Two scorpions under one white stone . . .

He would certainly have thought the portrait less than just. He was not conscious of having wilfully given pain to any human being. Probably he did not think of himself as a reactionary.

When he died at eighty-five, he was a pious, kindly old gentleman who wrote occasional harmless poetry and talked a great deal about the famous men he had known. He had been married twice; by his first wife, Ursula Mary Hammond, whom he married in 1791, he had six children; his second, Mary Ann Townshend, whom he married in his sixties, brought him a splendid fortune. Now he is remembered, if at all, by the scoffing lines:

> Pitt is to Addington
> As London is to Paddington.

It was a cruel stroke of fate that brought one of the most commonplace of Prime Ministers into such sharp contrast with one of the greatest.

The **CATO STREET CONSPIRATORS**, *on the Memorable night of the 23ᵈ of Febᵞ 1820, at the moment when Smithers the Police officer was Stabbed; NB The Scene faithfully represented from the Description of Mᵗ Ruthven, The View of the Interior correctly Sketched on the Spot*

26 The Cato Street Conspirators, who planned to murder the entire Cabinet in 1820, when Addington was Home Secretary in Lord Liverpool's ministry.

XVI

❧ WILLIAM WYNDHAM, ❧
Lord Grenville

1806–07

The son of one Prime Minister and the nephew of another, William Wyndham Grenville (born 24 October, 1759) grew up in a hotbed of politics and received the education (Eton and Christ Church, Oxford) which was held to fit a man for a high place in the state. His appearance was not prepossessing; his manners were shocking, and, as a third son, he was not particularly rich (£1,500 a year), but these were misfortunes which were scarcely noticed among the array of his assets. These included a rich political place, likely to be found for him sooner or later by one or other of his cousins. They would deem it unthinkable that a Grenville—any more than a Temple or a Lyttelton—could suffer want.

It was more important, perhaps, that he had no particular aptitude for public affairs, but that was a failing which a young man born in his sphere in life would dutifully overcome. Industry he had in full measure, a capacity for hard slogging. But he only seems to have felt at ease in his own family circle, which was ample enough. His rise in politics was smooth and rapid, as was to be expected from one with his name and background. At twenty-two (in 1782), he became MP for Buckingham—a family borough. It was a lucky moment, for his cousin, William Pitt, had just been made Chancellor of the Exchequer. Within a year, Grenville was Chief Secretary to his brother, Lord Temple, Lord Lieutenant of Ireland, and, when Pitt became Prime Minister in the following year (1783), he made Grenville Paymaster-General.

As the perquisites of that office were considerable, the young man was thenceforward spared the nagging anxieties of penury. At twenty-nine, he was elected Speaker of the House; three years later, he was a peer and Foreign Secretary (1791). In addition, he was appointed Ranger of Hyde Park, a cosy little sinecure worth £4,000 a year, to add to his post as Auditor of the Exchequer, also worth £4,000 a year. Now he was well enough off to marry but, characteristically, he did so within the cousinhood. His bride was the Hon. Anne Pitt. They settled down in a charming little property, Dropmore, in Buckinghamshire. There he built up a fine library and, when politics did not take up all his time, devoted himself to gardening and the classics. It was agreed among his friends that marriage had made him a great deal less uncouth than he had been. Lord Mornington wrote; "I cannot tell you with how much pleasure I saw your *ménage*. I told Pitt that matrimony had made three very important changes in you, which could not but affect your old friends—(1) a

27 William Wyndham, Lord Grenville, by John Hoppner.

brown lapelled coat instead of the eternal blue single-breasted, (2) strings in your shoes, (3) very good perfume in your hair powder.''

The French Revolution had the same effect on his opinions as it had on those of many men of liberal views and conservative temperament—it turned him towards repression. He expelled the French ambassador, Chauvelin, suspected of sedition; he supported the government in the Lords on the Habeas Corpus Suspension Bill, the Treasonable Practices Bill and the Seditious Meetings Bill—the legal armoury by which Pitt sought to ensure that revolutionary doctrines did not gain a foothold in Britain.

On the other hand, he remained true to the economic doctrine of Adam Smith, and protested when Pitt seemed to tamper with the market economy. Again, on the question of Catholic Emancipation, he was on the liberal side and resigned with Pitt in 1801 on this issue. He had been Foreign Secretary for close on ten years. He and Canning and Fox now led the Parliamentary campaign against the Addington administration which, in the end, brought it down. When Addington was obliged to resign, Grenville would not join the ministry which Pitt formed until Fox was included, and this the King would not have. From this time forward, Pitt and Grenville were not on friendly terms.

After Pitt's death in 1806, Grenville formed what was called the Ministry of All the Talents (1806–07) from the supposed brilliance of its members. Grenville took the premiership reluctantly, pointing out that he would have no increase in income through having to surrender the Auditorship. The difficulty was surmounted when Fox promised to bring in a bill by which the Auditorship would be conveyed to a trustee. It was a clever—perhaps too clever—device and, after it, Grenville became Prime Minister. But the ministry proved to be an ill-assorted team. "We are three in a bed," said Fox, who was one of the ministers. It lasted for fourteen months, after which the Catholic question came to the front once more and on that the King was as obdurate as ever.

Grenville, whom the King called "Popish", resigned; he spoke of the "infinite pleasure I derive from my emancipation". Probably he was sincere. His house, garden and library at Dropmore occupied his thoughts; his wife had inherited the Pitt estate at Boconnoc in Cornwall. Grenville was now a wealthy man. Now and then he spoke in the Lords, for instance, in favour of abolishing the death penalty for shoplifting. He remained faithful to Catholic relief and Free Trade. He died in 1834, after a stroke, aged seventy-four. He had no children.

Lord Liverpool, a Prime Minister who followed him, summed him up: "The most extraordinary character I ever knew . . . uncommon industry, but he never sees a subject with all its bearings . . . not an ill-tempered man but he has no feelings for others . . . in his outward manner, offensive to the last degree, rapacious with respect to himself and his family." It was severe but not altogether unjust.

XVII

❧ SPENCER PERCEVAL ☙

1809–12

It is not every day that a British Prime Minister is assassinated in the lobby of the House of Commons, but this fact has saved Spencer Perceval from being relegated to the long list of forgotten premiers. If it had not been for that horrid incident, on a May day in 1812, Perceval might have been remembered today as the smallest Prime Minister (with some competition from Lord John Russell), or the Prime Minister with the record number of children (but he was beaten by Grafton), or the one with the prettiest wife (but what of Lady Peel?), but it is unlikely that he would have gone down in history for any remarkable political achievement. To be fair, Perceval had not long to show what he could do, before the murderer's pistol ended the story.

He was born in 1762, the second son of the Earl of Egmont, by a second marriage. The result was that he failed to inherit either his father's earldom or his mother's barony and, in 1783, was left with the modest income of £200 a year to seek a livelihood at the Bar, after Harrow and Trinity College, Cambridge. He built up a good practice on the Midland Circuit but he was not the sort of young man mothers thought about for their daughters. So, when he met and fell in love with Jane Spencer-Wilson, he had to overcome some opposition from her family.

He was industrious, promising, a young barrister with a future, but undeniably poor at the time that he married in 1790. So poor that the young couple lived above a carpet shop in Bedford Row, London. What was more, children were arriving with relentless regularity—five in the first six years. Perceval took silk in 1796, which is always a daring step for a lawyer, and cast his eyes towards politics. His convictions were of a kind likely to find favour at that time: he was intensely conservative, an enthusiastic churchman, a firm believer in law and order, an opponent of anything that smacked of radicalism.

By this time, he was doing well at the Bar and had, thanks to the intercession of his cousin, Lord Northampton, gleaned a modest but useful sinecure at the Mint—Surveyor of the Meltings and Clerk of the Irons, value £120 a year. Not a great deal of money but, as it turned out, the Meltings and the Irons were only the first of a helpful series of the kind.

More important was the fact that he had caught the eye of William Pitt, who offered him the job of Chief Secretary for Ireland, with the promise that his financial future would be more comfortable. Perceval politely declined.

Already he could see a career opening up in politics and, in three months, he was elected MP for Northampton (1796), a borough where his family had some interest. He proved to be an effective debater, so much so that before Pitt fought his duel with Tierney, when he was asked who would succeed him if he were killed: "Perceval," he said, "seems to be the most able to cope with Mr Fox."

Meanwhile, his professional career flourished; he was Solicitor-General, then (in Addington's ministry) Attorney-General. He had disagreed with Pitt on the issue of Catholic Emancipation, to which, as a devout Church of England man, he was strongly opposed. When Pitt returned to office in 1804, Perceval agreed to continue as Attorney-General only if the Catholic question were not raised and if Fox were not a member of the government. When Pitt died, Perceval took over the leadership of the Opposition.

By this time his practice at the Bar was flourishing; in the top year his fees amounted to 5,000 guineas, which, with his income from other sources, made him reluctant to take a ministerial office which would prevent him continuing his legal career.

The Catholic question still hovered on the political horizon, threatening every ministry that tampered with it. Thus, it destroyed the Ministry of all the Talents, after which the aged Duke of Portland formed a government in which Perceval was Chancellor of the Exchequer. Two years later (1809), he was Prime Minister.

By this time he had earned the hatred of the Prince of Wales by taking his wife's side in the courts and the Whigs hoped that, when the Prince became Regent, he would dismiss Perceval. But one evening Creevey, the Diarist, walking past Perceval's house, smelt delicious odours coming from the kitchen. Perceval was entertaining the Prince Regent, who, putting the past aside, had decided to keep him in office as Prime Minister.

He ran into trouble at once over the Luddite riots, against which he deployed more troops than Wellington had in the Peninsula. For this and for his generally stern measures against disaffection, he was criticized. Sydney Smith wrote, "I say I fear he will pursue a policy destructive to the true interest of this country; and then you tell me he is faithful to Mrs Perceval and kind to the Master Percevals . . . I should prefer that he whipped his boys and saved the country."

It was true that his domestic life was blissful and fruitful (twelve children). In addition, his religious interest centred on the prophetic books of the Old Testament, in which he found political guidance. When the House of Commons had its annual service to repent for the execution of Charles I, Perceval looked round the church with disapproval: "The attendance is discreditably thin." On the Catholic issue he remained "sound": "Though it is a peculiarly sacred duty to His Majesty," he wrote to his constituents, "to defend the established religion of his kingdom, yet it must be felt by you to be the common duty and interest of us all."

From the political point of view, the murder of this amiable and upright reactionary was a total irrelevance. A bankrupt named John Bellingham had been imprisoned while trading in Russia. The British ambassador in St Petersburg refused to interfere with the course of Russian justice, with the result that Bellingham returned to Britain with a grievance against the government which, in due course, preyed on his sanity. His longing for vengeance centred on the Prime Minister.

Right Hon Spencer Perceval 1812.

28 Spencer Perceval, by G. F. Joseph.

On Monday, 11 May, 1812, a committee of the House of Commons was examining the effects on trade of the Orders in Council aimed at injuring French commerce when Lord Brougham complained that the Prime Minister was not present. Perceval was sent for and, while he was on his way, was shot dead in the lobby by Bellingham with a pistol he had concealed in his pocket. Bellingham was hanged a week later, his counsel's plea of insanity being rejected at the Old Bailey. To Perceval's widow, left with a large family and modest means, the House of Commons voted £50,000 and £2,000 a year.

Contemporary opinions about Perceval differed widely. "The model of a high-minded, high-principled, truthful, generous gentleman," thought an admirer. Lord Holland disagreed. To him the murder, atrocious as it was, was "a very fortunate event for the glory, happiness and independence of my country".

29 The assassination of Spencer Perceval.

THE ASSASSINATION OF THE RIGHT HON: SPENCER PERCEVAL,
In the Lobby leading to the House of Commons, May 11 1812.

XVIII

❧ ROBERT BANKS JENKINSON ❧
2nd Earl of Liverpool

1812–27

Naturally, Rothschild* was first to hear the news. Next morning, Wednesday, 21 June, he passed it on to the Cabinet. The Prime Minister did not believe it. In a great battle fought at Waterloo, Napoleon had been decisively beaten. It was too good to be true. Not until the evening was the Prime Minister, Lord Liverpool, convinced of it. He was the sort of sensible, cautious Englishman who has a natural tendency towards pessimism and who wants to be certain that good news is true before ordering the salute to be fired.

He was born (7 June, 1770) Robert Jenkinson, son of Charles Jenkinson, a Tory country gentleman who became, in 1786, Lord Hawkesbury. Educated at Charterhouse and Christ Church, Oxford, Robert Jenkinson went abroad in 1789, travelling in France, Germany and Italy. As it chanced, then, he was an eye-witness of the symbolic event which marked the passing of the old world. He saw the Paris mob attack the Bastille.

While he and his young companions roamed the Continent, broadening their knowledge of the world, political friends were at work on his behalf at home. The electors of the pocket borough of Appleby, a property of the Lowther family, discovered that he, and only he, should be their MP. The boy was not yet twenty-one.

He was a shy, serious, awkward youth with few social graces, and his maiden speech in Parliament was the kind of painful, over-prepared thing that might have been predicted. He was speaking for the government against a motion of Whitbread's, censuring the ministry for increasing the size of the navy. Pitt heard the speech and affected to be impressed by it. More important, he gave the boy a seat on the India Board. From that moment until the day of his last illness, Jenkinson spent only thirteen months out of office.

He went abroad once more, visiting Coblenz and associating with the leaders of the French *émigrés*. Not surprisingly, on his return to England, he spoke strongly against Parliamentary Reform, which, as he thought, might open the door for revolution in Britain. He was, too, in favour of Pitt's measures against "sedition". When Louis XVI was excuted, Jenkinson advocated an immediate declaration of war on France.

---

*Nathan Mayer Rothschild (1777–1836), general merchant and financier, founder of the London branch of the firm.

30 Robert Jenkinson, 2nd Earl of Liverpool, by Sir Thomas Lawrence.

These were days in which a man needed little imagination to hear the tumbrils rumbling down St James's Street.

The outbreak of the war with France upset any political plans Jenkinson may have had. He become colonel of a yeomanry regiment, the Cinque Ports Fencible Cavalry, and left for garrison duty in Scotland, a country for which his enthusiasm was qualified. The style of living there was gross, as he thought, although hospitality was warm. There was too much drink for his taste.

He married (1794) the Earl of Bristol's daughter, Lady Louisa Hervey, and began to resume his part in public life. He and his father opposed Pitt's policy of admitting American ships to the West Indian trade but neither of them carried opposition to the point of resigning and, in reward for this loyalty, the father was made Earl of Liverpool while the son became Master of the Mint, a post worth £3,000 a year. Things were now moving fast for the young man. Pitt resigned the premiership in 1801 and, when Addington took over the government, Jenkinson, who, like Addington, opposed Catholic Emancipation, became Foreign Secretary.

31 Luddite riots, by Hablot Browne. *"Maddened men, armed with sword and firebrand ... rushed forth on errands of terror and destruction."*

As such he was in office when the Peace of Amiens was negotiated. But very soon he was convinced that a renewal of the war was inevitable. In particular, he opposed the evacuation of Malta, which had been agreed under the Peace. Reluctantly, he became a peer, as Lord Hawkesbury, and Leader of the House of Lords. He was made Home Secretary when Pitt came back to power. It had been a dizzy ascent for a man of thirty-three. But a height more exalted was before him.

When Pitt died, Jenkinson was offered the post of Prime Minister but he did not feel confident that he could command a Cabinet—he was a man of nervous temperament—and settled for the place of Lord Warden of the Cinque Ports. It was worth £3,000 a year, a fact which led Lord Sheffield to remark acidly, "This Jenkinson craving disposition will revolt the whole country." But the "whole country" remained unperturbed.

In Spencer Perceval's ministry, Jenkinson, who had, on his father's death, become Earl of Liverpool, was Secretary of War and the Colonies, and therefore responsible for the army during Wellington's campaign in the Peninsula. He brought a good deal of common sense to bear on strategic problems, believing, for instance, that Britain should concentrate her military effort on the Spanish War. He gave unquestioning support to Wellington.

In 1812, when Perceval was assassinated, Liverpool became Prime Minister, a position which he held for the next fifteen years. He was, therefore, at the head of the government during the last phase of the war against Napoleon and it is a notable tribute to his conciliatory temperament that he was able to hold together a coalition containing men of strong wills and diverse opinions, Canning, Castlereagh and Brougham, for instance. The principle on which he selected his Cabinet colleagues was a simple one: each man came in as an individual, not as the representative of a faction: He said, "I cannot bear the idea of the Cabinet being a connection of little knots of parties." On one occasion he asserted himself with effect. When the King sought to put an absolute ban on Canning as a Cabinet minister, having an intense personal dislike for him, Liverpool objected. He said that if that principle were applied, he would resign.

After the long and terrible war with Napoleon was over, his government faced the problems of peace: social discontent and economic depression, as expressed in the Luddite riots, when workmen broke up labour-saving machinery. On these matters Liverpool's ideas were benevolent but old-fashioned. He thought that government could not do much to improve the lot of the working classes; if ministers tried to help, they would probably do more harm than good. In consequence, what was done was cautious and on a small scale: he spent a million pounds on building churches; he supported a bill which gave protection to children in the cotton mills; he favoured state loans to foster work-creating schemes. Consistent with this general outlook was his firm policy of suppressing disorder when it appeared, as at the incident which became known as Peterloo.

But the burden of work was heavy and took a toll of his strength. In 1821, his wife died and he married Mary Chester in the following year. However, though in failing health, he held his turbulent Cabinet together for five more years. When he was about to make a speech, he used to take a whiff of ether beforehand.

In February, 1827, he paid the price of his overwork: he had a severe stroke. In

32 *Massacre at St Peter's or "Britons Strike Home"!* by George Cruikshank, 1819. This incident became known as Peterloo.

December, 1828, he died. As a Prime Minister he had been useful, if not inspiring: he had favoured small reforms, but had distrusted sweeping schemes of change, whether political or economic. He remained to the end a country gentleman, who believed in his own kind: the county MPs, "if not the ablest members of the House, may be trusted for the most part in periods of difficulty and danger".

XIX

❧ GEORGE CANNING ❧

1827

Charm, wit, intelligence, convictions—George Canning had all of these qualifications for success in politics. He even had, or married, money. What was there about him, then, which made a slight shadow cross the brows of his contemporaries when his name was mentioned?

There was the faintest doubt whether Canning's origins were quite respectable. The circumstances were these: his father, also George Canning, came to London from Ireland after an obscure family quarrel over an unfortunate attachment he had formed. He had an allowance of £150 a year, barely enough for a gentleman to keep body and soul together. He wrote for the press, married a beautiful Irish girl, Mary Anne Costello, and died in poverty. His widow then went on the stage, without success. She lived with an actor, who turned out to be a rogue and who deserted her and set her son, George (born 11 April, 1770, in Dublin), "on the road to the gallows". Mary Anne found another friend, by whom she had several children.

However, George had a rich uncle, a City banker, Stratford Canning, who came to the rescue and gave him the conventional education of a young man of family, i.e. Eton and Christ Church. Meanwhile, his mother married again, a silk mercer named Richard Hunn, who also went on the stage. Mary Anne was always a source of worry to her son.

When he was at school, Canning edited a school magazine, the *Microcosm*, of which he was able to sell the copyright to a publisher for £50. Obviously, he was a boy of exceptional gifts. Whether he had the sincerity of his opinions, the seriousness which is essential to the young man in politics, was another matter. Canning's wit in some ways was against him. Men laughed at his brilliance and remembered his mother, the actress. He thought of himself as an Irishman and was a member of the Irish Club in London.

Coming from a Whig family, he became a Tory. Some critics thought the change too abrupt:

> The turning of coats so common is grown
> That no one thinks now to attack it;
> But never yet has an instance been known
> Of a schoolboy turning his jacket.*

---

* Temperley. *Life of Canning*, p. 33.

It was said (by Sir Walter Scott among others) that Godwin the Radical had called on Canning in the Temple one day and told him that the English Jacobins meant to make him their leader when the Revolution came. And that this alarming prospect drove him into the arms of the Tories. It was a time when, owing to events on the Continent, the Tories were becoming more Tory and the Whigs were splitting into those who, without condoning the Terror, tolerated the French Revolution (e.g. Lord Holland), and those who were appalled by it.

What is certain is that Canning liked the Toryism he encountered at Oxford, and was soon one of the sprightliest contributors to a political fortnightly, the *Anti-Jacobin*. He practised at the Bar and, through the influence of William Pitt, became MP for Newport, Isle of Wight, in 1794. When he spoke in the House, his gestures were thought to be excessive and his manner too effusive for some tastes. His aggressive style in debates made him many enemies.

It seems, although it is not certain, that he had an affair with Caroline of Brunswick, the estranged wife of the Prince of Wales, a dangerous liaison from which

33 Queen Caroline of Brunswick, by Sir Thomas Lawrence.

he was lucky to escape with nothing more serious than some disturbance to his emotions.

But it was important that an ambitious young man making his career in politics should have some financial backing. In 1800, Canning fell in love with Joan Scott, an heiress, daughter of General Scott, who had made half a million at hazard. Canning married her and lived happily ever after (four children). Her fortune, £100,000, enabled him to devote himself to public life. He was also given half the revenue of the Paymaster-General, so that he could afford to retire when Pitt broke with the King on the question of Catholic Emancipation, a question on which Canning's views were liberal. Canning resigned, loyally, and reluctantly.

Returning to Parliament as MP for Tralee, one of the rottenest of the Irish boroughs, he did a great deal to bring down the Addington administration and was disappointed when Pitt, in office again after the renewal of the war against Napoleon, rewarded him only with the Treasurership of the Navy. In this post he remained until the death of Pitt. "I must not again be the child of favour," he told his wife. Three years and two governments later, he was Foreign Secretary. He was thirty-seven. By this time, his hectoring style in Parliament was growing calmer.

Events in Europe at this moment took a dramatic turn against Britain. Napoleon and the Tsar met on a raft in the river Niemen and signed a treaty which contained a secret clause: France was to occupy part of Denmark and seize the Danish Fleet. So Canning was told by his spies. Canning did not wait on the development of events. He arranged to send troops and a naval force to Copenhagen. The King was horrified by this daring and unscrupulous act. The Opposition held their fire, waiting for it to fail. Canning wrote to his wife, "The measure is a bold one and, if it fails, why, we must be impeached, I suppose—and dearest dear will have a box at the trial." After three days' bombardment of Copenhagen, the Danes agreed to surrender their fleet. The gamble had come off.

Napoleon's plan to build a northern coalition against England had failed. But British military projects that followed were also failures. Canning became convinced that Castlereagh, the War Minister, must go. He worked constantly to this end, with the result that Castlereagh was convinced that he was a disloyal colleague and sent him a challenge. The two men fought a duel on Putney Heath. Canning's shot missed and Castlereagh's wounded him slightly in the thigh. Castlereagh helped Canning to his surgeon. The wounded man sent an amusing account of the duel to friends, recommending Castlereagh as the operator, should they wish to repeat the experiment.

The Duke of Portland, who as Prime Minister had spent most of his time in Cabinet fast asleep, died in 1809 and was succeeded as Prime Minister by Spencer Perceval, whom Canning refused to serve under, although Perceval was eight years older than he. He thought that, with Whig support, he might be sent for by the King. "He considers politics as a game," said a friend, "and has no regard for principle if it interferes with his object of achieving power."

Three years later, when Perceval was assassinated, Canning and Castlereagh made up their quarrel.

In 1812 Canning was elected for Liverpool on the slave trade vote. When Lord Liverpool offered him the Foreign Office in that year, he refused, having heard that

Castlereagh was to be Leader of the House of Commons. With all his gifts, Canning was plagued by a jealous temperament and an uncontrollable passion for intrigue. In 1814, he was ambassador to Lisbon, an appointment which the Whigs regarded as an outrageous political "job".

He came back into the government as President of the Board of Control (which supervised the East India Company and evolved into the India Office) and was in that post when George IV came to the throne and the question arose of what was to be done about his consort, Caroline of Brunswick. To Canning, whose friendship with Caroline was known, this was embarrassing. he resigned when the Queen was tried. The public were on the Queen's side. Only a minority approved the quatrain written against her:

> Sweetest Queen, we thee implore
> Go away, and sin no more.
> But if that effort be too great,
> Go away at any rate.

She defeated the King's attempt to divorce her but died not long afterwards, mourned by Canning: "She had great and good qualities—with all her faults."

Canning's wit gave him the reputation of flippancy, in addition to the ambition which the public held against him. He was distrusted by the great property owners. By 1822, he had given up the political struggle in despair and was about to go to India as Governor-General when there was a sensational turn in events. Castlereagh committed suicide and the Foreign Office fell vacant. The King was unwilling to accept the fact that Canning, his wife's friend and, in the opinion of many, her lover, was the obvious man for the post. Was he not bound on his honour to turn such a man down? The Duke of Wellington, consulted on the matter, insisted that, on the contrary, the King's duty was to appoint Canning.

Canning said, after kissing hands, that his appointment was like receiving an entry card to Almack's Club and finding the words written on the back, "Admit the rogue".

As a Foreign Secretary, he soon showed himself a dominant figure, keeping the King amused by his wit, pleasing Lord Liverpool, the Prime Minister, by his command of the House of Commons, and winning respect for his extraordinary industry, e.g. he could dictate two dispatches simultaneously, one on Greek, the other on South American affairs. In addition, he pleased George IV by appointing Lord Francis Conyngham, a son of the royal mistress, Lady Conyngham, to a post in the Foreign Office! One of the lady's ex-lovers, Lord Ponsonby, was posted to South America out of the reach of royal suspicion. Canning could hardly have done more to please his sovereign. His policy was determined and, for a Tory, unconventional.

He would have nothing to do with the clique of reactionary powers who were trying to keep Europe in chains to autocracy. He sent the Duke of Wellington to the Congress of Verona to make it plain that Britain would not collaborate with Bourbon France in an invasion of Spain to suppress the progressive forces there. On the contrary. When the time came and Spain, by this time conquered by reaction, proposed to overthrow the democratic government of Portugal, Canning sent British troops to help the Portuguese.

He was at once an isolationist, an interventionist and a nationalist. "For Europe," he said, "read England." The people liked his independent, energetic and daring policy; the King's entourage were bitterly opposed to it; the King himself was alarmed about it until it was clear that Canning was succeeding.

It was on South America that he made his most spectacular break with Britain's European allies. Spain's South American colonies had broken from her. Europe would, at her leisure, recognize their independence. Canning would not wait on the others. If Britain acted independently and at once, she could hope to pick up a rich trade. And to this bold course he eventually won round the Cabinet.

"I called the New World into existence," he told the House of Commons, "to redress the balance of the Old." It was typical of the man, in the confident mood of 1826, to which also belongs his famous verse, sent in cypher to the Ambassador at The Hague:

> In matters of commerce the fault of the Dutch
> Is offering too little and asking too much.

The Secretary of the Embassay at The Hague read the message twice and said, "It is oddly worded." He had not noticed that it was in rhyme. Just then, the Dutch government was being tiresome over a proposed reciprocal lowering of duties, one of the ingredients of Canning's Free Trade policy.

In the following year, Liverpool suffered a severe stroke and it was clear that he would never recover. The right wing of the Tories realized with alarm that Canning was the most likely successor. And Canning would certainly press for Catholic Emancipation, on which he was at odds with half of the party. In the circumstances, the right wing urged the King to appoint Wellington. Canning's retort did not lack subtlety: "Sir, your father broke the domination of the Whigs. I hope your Majesty will not endure that of the Tories." The King flushed. "I'll be damned if I do," he said.

Canning became Prime Minister in 1827, aged fifty-seven. He was already a dying man, dependent on laudanum.

At once, he ran into trouble, Wellington had disliked him since the Congress of Verona (1822), at which, much against his liking, he had been compelled, as Britain's representative, to carry out Canning's policy. The European monarchies were bent on invading Spain in aid of the Bourbons. Wellington, who approved of this project, had the painful task of informing the Congress that Britain would have no part in this intervention. Accordingly, Wellington felt humiliated. Now he refused to serve in Canning's government. What is more, he resigned as Commander-in-Chief. Sir Robert Peel would not serve. By bringing in Whigs, Canning had made new difficulties for himself. Lord Grey, whom Canning had baited long ago, subjected him to every sort of abuse. Catholic Emancipation was held up. His proposed reform of the Corn Laws was frustrated.

In foreign affairs he was more successful: he made an alliance with Russia and France, aimed at saving the Greeks, struggling for their independence against Turkey. The alliance achieved its purpose when the Turkish fleet was destroyed at Navarino. But by the time the news reached England, Canning was dead.

His health, which had been failing for some years, grew rapidly worse after he caught a chill at the Duke of York's funeral at Windsor. Suffering from agonizing lumbago, he took refuge in the Duke of Devonshire's villa at Chiswick. There he died, on 8 August, 1827, having been Prime Minister for just a hundred days. He was buried in Westminster Abbey; his widow was made a viscountess. The Duke of Wellington wrote, "Mr Canning's death will not do all the good it might have done at a later period. But it is still a great public advantage."

Canning, who was Prime Minister for a shorter time than any other, was a strange mixture of opinions—a Liberal in such matters as foreign affairs and Catholic Emancipation, but a conventional Tory when it came to dealing with the rising tide of social unrest. He might, as Greville said, have been able to arrest the torrent of Reform but, "the Tories, idiots that they were, hunted him to death with their besotted and ignorant hostility". He had said, a few weeks before his death, "we are on the brink of a great struggle between property and population." It "is only to be averted by the most liberal legislation". The stage was being set for the drama of Reform.

XX

🪶 FREDERICK JOHN ROBINSON, Viscount Goderich 🪶

1827–28

If anyone were hesitating about embarking on a political career on the grounds of his intellectual insufficiency or weakness of character, a study of the life of Fred Robinson would quickly end such poor-spirited fears and produce a surge of self-confidence. It might, of course, be argued that, since Robinson's day (MP in 1806), the standards of political life have grown more severe. But this, too, seems at best uncertain.

The achievements of Robinson—Chancellor of the Exchequer, Prime Minister, Viscount, and finally, Earl—show what can be done in public life by a man who has a plump, dimpled face, pleasant manners, a vein of unconscious humour and not much else. He was a well of good-natured optimism, spreading around him a kind of fatuous euphoria, which was very welcome in grim times.

The Robinsons were a rich Yorkshire family which for generations had been in politics and had acquired the barony of Grantham. Frederick (born 30 October, 1782) went to Harrow and to St John's College, Cambridge. By 1806, aged twenty-four, he was an MP for an Irish county which, in the following year, he exchanged for Ripon. In 1814, he married Lady Sarah Hobart and had one son who survived childhood. In the year of Waterloo, he introduced a bill which restricted the import of corn, as a result of which an angry crowd attacked his London home; three years later, the Prime Minister of the day, Lord Liverpool, made him Chancellor of the Exchequer. "Why Fred Robinson is in the Cabinet," grumbled Henry Legge, MP, "I don't know, nor do I recollect to whom he is supposed more particularly to belong." But Robinson went on for four years, producing a series of optimistic Budgets which earned him the nickname "Prosperity Robinson". The country was booming at that time and Robinson's cheerful free trade policy thrived with it.

He had a piece of luck in 1824 when the revenue was unexpectedly augmented by the repayment of part of an Austrian loan. This windfall he spent with unusual imagination—£500,000 on new churches, £300,000 on the restoration of Windsor Castle and £57,000 on acquiring the Angerstein collection of pictures, the beginning of what is now the National Gallery. Even when a trade recession came in the following year, his reputation survived it. When Canning came to power, he made Robinson Secretary for War and the Colonies and George IV created him a peer, as Viscount Goderich.

As Colonial Secretary, he was not a success. William Cobbett called him "Goody

34 Frederick Robinson, Viscount Goderich, by Sir Thomas Lawrence.

Goderich" because of his lack of force of character. The name stuck. A few months later, Canning died. His followers searched for "a man of rank, property and consideration" and thought of the Duke of Portland, who had taken no part in politics, but seemed, in other ways, the right sort of man. However, George IV in 1827 choose Goderich to succeed, thinking, no doubt, that he would be an obedient servant. Nobody questioned the King's right to choose his own Prime Minister but on this occasion the King went further, excluding some men he disliked from the new government and insisting that others should be included. In consequence, Goderich had no authority in his own Cabinet, and little respect in Parliament.

Was he a Prime Minister in any real sense of the word? He did not think so himself. "On the contrary," he said, "quite the reverse." After a few months, during which he tried to hold together a ministry rent by confusions and rivalries, without party discipline and, above all, without a firm control by its nominal leader, Goderich threw in his hand. He could not make up his mind which policy Britain should follow in the Eastern Mediterranean. In a state of deep depression, following the death of a favourite child, he felt himself unable to keep the peace between wrangling colleagues and, in floods of tears, announced his resignation to the King. The King lent "the blubbering fool" a handkerchief and accepted his resignation. Goderich's term of office had lasted less than a year. He was followed by the Duke of Wellington, a statesman of a very different calibre.

But Goderich's career in politics was not ended. Weak and likeable, with few opinions that he was not willing to sacrifice for a place–"His political convictions," said Lord Crewe, "were limited to those announced by the diverse governments of which he was a member"—he was the kind of man who lasts longer in public life than his abilities merit and is ready to endure any number of personal humiliations, provided he can stay in the political game. During the time he was Prime Minister, he never met Parliament. A unique distinction.

When Lord Grey became Prime Minister in 1830, Goderich was given the War Office and, two years later, was made Earl of Ripon and a Knight of the Garter. The earldom he took because he needed the rank in order to get the Garter, which he wanted. In Peel's government he was President of the Board of Trade and, later, of the India Board. He died in 1859, aged seventy-six.

So passed on a Prime Minister who can hardly be said to have left a deep impression on history, although he was in office of one kind and another for thirty years. Disraeli called him "a transient and embarrassed phantom". It is not a kind description, but not unjust.

XXI

❧ ARTHUR WELLESLEY, Duke of Wellington ❧

1828–30

The King was in bed at Windsor, dressed in a dirty silk jacket and a turban nightcap, one as greasy as the other. "Arthur," he said to his visitor, the Duke of Wellington, "the Cabinet is defunct." In other words, the ministry of Viscount Goderich was, on that day in 1828, about to come to an end. Who was to succeed? Beyond all doubt, Arthur Wellesley was the man for the job. With a sinking heart, the Duke recognized where his duty lay.

He was fifty-nine years old, born in Dublin on 29 April, 1769, fourth son of an Irish peer, the Earl of Mornington. After Eton and a spell at a French military academy at Angers, he had joined the army and spent the ten years after 1794 on service in India. After that came a time in politics, as Chief Secretary of Ireland. In 1807, he married Catherine Pakenham, daughter of the Earl of Longford, by whom he had two sons. In July, 1807, he was given the command of the British forces in the Peninsula, with the task of driving Napoleon's brother, Joseph Bonaparte, out of Spain. This he duly did, in spite of feuds among his Spanish allies and an absence of steady support from his own government. Napoleon abdicated and Wellesley, already a field marshal, became Duke of Wellington, KG and British ambassador in Paris.

The fact that he was Commander-in-Chief at the final defeat of Napoleon at Waterloo made him the most illustrious Briton of his day, a man whom his fellow-countrymen looked up to with awe. He was loaded with foreign decorations and titles and given £500,000 by the British government.

Two years after Waterloo, he entered politics as Master-General of the Ordnance in Lord Liverpool's government. He was a trim, erect figure, with an eagle nose and a curt, no-nonsense style which has become the British army's contribution to the art of conversation.

His wife, Catherine, and he were temperamentally unsuited to one another. His sons also were a problem to him.

"The Beau", as he was called in society, had been well-known as a busy social figure in London, fond of the company of pretty women and a notable clubman. Indeed, it was said that he had founded one club in order to have the pleasure of blackballing his son from it. His politics were those of his class and profession, those of an Irish Protestant aristocrat, an officer who believed that orders must be obeyed and indiscipline must be sternly punished.

Canning's policy as Foreign Secretary was to recognize the former Spanish

35 Arthur Wellesley, Duke of Wellington, by B. R. Haydon.

colonies which, by rebellion, had become South American republics. When Canning became Prime Minister in 1827, Wellington resigned from the Cabinet and the post of Commander-in-Chief. The latter resignation was regarded by the King as a personal affront.

When Canning died after he had been in office a hundred days, Wellington thought he might be called to succeed; on the critical weekend he had arranged to stay with his friend, Mrs Arbuthnot; he cancelled the appointment: "I think it is best to be found at home." Then, at his house at Stratfield Saye, he heard that Viscount Goderich had gone to the King. "Our lord and master hates Peel and me," Wellington concluded, "and he will adopt any resource rather than send for us." When, however, the King invited him to resume his post as Commander-in-Chief of the army, he accepted.

The situation did not last very long. Goderich turned out to be an exceptionally weak Prime Minister, which was exactly what the King wanted, being convinced that he himself was capable of governing the country alone. At last, however, a naval war broke out in the Mediterranean, with Russia and Britain united against Turkey on behalf of the Greek insurgents. The British Cabinet was "quite at sixes and sevens; some for peace, some for war", as Mrs Arbuthnot reported. It was plain that Goderich would not do.

It was then that George IV summoned Wellington to Windsor and, in his greasy jacket and turban, insisted that he should be Prime Minister. Wellington was aware that he was taking on a job for which he had no training and no liking. "There is

36 *A Sketch in the Park*. **The Duke of Wellington and Mrs Arbuthnot.**

nobody who dislikes as much as I do and who knows as little of party management," he wrote. "I hate it."

He had no liking for popularity: like Castlereagh, he preferred its opposite—"it is so much more convenient and gentlemanlike." To crown all, he had no talent for public speaking. His opinion about himself was widely shared in the newspapers. The *Manchester Guardian* spoke of his "strong bias to arbitrary power, utter ignorance of the principles of philosophical legislation, inveterate prejudices, mediocre abilities, unteachable disposition."

On the last complaint, the Duke soon proved the newspaper wrong. He made Peel, who was not an aristocrat, the Home Secretary in his Cabinet and pressed on with Catholic relief, a cause of which he personally disapproved. He was not helped by a dispute in the royal family. The Duke of Cumberland, of whom the King was afraid, opposed any pro-Catholic measure; the Dukes of Clarence and Sussex favoured it. The House of Lords witnessed an unseemly fraternal brawl. Clarence called Cumberland "factious and infamous". The royal dukes were, as Wellington had told Greville ten years before, "the damnedest millstone about the necks of any government that can be imagined. They have insulted—personally insulted—two-thirds of the gentlemen of England."

The King, torn between his brothers, wept for his Protestant conscience and sought comfort in brandy and water. Catholic Emancipation was achieved to a large extent because of the Duke's unique prestige. "He can address the King," said Greville, "in a style which no other minister could adopt . . . The King stands completely in awe of him. The greatest ministers have been obliged to bend to the King or the aristocracy or the Commons, but he commands them all."

In the course of the debates on the subject, a melodramatic interlude occurred. The Duke thought that Lord Winchelsea had made a remark reflecting on his honour. He sent a challenge. The two met with pistols on Battersea Field. The Duke intended to give his adversary a leg wound. Winchelsea had promised not to fire at the Duke. As a result neither was hurt, whereupon Winchelsea apologized for his remark, the Duke touched his hat, said "Good morning" and rode back to London.

It was a ridiculous episode and quite out of character for the Duke. "Ill-advised man," said Jeremy Bentham. "Think of the confusion into which the whole fabric of government would have been thrown, had you been killed."

There was now an urgent need for a much wider measure of franchise reform not confined to the religious issue, amounting to a revolution in the electoral system in Britain, with the extinction of many small country constituencies which had become obsolete and corrupt and the enfranchisement of many town dwellers.

The reason was the growing industrial distress, popular discontent and rural disorder. Meanwhile, across the Channel, a revolutionary outbreak drove King Charles X from the throne and installed his cousin, Louis Philippe. Would this be imitated in Britain?

When George IV died and the Duke of Clarence became King William IV, a general election was required by law. The result was confused but Wellington interpreted it as a signal for him to go.

He resigned (1830) and was never Prime Minister again. He would go down to the country, he said, and do what he could to restore law and order. He would never lead a political faction. Meanwhile he was heaped with the dignities reserved for the retired statesman, e.g. Governor of the Charterhouse, Elder Brother of Trinity House. He was already Constable of the Tower and Lord Warden of the Cinque Ports.

He was succeeded as Prime Minister by Lord Grey, who believed devoutly in Parliamentary Reform. During the debates on the Reform Bill, the Duke was prominent as an opponent. He was widely regarded as an extreme reactionary, an "ultra" as the term went then. A mob raged outside Apsley House, his London home, until one of his servants fired a blunderbuss over their heads, upon which the rioters dispersed. However, his windows had been broken. He installed iron shutters to protect them.

He was hanged in effigy in Seven Dials, a notorious London slum area. But such demonstrations of popular disapproval did not disturb him unduly. Years afterwards, when the fickle public were cheering him once more, he tipped his hat towards the iron shutters with an ironical bow.

37 *Taking an airing in Hyde Park. A portrait. Framed but not yet glazed.* **A prominent opponent of the Reform Bill, the Duke of Wellington had the windows of his London home, Apsley House, broken by angry rioters.**

When Grey's government was defeated in the Lords in 1832, Wellington was again asked to form an administration. When he failed in this, Grey came in and the Reform Bill was finally passed. Grey (see pp. 106) was followed by Melbourne who, to the rage of the Whigs, was dismissed two years later, at a time when Sir Robert Peel was on holiday in Italy. Wellington, summoned by the King, was acting Prime Minister for three weeks in 1834. Until Peel arrived, he was in effect First Lord of the Treasury, Home Secretary, Foreign Secretary and Minister of War!

"His Highness, the Dictator," said Grey, "is concentrating in himself all the power of the state." The Whig Duke of Bedford said that the choice was between anarchy and despotism and he preferred anarchy. "If we have anarchy," replied Wellington, "I'll have Woburn" (Bedford's place).

In this interval he was happy doing all the business of government without having to consult the wishes of his colleagues; the trouble was that essential decisions of policy often had to wait while the head of government was bogged down in details of administration.

The burden of work came at a moment when he was glad of the distraction it offered. His dear friend of twenty years, Mrs Arbuthnot, had died of cholera.

It was she who had commented previously "that it can never be right that the First Lord of the Treasury should be consulted as to who should be Colonel of the Life Guards".

Peel landed in England on 9 December, and Wellington gave up all his offices, except the Foreign Secretaryship. When Peel went out and Melbourne came in, Wellington was out of office. He had been a minister for the last time. Many times he was asked to serve, sometimes he was tempted, but—apart from anything else—increasing deafness made it impossible. The magic of his name remained.

When he was seventy-one, the King of Prussia asked him to command the armies of the German Confederation. Europe had not yet produced a soldier to match his fame. Then, in 1837, William IV died and a strong-willed girl named Victoria was Queen. She might have been expected to turn to the old war-horse but, instead, she succumbed to the charm and kindness of Lord Melbourne.

As the years passed, the Duke's influence in Parliament grew less; when Peel and the Tories came back to power in 1841, Wellington had a seat in the Cabinet, although he had no Department of State. But in the hours of crisis his steadying voice was ready to moderate counsels. "The King's"—later, the Queen's—"government must go on", and he was the servant retained to see that it was so.

"He was willing," wrote Lord Rosebery, "to press any measure of any character that might be considered necessary in the public interest, without reference to his own opinions. He emancipated Roman Catholics in the teeth of his former professions: he was accessory to the repeal of the Corn Laws, a repeal to which he was extremely averse: he was ready to pass a Reform Bill which he regarded as the ruin of the country. He cannot therefore be regarded as a party politician at all."*

He was a prince in the Netherlands, a duke in France, Spain and Portugal, a marshal of seven European armies and a Knight of twenty-four orders, in addition to his British honours. It is probable, however, that none of these distinctions were equal in his mind to being an English—or Irish—gentleman. One day, when he was

---

* Rosebery. *Lord Randolph Churchill*, p. 122.

38 The Duke of Wellington's funeral procession passing Apsley House. Lithograph by T. Picken.

old, a man helped him across Hyde Park Corner. "My Lord," he said, "never did I hope to reach the day when I might be of some assistance to the greatest man that ever lived."

"Don't be a damned fool," said the Duke of Wellington.

He died peacefully on 14 September, 1852, at Walmer Castle, which Queen Victoria called the most uncomfortable house she was ever in and which Lord Curzon called "that charnel house". The Duke's funeral procession from Chelsea Hospital to St Paul's was a splendid spectacle, witnessed by a vast crowd, although the huge funeral car, the design of which was inspired by the Prince Consort, was thought by some judges to be abominably ugly.

XXII

❧ CHARLES, 2nd Earl Grey ❧

1830–34

As a young man of a family of Northumbrian landed gentry, born 13 March, 1764, Charles Grey was elected MP for Northumberland in 1786. At the time he was on the Grand Tour, after being educated at Eton and Trinity, Cambridge. He represented Northumberland for the next twenty years. His father, a soldier, had by then become a general, a Privy Councillor and (1801) a peer. The Greys were moderate Tories, but young Charles drifted towards the Whigs, the faction of Charles James Fox and the "Friends of the People", who hoped, by promoting a measure of moderate reform, to avoid the danger of radical reform. Of this movement, Grey became the leader. Later, he regarded his association with the Friends as a boyish folly.

He was opposed to the war against the French which the younger Pitt was conducting, but his chief interest was in Parliamentary Reform. Young Grey made an impressive debut in the House of Commons: his first speech had "an éclat that has not been equalled in my recollection", Addington reported. He was, too, a young man of independent character, opposing Pitt on the suspension of Habeas Corpus and the rest of the Six Acts invoked to defend society against the wave of disorder that followed the French Revolution. He fell out with the Prince of Wales, whose grant he wanted to reduce from £65,000 to £40,000; and he resisted the project for a Parliamentary Union with Ireland.

Then, in 1800, he seemed to lose his interest in the Reform movement. He lived more and more in the family estate at Howick in Northumberland and resisted the attempts of Fox to persuade him to come nearer London. With his wife, Elizabeth Ponsonby (whom he married in 1784), and their brood of fifteen children, he enjoyed life in his northern fastness, four days' journey from London.

As a handsome and elegant young man, he had pursued the beauties of the Whig drawing rooms in Mayfair; he had been the lover of the Duchess of Devonshire; he had known the heady appeal of the Prince of Wales's set at Carlton House. Now all that was changed. London, he decided, did not agree with his health; in Northumberland, he was happy with his wife and children. "If idleness is the best gift of God to man," he told his leader, Fox, "there was never anybody so highly favoured of heaven." The Parliamentary movement for Reform, linked as it was with a demand for peace with post-Revolution France, wilted during the years of French military expansion on the Continent. Grey, in 1807, he found the whole idea of a political career repulsive to him. Then his friends, the Foxites, overthrew the government and formed the short-lived administration, misnamed the Ministry of

39 Georgiana, Duchess of Devonshire with her daughter, by Sir Joshua Reynolds.

All the Talents. Grey had become the First Lord of the Admiralty in 1806 and then Foreign Secretary. He was not long in office, although he managed to push a bill through Parliament abolishing the slave trade.

In March, 1807, Grey asked leave to bring in a bill which would have allowed Catholics into the army and navy. The King would not have it and dismissed the ministers. Grey was now in Opposition, and remained there for almost a quarter of a century.

He had succeeded to his father's peerage in 1828 and to the family baronetcy and the properties that went with it. He enjoyed life in the country. His wife's death in 1824 was, in fact, one of the blows that brought to an end an indolent way of life. But until the death of George IV, he could not hope for a place in government. He had criticized the King violently over the repudiation of Mrs Fitzherbert, he had denounced Lady Hertford, then the reigning mistress, as an "unseen and pestilent influence that lurked behind the throne". These were offences which could not be forgiven.

But, in 1830, the King died and the Duke of Wellington's Tory government was defeated in a general election. The whole picture was changed. William IV sent for Grey. By then he was a man of sixty-six, who had held no office for twenty-four years. His Cabinet was, of necessity, composed largely of men belonging to a new generation, men he hardly knew: Whigs, older (Holland) and younger (Althorp,

40 Charles, 2nd Earl Grey. After Sir Thomas Lawrence.

Sir Robert Walpole. Studio of J.B. van Loo

John Stuart, 3rd Earl of Bute, by J. Reynolds

The House of Lords: *The Trial of Queen Caroline, 1820,* by G. Hayter

The Death of the Earl of Chatham, by J.S. Copley

George Canning, by T. Lawrence

Arthur Wellesley, Duke of Wellington, celebrating the birthday of his godson, Prince Arthur, and the opening of the Great Exhibition. *First of May, 1851*, by F. Winterhalter. Reproduced by gracious permission of Her Majesty the Queen.

The House of Commons, 1833, by G. Hayter

William Lamb, 2nd Viscount Melbourne, by T. Lawrence

The Burning of the Houses of Parliament, 1834, by J.M.W. Turner

Sir Robert Peel, 2nd Baronet, by J. Linnell

Benjamin Disraeli, Earl of Beaconsfield, by J.E. Millais

William Ewart Gladstone, by J.E. Millais

Robert Gascoyne-Cecil, 3rd Marquis of Salisbury, by J.E. Millais

David Lloyd George, by W. Orpen

Stanley, Graham); Canningites, like Melbourne and Palmerston; a Radical (Durham, Grey's son-in-law) and a Tory (Richmond), and Brougham, an eccentric and contentious character, who was Lord Chancellor. It was an aristocratic gathering, every member of which had an hereditary title, and it owned, Grey said, more acres of English land than any of its predecessors. It put on the Statute Book, before Grey resigned four years later, what was probably the most important single piece of legislation of the century—the Reform Bill. By it he proposed to wipe out sixty boroughs and halve the membership of others, distributing the seats which they lost among other areas which had been under-represented or not represented at all. The effect was that the existing number of half-a-million voters was almost doubled.

His introduction of the bill to the Commons on 1 March, 1831, was the signal for an immense political upheaval in the country. The King had to be persuaded not to oppose; the Radicals conceded that this measure, which they were bound to regard as inadequate, was the best that they could get in the circumstances. The middle sections of opinion, represented in the government by Lord Brougham, said that the alternative to it was anarchy. In this bill, Grey, after long years spent in rural seclusion, realized the aim of his youth.

The progress of the bill through Parliament was dramatic. The Second Reading was carried by a single vote. Grey addressed the House in the stately periods of a bygone age. Brougham, the Lord Chancellor, ended his speech with a peroration in which, falling on his knees and with outstretched hands, he implored the peers not to throw out the bill. Unluckily, in order to stimulate his eloquence, he had, during his speech, drunk a whole bottle of mulled port, with the result that once on his knees he found he was unable to get up until assisted by his embarrassed colleagues.

In spite of Brougham and Grey, a destructive amendment was carried. At once, Grey asked the King to dissolve Parliament. The King agreed. The Reformers won the subsequent general election. A second Reform Bill was presented to Parliament, was carried in the Commons and sent to the Lords, who rejected it by forty-one votes. The King asked Grey not to resign but, at the same time, said that he would not consent to the bill being passed by the creation of new peers.

The Cabinet was split between those who wanted a weaker bill and those who demanded that the King should create enough peers to ensure that the bill got through as it stood. Cabinet meetings were rowdy. Lord Durham, very rich, very rude ("Radical Jack"), screamed abuse at his father-in-law, Grey. "If I'd been Lord Grey," commented Lord Melbourne, "I'd have knocked him down." But it was Grey's duty, and achievement, to keep the Cabinet together.

Meanwhile the country seethed with disaffection. Grey was unwilling to make any major concessions on the bill while, on the creation of new peers, he was in two minds. In Queen Anne's reign a dozen peers had been created to save Harley's government; now a much greater number would be needed to save the country from the social upheaval which, as Grey saw it, would come if Reform was defeated. And the King was reluctant to make new peers, certainly on the scale that was needed to see the bill through the Lords.

Grey's amended bill passed the Lords by nine votes, in April, 1832; a wrecking motion was carried soon after. Grey then offered the King a choice between the government's resignation and the creation of peers. The King preferred the first but, when the Duke of Wellington reported that he could not form a government, wrote a letter agreeing to create enough peers to pass the bill, first calling up peers' eldest sons. Faced by this promise, or threat, many peers abstained from voting and the bill was passed. The Tory seats in the Lords were empty that day. It was the supreme achievement of Grey's ministry and of his long career in politics.

London had for long been uncongenial to him. Now his health began to wilt. The tension in which he had lived during the long struggle to save his bill from King, peers and Radicals, while revolution growled in the streets outside—this began to tell. He resigned in July, 1834, and was succeeded by Lord Melbourne. Yet the Reform Act, although undoubtedly the chief work of his government, was not its sole accomplishment. Slavery was abolished in the British Empire by an Act of 1833, two million pounds compensation being paid to the slave-owners. In the same year the first effective Factory Act was passed. When Grey drove north in his coach to his beloved Howick, he could look back on a tremendous burst of legislation which had transformed, in a matter of months, the structure—and, as it proved—the nature of British politics, and had opened the door to a new era of change. Change, and not tranquillity. The hopes that Grey had cherished that the improved electoral system would appease social animosities were not realized.

Problems remained, but they were problems for a new generation. King William, the silly old man who sat on Britain's throne, chose Lord Melbourne as his new Prime Minister and Grey left politics for ever. Grey was an old man now, although still, as Creevey thought, "the best dressed and handsomest man in England!" He died at Howick (17 July, 1845), ten years after his resignation, and was survived by ten of his fifteen children.

41 The Reform Banquet, 1832, by B. R. Haydon.

XXIII

❧ WILLIAM LAMB, 2nd Viscount Melbourne ❧

1834; 1835–39; 1839–41

"I think it's a damned bore," said Lord Melbourne to his low-life friend, Tom Young. "I am in many minds as to what to do."

King William IV had just invited him to call to discuss forming a government.

"If it only lasts three months," Young replied, "it will be worth while to have been Prime Minister of England." "By God, that's true," said Melbourne. "I'll go."

And so a Prime Minister was made from unlikely material. He lasted, not three months, but six years.

Unlikely except, of course, that he was a Whig and the Whigs had, by that time (1834), come back to what they regarded as their natural place in the scheme of things, as rulers of England.

The Whigs were not, strictly speaking, a party, rather a caste. They were aristocratic, for instance, regarding the royal family without undue respect; rich; tolerant; insolent; easy-going in morals; anti-clerical. "Things have come to a pretty pass," said Melbourne, "when religion is allowed to invade the sphere of private life." Whigs believed passionately in liberty and not much else.

Their headquarters were Brooks's Club and a few great houses, for instance, Devonshire House, Panshanger, Holland House. Indulgent hostesses, who combined an interest in politics with a talent for flirtation, were essential to the Whig system.

William Lamb (born 15 March, 1779), who, in due course, became Lord Melbourne, was indolent, clever and very good-looking. The Lambs were not of the old Whig aristocracy, the family having been founded three generations before by a successful Nottingham attorney. William Lamb's father, the first Lord Melbourne, bought his way into Parliament; his mother, Elizabeth Milbanke, had six children, of whom only one, the eldest, was certainly a Lamb. Elizabeth was, Byron said, "a sort of modern Aspasia". "Not chaste, not chaste," her son, William, conceded. William's father was probably the rich, eccentric Lord Egremont; his brother, George, was reputedly sired by the Prince of Wales. The parentage of others is hazier. The family, perhaps for that reason, was a happy one.

William, after Eton and Cambridge, spent two years at Glasgow University—for the war with France put the Grand Tour out of the question. Glasgow, he found a dirty town; as for his fellow-students—"the truth is," he told his mother, "that the Scotch universities are very much calculated to make a man vain, important and pedantic . . . you cannot have the advantages of study and the world together."

42 Lady Caroline Lamb, by Thomas Phillips.

William was heading for the Bar—he had one brief, at a guinea, when the death of his eldest brother made him heir to the peerage. From that moment, it was clear that politics was likely to be his destiny.

As a youth, he shared all the prejudices of a follower of Fox. Thus, he hoped that Napoleon would beat the British. Aged twenty-six, he was MP for Leominster.

By that time he was married to Lady Caroline Ponsonby, pretty, blonde and wild, the daughter of Lady Bessborough. The marriage was a disaster: "he good-natured, eccentric and not nice; she profligate, romantic and comical" (Greville). The girl's wildness developed into something like madness. Their only child, Augustus, was a mental defective.

One evening in 1812, Caroline met Lord Byron at a party and decided that he was "mad, bad and dangerous to know", in other words, that he must become her lover. This he did. In a very short time, the ensuing liaison was all the talk of the fashionable world and Byron, who had no intention of settling down to a steady life of fashionable adultery, found himself in the clutches of a woman's reckless passion. From it, he escaped with some difficulty, while Caroline went on to adventures steadily less respectable and more absurd.

William Lamb watched the business with cynical distaste and with a sympathy with his wife's vagaries that went far beyond the limits of tolerance expected of a Whig nobleman. Even her authorship of a novel, *Glenarvon*, which was a thinly veiled account of her affair with Byron and contained unkind portraits of the Melbourne family and their friends—although it led to Caroline's exclusion from polite society, i.e. Almack's—did not bring about a separation. He remained captivated by the impossible woman. It was part of the casualness, indolence, flippancy, which, it seemed, would prevent him getting anywhere in public life. His brother-in-law, Lord Palmerston, complained that "he ate too much and took no exercise".*

Meanwhile, like other men of his time and class, Melbourne experienced the shock of the French Revolution, which showed that "Progress" could have an ugly face. Anyone who doubts the turmoil that events in Paris caused in British opinion at the time has only to read the letters of Horace Walpole (who had sympathized with the American Revolution). "Indeed, Madam," he wrote to Lady Ossory, "there is not a word left in my dictionary that can express what I feel. Savages, barbarians etc. were terms for poor ignorant Indians, Blacks and Hyenas . . . It remained for the enlightened eighteenth century to baffle language and invent horrors that can be found in no vocabulary."† And so on, in mounting indignation. The Whigs were divided into those who would resist France and those who were against making war on her. Lamb, as a moderate, divided in his sympathies, believed that Canning would provide the kind of government he wanted. But, in 1812, the Prince Regent opted for the Tories and the House of Commons agreed with him. Canning was excluded in favour of Lord Liverpool. Lamb resigned his seat in August of that year. It was just

---

* But Palmerston's own performance at the table was not to be despised. In the last year of his life he ate, at one sitting: two plates of turtle soup; cod with oyster sauce; pâté; two slices of roast mutton; a slice of ham; pheasant; pudding; jelly; dressed oranges and half a large pear.

† R. W. Ketton-Cremer. *Horace Walpole*, p. 305.

four months after *Childe Harold* had made Byron the most famous poet in Europe and a magnet attracting every nymphomaniac in London. It was well that Lamb was out of politics during the next four years, at the end of which *Glenarvon* appeared. On this, Lamb swore he would never see Caroline again—a promise he did not keep.

He became MP for Northampton. Caroline did not die until January, 1828. By that time, Lamb was Secretary for Ireland in Canning's government; he was Lord Melbourne, having inherited the title from his father in 1828. It seemed that, after all his miseries, he was going to realize the political promise which George IV and Castlereagh had predicted for him. But the easy-going, ironical nature which had enabled him to survive his marriage still counted against him.

He remained in Dublin for a year, just long enough for him to embark on an affair with a beautiful lady, the wife of an Irish peer who was also a clergyman, Lord Branden. The husband was willing to overlook his wife's transgression, provided Melbourne would arrange that he should be made a bishop. But this proved to be unnecessary. The evidence against Melbourne was flimsy and the judge dismissed the case. How deep the affair went is not certain, although it should be noted that Melbourne left Lady Branden an annuity in his will.

While he was in Ireland, the ministries of Canning and Goderich ran their course and, when it was plain that the Duke of Wellington, the succeeding Prime Minister, had brought in a purely Tory régime, Melbourne resigned.

In 1830, he was Home Secretary in Lord Grey's government, responsible for law and order in the country during the riotous days of the Reform Bill, a measure about which his scepticism was extreme. It would lead, he thought, to the complete destruction of free speech; besides bringing about rule by the middle classes, which would be worse than rule by the aristocracy. "All his notions were aristocratic and he has not a particle of sympathy for what was called Progressive Reform."* The rotten boroughs were, as he saw it, essential to carrying on a government. But what was inevitable, as Reform was, must be accepted. As a Canningite, a middle-of-the-road man, he was convinced of that. In any case, his hands were full keeping agitation and disorder within bounds. This he did with the utmost thoroughness.

When Grey gave up in 1834, Melbourne became Prime Minister, as "the only man of whom none of us would be jealous", as Lord Durham said. His popularity stemmed from his manifest lack of ambition. Dissensions in the Cabinet and the death of Earl Spencer, which meant that Lord Althorp must go to the Lords, gave the King the excuse to dismiss the government in November, 1834, a coup which Melbourne greeted with laughter; that night he went off to the theatre with the greatest nonchalance in the world. "I am not surprised at his [the King's] decision," he told Lord Grey, "nor do I know that I can entirely condemn it."

Peel came into office and the Tories won a general election, but not by a big enough margin over the other parties to give Peel a majority in the House. In consequence, Melbourne became a reluctant Prime Minister once more in March, 1835.

Two difficulties faced him in forming his Cabinet: Lord Durham and Lord Brougham, the first wealthy and contentious, a disloyal colleague; the second an uncouth, rowdy Scots lawyer, "leaving a trail of bad faith and bad blood wherever he

---

* Charles Greville. *Diary.*

**43 The Hon. Mrs Norton,
by Landseer.**

went".* Both men were likely to be sources of trouble to Melbourne, as they had been to Grey. He sent the one to Canada and to the other he refused—to Brougham's incredulous rage—the Lord Chancellorship.

Melbourne set up new standards in the distribution of higher patronage ("Confound it, does he want a Garter for his *other* leg?"). For a man whose religious feelings were not strong, he was unusually fastidious in appointing the bishops, who, he said, "positively died to vex me".†

His government was disliked by the King and was not strengthened when Melbourne appeared for the second time as co-respondent in a divorce case, this time in an action brought by the Hon. George Norton against his wife, Caroline, the beautiful grand-daughter of the great Sheridan.

This lady lived in a charming little flat in Storey's Gate, a few minutes from the Houses of Parliament. She supported herself by writing. Every evening, on his way home, Melbourne called in to see her. Sometimes she came to see him in the house he

---

* David Cecil. *Melbourne*, p. 294.
† Norman Gash, *Politics in the Age of Peel.* p. 344.

had taken in South Street. It seems, however, that, against appearances, their relations did not go beyond friendship.

Resisting one lover, Mrs Norton had said, "Adultery is a crime, not a recreation." It is likely that she applied the same stern principle to her dealings with Melbourne. Norton's action against his wife was weakened by the fact that he had ushered Melbourne to her bedroom when she was ill and he had accompanied her to Melbourne's house in South Street. In the court, Melbourne was acquitted.

But his brother wrote to his sister, "Do not let William think himself invulnerable for having got off again this time. No man's luck can go further." The Lamb family was, apparently, not as convinced as the judge of William's innocence.

In June, 1837, the political scene changed for Melbourne and Britain. King William died and was succeeded by Queen Victoria, an impulsive, naïve and strong-willed girl of eighteen. Melbourne became her guide and mentor, and she filled an empty niche in his emotional life. One woman had hurt him deeply, no other had taken her place. He had fathered one child, who had died mad. Now this girl, whose youth and immaturity were so touchingly disproportionate to the greatness of her destiny, came as one who appealed to his loyalty and his affection. For no Tory was more romantic at heart than this Whig.

So the strange, cynical old man, who had lounged in Brooks's and exchanged epigrams with Lady Holland, who could look back on Devonshire House at its most alluring and Carlton House at its most raffish, responded with all the warmth of his nature to a strait-laced girl.

To train a queen at that moment in Britain's political development was no easy task—she could not be a sovereign as George III had been, or even as William IV had been; the ground was moving fast under the throne. But what could she be, what should she try to be? Only the girl herself, with her excitable, obstinate nature, could —and did—supply the answer. But, in the process, the calming and reassuring counsels of her Prime Minister were incalculably useful, the man who was seen by one of his successors* at her coronation, "with his coronet cocked over his nose, his robe under his feet and holding the great sword of state like a butcher".

He could be candid with the girl, as when she wanted to make Prince Albert a King Consort and Melbourne, who knew his people, said, "For God's sake, let's have no more of it, Ma'am. If you once get the English people into the way of making Kings, you'll get them into the way of unmaking them." For titles and honours he had the cool disparagement of the aristocrat. "The Garter!" he exclaimed. "What would be the good of my taking it? I cannot bribe myself." However, he had one word of praise for the Garter: "there is no damned merit in it."

The serious Queen was getting her first lessons in statecraft from an elderly man who combined the no-nonsense approach of the old Whig nobility (suitably bowdlerized for young ears) with the charm of an affectionate uncle. He was a wonderful tutor for an inexperienced monarch. It was, perhaps, the greatest service he rendered as a Prime Minister.

Apart from that, his administration was not a spectacular success. In the deplorable business where Lady Flora Hastings, lady-in-waiting to the Queen's

---

* Disraeli.

44 Queen Victoria riding out with Lord Melbourne, by Sir Francis Grant.

disturbed mother, the Duchess of Kent, was supposed, wrongly, to be pregnant, Melbourne did not, or could not, prevent Victoria from rushing into uncharitable assumptions. When these were proved to be mistaken, the Queen's popularity suffered. It was one of those occasions in which Melbourne, as a man of the world, might have saved his charge from making a blunder.

In due course, what was inevitable happened. The Queen fell in love and married. Melbourne's reign as her mentor was over. In 1841 he resigned and appealed to the country. The country rejected him. Seven years later, he died (5 November, 1848), after a stroke.

He had been a statesman in a period of tumultuous and perilous transition, when the smouldering fire of discontent might easily have flared up into revolution. That it did not do so is, in some measure, due to the mixture of dexterous retreat and firm repression which he applied to the changing situation, and which conformed to his temperament, composed as it was of indolence and intelligence. He cannot be said to have contributed greatly to constitutional development, with one possible exception.

When the Corn Laws were being discussed, he shouted up the stairs to his colleagues, after a Cabinet dinner: "Now, is it to lower the price of corn, or isn't it? It is not much matter which we say, but mind, we must all say *the same*." In that remark can be found in the embryo the doctrine of the collective responsibility of the Cabinet.

> For a patriot too cool, for a drudge disobedient,
> And too fond of the right to pursue the expedient.

Goldsmith's lines on Burke might be applied to Melbourne. Fond of his family and plundered by his servants, he was also jealous and touchy, "mortified" (for example) "at not being asked to join Lord John Russell's government".

With Melbourne, the Whig aristocracy bowed out. The future lay with the manufacturers and the middle class, whose representative man was Sir Robert Peel.

XXIV

❧ SIR ROBERT PEEL, 2nd Baronet ❧

1834–35; 1841–46

Autumn, 1830. Britain was in ferment. Wellington's ministry had collapsed. From France there had come, that summer, ominous news of revolution. Would it cross the Channel? Already there had been rioting. A man of forty-two wrote from his Staffordshire property:

"There is yet hope that, by diligently reading the lessons that have been written in blood at Bristol, that class of People which has neither Property nor sense may learn the risk or rather the certain price of revolutions . . . I wish you would come and see us here and watch the tardy progress of my new house. I am just importing carbines, as I mean to defend my old one as long as I can."

The writer, Sir Robert Peel, Bart, was not the only man who was taking precautions just then. The Duke of Newcastle had mobilized two hundred men and ten cannon to defend his house at Clumber. At Belvoir, an artillery sergeant drilled the Duke of Rutland's servants every day.

Peel was not one of the old aristocracy, Whig or Tory. He was the son of the industrial revolution, his father having made a vast fortune in cotton manufacture, a fact which Peel's political enemies did not forget. "Spinning Jenny," they said. Sir Robert Peel was born on 5 February, 1788, at Chamber Hall, Bury, of a Lancashire family which had been in the cotton industry from the beginning, and he had been at school (Harrow) with Byron and Palmerston: after that, he was at Christ Church (double first in Classics and Mathematics). In 1809, aged twenty-one, he was MP for the pocket borough of Cashel, Tipperary. Next year he was Under-Secretary for the Colonies and War.

When Lord Liverpool became Prime Minister, he made Peel Chief Secretary for Ireland, in which post he served for six years.

In a period when war and revolution made a policy of repression seem the merest necessity of good government, young Peel was as firm as anyone. In Ireland, he was known as "Orange Peel". He said of the Peterloo incident* that "it was better that blood should have been shed than that the meeting should have proceeded". His political aphorisms revealed a conservative temperament and a deep distrust of enthusiasm: "No government can exist which does not control and restrain the popular sentiments . . . The longer I live, the more clearly do I see the folly of yielding a rash and precipitate assent to any political measure."

---

* When yeomanry charged a crowd at St Peter's Fields, Manchester, killing a dozen (16 August 1819).

It was not difficult to guess where a man holding these opinions would be likely to stand in an age of tempestuous and accelerating change. He was, inevitably, a Tory, but, as it turned out, a reforming Tory, who knew that the industrial England which was growing up was different from the agricultural community of squires and peasants that had preceded it.

As Home Secretary (1822) he ended the system of espionage which the government had employed against workmen; he abolished the death penalty for a hundred crimes; he organized an efficient civilian police force.

By that time, he had married Julia Floyd, a young woman of great beauty to whom he remained devoted for the rest of his life. They had five sons and two daughters. He was listened to with great respect in the Commons, but his relations with his fellow-members remained stiff and formal. When she came to the throne, Queen Victoria found him unattractive, perhaps because his manner seemed cold after the avuncular ease of Lord Melbourne.

45 Julia, Lady Peel, by Sir Thomas Lawrence.

On the great question of Catholic Emancipation, he remained unconvinced of the need for reform. But he was a man who could be taught by events; as his great admirer, the French statesman Guizot, said, he was "a man of essentially practical mind, consulting facts at every step as the mariner consults the face of heaven". In time, the imminent danger of civil war in Ireland convinced him that it was necessary to make concessions to Catholic feeling. He prepared the bills that were required, resigned his seat and was re-elected. After this obeisance to constitutional niceties, he got his bill through. He was at this time Home Secretary in the Duke of Wellington's government. The Duke looked on his colleague with less than complete enthusiasm: "How are we to get on? I have no small talk and Peel has no manners."

With or without manners, the old soldier and the man from cotton Lancashire worked together until the Duke's government was defeated in 1830 and the Whigs, with Lord Grey at their head, came into power. At the same time, Peel inherited his father's fortune. He was now one of the richest men in England, proud owner of a fine estate at Drayton in Staffordshire, which he was steadily improving and on which he was building a new and splendid house.

The Reform Bill went through, the Tory peers having agreed not to embarrass William IV by forcing him to create enough new peers to pass it. After a general election, Peel found himself back in the House of Commons, leading a sadly diminished Tory party. He did so with success. In 1834, Greville said of him, "Peel's is an enviable position; in the prime of life, with an immense fortune, *facile princeps* in the House of Commons, universally regarded as the ablest man . . . the moment he rises all is silence, and he is sure of being heard with profound attention and respect." These events followed with bewildering speed: Grey resigned, Melbourne was dismissed and a courier was sent to find Peel, who was at that time on holiday somewhere in Italy. Finally, he was located in Rome and he returned to London in haste.

He was in office as Prime Minister (1834) for just a hundred days. It seemed to be a momentous change from the old days of the aristocracy, but—"What was the grand charge against myself—that the King had sent for the son of a cotton-spinner in order to make him Prime Minister . . . Ought it not make you, gentlemen, do all you can to reserve to other sons of other cotton-spinners the same opportunities of arriving at the like honourable destination?"

In opposition once more (1835) Peel devoted himself to the problem of building up a strong, moderate Conservative party. He attracted Stanley, Disraeli and Gladstone and, by 1838, was asked by Queen Victoria to form a government. However, there was a disagreement between the young monarch and the Conservative leader. She wanted to keep unchanged the ladies of her household; he insisted that they—some of whom were wives or daughters of his political opponents—should be changed. On this trifling issue, Peel was excluded from office and Melbourne resumed his sway. The crisis showed the character and the limitations of the two leading personages: the young Queen, angry and bewildered at having lost her much loved guide, Melbourne; the middle-class politician, conscious of the Queen's dislike of him and stubbornly refusing to yield to her on any point, however minor, which might contain an element of principle. Even when it was all over, when Melbourne for the second time had been driven from office, when the Prince Consort had appeared on the scene and had smoothed out the disagreements over Court appointments, the two were uncomfortable with one another: "He is shy with me, and makes me shy with him," she said, while Greville, watching at a Privy Council, observed that Peel could not help putting himself into "his accustomed attitude of a dancing master giving a lesson". Looking back as an old woman on the episode of her Bedchamber ladies, the Queen said, "Yes, I was very hot about it and so were my ladies; but I was very young, only twenty, and never should have acted so again. Yes, it was a mistake!"

As Prime Minister in 1841, Peel had graver problems to deal with than a sulky and scared young Queen. There was widespread distress in the industrial areas; Chartism; anti-Corn Law propaganda. Peel's first Budget imposed an income tax of sevenpence in the pound and big cuts in indirect taxes. It was immediately popular. He followed it with a succession of Budgets which continued the progress towards Free Trade.

The most critical decision he made was to repeal the Corn Laws, which prohibited the import of foreign wheat except when the price was unusually high in the home market. In 1842, he altered the scale of duty on wheat imports, so that the price of corn was reduced. The reduction was not thought to be enough. In that year, there was widespread distress in the country and disturbances resembling those of 1830. Peel was particularly worried because his wife and children were in Staffordshire and when he went to see her he was alarmed by a false report that the Queen had been assassinated.

Busy organizing the defence of public order in London, where a mob was in the streets, Peel begged his wife to come to town, which he thought was safer than Staffordshire: "Do not run the slightest risk, for your presence could not add to the security of the house." Julia, his wife, reassured him: "Mr Bonham sent us some carbines and ammunition by a most trustworthy person." The crisis passed, but three years later, in 1845, Peel faced an even graver situation: the English wheat harvest was ruined. The Irish potato crop was attacked by disease. In these conditions, he determined to abolish all protection for agriculture; to repeal the Corn Laws. It was an extraordinarily bold step for a Conservative Prime Minister, the traditional guardian of the landed interest. On the Tory benches there was dismay. The Duke of Wellington grumbled, "Rotten potatoes have done it all. They have put Peel in his damned fright." And Melbourne complained to the Queen, "Ma'am, it's a damned dishonest act." The Queen was amused.

With the help of his political opponents he passed the necessary bills. He was instantly popular in the country. There were cheers in London and glowing leading articles in the provincial press.

Peel's belief was that social legislation, like charity, was not the way to tackle the misery in the industrial areas: "We must make this country a cheap country for living." In the meantime, the turmoil persisted. Peel's private secretary was shot and killed in Whitehall by a deranged Scotsman, who had arrived in London for the purpose of killing the Prime Minister. Peel assured the Queen that he was not anxious for his own safety: he walked home every night from the House of Commons and had not "met with any obstruction". However, Lady Peel, shocked and worried, took to her bed.

Peel was the first of a new kind of political leader. He was an earnest, strenuous, devout Low Church Anglican; for him, politics was essentially a moral exercise, a fact which distinguished him from Melbourne, Wellington and Palmerston, and which was at the root of his deep concern with the industrial population and its miseries. He was, it may be said, the first truly Victorian Prime Minister, imbued by nature with the serious vein of feeling which was expressed in a contemporary revival of religion among Anglicans and Nonconformists alike. Peel was essentially middle class, the product of a business community, as familiar with ledgers as with the classics. He had seen the country through two great crises, the Reform Bill and the repeal of the Corn Laws. He had done so by estranging half of his party. But a political situation had been created which an adroit and ruthless rival could exploit against him. This rival in due course appeared. Disraeli. He had a profound respect for Peel's gift as a Parliamentarian, who "played on the House of Commons as on an old fiddle", but he understood the basic weakness of Peel's position as a Conservative leader in the age that was opening. There was an element of personal animosity in Disraeli's onslaught. Peel had refused to give him office. He attacked Peel on the ground that he had been elected as a Conservative and had pursued Liberal policies.

The limitations which Peel's temperament and prejudices put upon his action as a party leader were revealed after the repeal of the Corn Laws in 1846, when Cobden urged him to dissolve Parliament and go to the country with the slogan, "Peel and Free Trade". Peel replied that, if he had come to embody an idea, he must be careful not to use his power for any personal object.

He was, at last, defeated in the House. When the result of the voting was whispered to him, he was watched by an interested observer.*

"Sir Robert did not reply, or even turn his head. He looked very grave, and extended his chin as was his habit when he was annoyed, and cared not to speak. He began to comprehend his position." He resigned, surprised and, it may be, shocked by the violence of Disraeli's attack on him. It is certain, too, that he was exhausted by the burdens that had fallen on him as Prime Minister. He retired to his country seat and did not attend Parliament often.

Thomas Carlyle met him about this time and wrote in his diary, "I consider him by far our first Public Man, which indeed is saying little, and hope that England in these frightful times may get some good of him."

In 1850, a skittish horse threw him over its head on Constitution Hill and he died two days later in his house in Whitehall Gardens (2 July, 1850).

"For a quarter of a century at least," Godwin Smith wrote of him, "he was without question the first public servant of England."

---

* Disraeli.

XXV

⚜ LORD JOHN RUSSELL ⚜

1846–52; 1865–66

The Russells, as a woman member of the family once confessed, "are very odd people". They are a class of aristocratic rebels, who can never forget that once they made a revolution. Lord John Russell was not the least strange of them. He was born (18 August, 1792) in Hertford Street, Westminster, third son of the sixth Duke of Bedford, and grew to be a frail little man, just 5 feet 4¾ inches tall, weighing eight stone. In later life, for obvious reasons, he was a caricaturist's joy. When he stood for Parliament the electors thought him too short, but accepted his explanation that he had been taller but "was worn away by the anxieties and struggles of the Reform Bill". After a year at Westminster School, where he found life was hard, his education was entrusted to a chaplain; aged seventeen, he was sent reluctantly to Edinburgh University, which, to his surprise, he liked very much. This was followed by extensive travels in Southern Europe, during which he rode with Wellington at Torres Vedras and had a long conversation with Napoleon on Elba. On that occasion, according to a family tradition, Lord John, aged twenty-two, told Napoleon at length about the Russell family; Napoleon made no comment, but went to a corner of the room and relieved himself. Lord John's account of the interview allows Napoleon a greater share of the conversation. What Napoleon thought about his visitor is unknown, but it is clear, however, that Lord John was, even at that age, a self-sufficient young man.

After all, he was already an MP (Whig) for the family borough of Tavistock. However, his health at that time was bad, and he spent more time on foreign travel or in writing than he did at the House of Commons. He lost Tavistock in the election of 1830, the local Wesleyans having taken exception to a remark of his on prayer. He published a novel, *The Nun of Arronca*, and a five-act play in blank verse, *Don Carlos*, which was never acted. Disraeli, years later, said the novel was "the feeblest romance in our literature" and *Don Carlos* was "the feeblest tragedy in our language". About the same time, Russell wrote a biography of his ancestor, Lord William Russell, executed in 1683, after the discovery of the Rye House Plot, which was aimed at the murder of Charles II and his brother James.

In those years, the frail little man was occupying himself much as other young men did: pursuing women and seeking the hand in marriage of girls of his own class. There is talk, but hardly any evidence, of illegitimate children. He was turned down by Lady Holland's daughter and by Lady Emily Cowper.

46 Lord John Russell, by Sir Francis Grant.

Intellectually and socially, Lord John was more than presentable; but as a person he was awkward and hard to live with. As his brother told him: "You are a man of settled pursuits and habits—a gidding, flirting, dressing, ball-going wife would be the devil." The impression he made on his male contemporaries was that of an exaggerated coolness. Sydney Smith described the impression he gave: "He would perform the operation for the stone, build St Paul's, or assume the command of the Channel Fleet and no one would discover from his manner that the patient had died, the church tumbled down and the Fleet had been knocked to atoms." Forty years later, Lord John still resented the gibe.

He was extraordinarily touchy when anyone else was given the credit (e.g., for the Reform Bill) which he thought was his due. It was his speech introducing the bill which made him well known; indeed, it may be said that then, in 1832, when he was forty, his popularity was at its peak. In 1835 there was an election and in Devonshire, where his constituency was situated, Lord John fell madly in love with a beautiful little widow named Lady Ribblesdale. After a headlong courtship, he married her. He was forty-three. By her he had two daughters. She died in 1838.

The election did not go well. On one of the Whigs' flanks, Peel's Tories strengthened their hold; on the other, the Radicals made gains. Peel became Prime Minister until Melbourne replaced him, with Lord John as his Home Secretary and Leader of the Commons. His manners made him unpopular in the House.

> "Next, cool and all unconscious of reproach,
> Comes the calm of Johnny who upset the coach,"

wrote Lord Lytton in the *New Timon*. He was disliked, too, by King William, who believed that he was bent on undermining the rights of the church in Ireland. In 1846, the Irish Famine and the failure of the grain crops in England produced a collapse of the Peel government and Lord John became Prime Minister, dedicated to a Free Trade policy, although he had only about 250 supporters in the House of Commons. However, the Opposition was hopelessly divided.

The Irish Famine was followed by a financial panic; gold had poured out of the country to buy corn in Russia and America; in consequence there was a run on the banks in 1847. Lord John, who did not understand finance, explained what was happening to the Prince Consort. Peel was called in, who explained the workings of the Bank Act to both of them. Chartism surged up; in London, a monster demonstration was held on Kensington Common. At this critical moment, the Home Secretary, Sir George Grey, kept cool; Wellington promised to leave plenty of room for the Chartists to run away; 175,000 special constables were enrolled, the troops remained loyal. Lord John blocked the windows of his London house with Blue Books. However, the Chartists' leader, Feargus O'Connor, as alarmed as anybody by the way matters were developing, promised that all would end quietly, and so it did.

What is more, he tipped the government off about a plot to assassinate Lord John. No wonder the Queen hoped that the "glorious example of this country would be a check to the wicked example set by France".

In these disturbed conditions, Lord John and his ministers, alienated from the Radicals, reached out towards the Peelites. In vain. The Peelites thought that the day would come when they would gain power without any need of alliance with Lord John. In 1841, Lord John had married for the second time, Lady Fanny Elliot, by whom he had three sons and a daughter.

By the end of 1851, the Foreign Secretary, Palmerston, had alarmed the Queen and annoyed Lord John by the truculent foreign policy which he carried on without consulting his colleagues. When he approved the *coup d'état* of Louis Napoleon, the Prime Minister dismissed him. He was warned, "Palmerston never forgives." And so it was. Palmerston defeated the government on an unimportant bill and Lord John threw in his hand.

"The complaint is," said his brother, the Duke of Bedford, "that you were not sufficiently Prime Minister." There had been too much independence among Cabinet ministers. Moreover, Lord John had been careless and idle in dealing with his official business. The Queen complained of his bad manners. And his own followers found him aloof and cold. He had not the gifts of a great popular leader. A Derby-Disraeli ministry came in 1852, and was followed in the same year by one headed by Lord Aberdeen, a taciturn Scot, who hammered together a coalition government in which Lord John, having been offered the Foreign Office, which he refused—too much work—served as Leader in the Commons.

Before long the new Cabinet was in trouble at home and abroad: Lord John believed that Aberdeen had promised to make way for him; Aberdeen did not. The Queen took a dislike to Lady John and was annoyed when Lord John refused to attend her at Balmoral. More important, Britain had drifted into a war with Russia, which, it was all too clear, was going badly. When an MP named Roebuck brought in a motion to enquire into the conduct of the war, Lord John told the Queen and Aberdeen that he could not resist the motion and must resign. Roebuck's motion was carried and the coalition fell. Lord John, through ill-temper and wilfulness, had ruined himself. This the Queen saw at once. The new government, Palmerston's, sent him to Vienna to negotiate a peace settlement. The mission was a failure.

When Orsini threw a bomb at Napoleon III, Palmerston proposed to legislate against conspiracies to murder which were hatched on British soil. Parts of the bomb had been made in Britain. But the British public reacted furiously against the violent anti-British campaign in the Paris press and Lord John saw a chance of revenging himself on Palmerston. The government fell, and the Queen sent for Derby, whose ministry lasted only a matter of months. Palmerston and Lord John were publicly reconciled at a meeting in Willis's Rooms which can be regarded as the birth of the modern Liberal Party.

Forced to choose between two men she disliked, the Queen chose Palmerston. Lord John became his Foreign Secretary (1859) and, to the surprise of all, recovered his good temper at once. At that time, the great question in Europe was the liberation of Italy from the Austrians and its unification under Cavour. Lord John was strongly pro-Italian, as both Palmerston and Gladstone were. But the issue was not simple.

The Palmerston government came into being at a moment when the French had defeated the Austrians at Magenta and Solferino. A French suzerainty in Italy would be no more pleasing than an Austrian one. The matter became even more complicated when the French arranged with the Austrians to carve up Italy between them. However, it proved to be an unworkable plan, especially as Napoleon III seemed not to know whether he was on the side of the Italians, the Pope or Austria.

Events moved quickly: Napoleon grabbed Nice and Savoy; Garibaldi conquered Naples; Cavour occupied the Papal territories and Lord John, without consulting his colleagues, wrote a dispatch announcing that the government turned "their eyes to the gratifying prospect of a people building up the edifice of their liberties." By that declaration, Lord John identified Britain with the birth of modern Italy. Soon afterwards he became Earl Russell, but stayed at the Foreign Office. He was there when the American Civil War broke out and the cruiser *Alabama* left Birkenhead to prey on northern commerce.

Russell was able to plead later on that he had acted in good faith when he had allowed the *Alabama* to leave Liverpool; but eventually Britain had to pay fifteen million dollars damages. Russell, like Gladstone, was convinced that the South would win the war. Again, in the dispute between Germany and Denmark over Schleswig-Holstein, Russell and Palmerston managed to have the worst of both worlds, first threatening Bismarck, then having their bluff called in the most humiliating manner.

When Palmerston died in 1865, Russell became Prime Minister for the second time with Gladstone as Leader in the Commons. This Cabinet ended eight months later; it fell, hopelessly split on the issue of Reform of the franchise. Russell was followed by Gladstone. The issue of Reform had, however, been raised and could not in the end be denied.

Russell lived another ten years, as incapable as ever of refraining from criticizing a political friend or from claiming that he was denied his due share of this or that measure. He was a remarkable man but, in spirit as in stature, a small one; splenetic, sometimes spiteful, quite unable to control a jealous temper. As an aristocrat, he disliked the necessity of placating his followers, even of being civil to them. he was a man of the old school, preparing the way for democracy without any particular affection for it.

Having enjoyed, and nursed, bad health all his life, he died at Pembroke Lodge, Richmond, on 28 May, 1878, in his eighty-sixth year.

XXVI

❦ EDWARD GEOFFREY STANLEY, 14th Earl of Derby ❧

1852; 1858–59; 1866–68

Racing, gambling, the Garter and gout all figured in the life of Edward Stanley, fourteenth Earl of Derby, born 29 March, 1799. But of how many Prime Ministers could it be said that his translation of the *Iliad* ran to six editions? Or that he regarded Disraeli's company at Knowsley as a bore because the need to talk politics with his guest interrupted the pleasure of translating from the Greek? As for racing, Greville, the diarist, who knew and distrusted him, thought that his conduct on the turf was tinged with sharp practice, but racing was a nobleman's indulgence; it was one in which Derby netted £100,000 in stake money. His political career may not resound with brilliant achievement but most people have heard of the "Rupert of Debate" and some of them may know that the nickname belongs to Derby. It was invented by Disraeli, at one time Derby's opponent, later his exasperated ally: "The noble Lord is the Prince Rupert of Parliamentary discussion; his charge is resistless; but when he returns from pursuit he always finds his camp in the possession of the enemy."*

The fourteenth Earl of Derby, as he became on his father's death in 1851, was head of the house of Stanley and therefore of a family important and wealthy in Lancashire since Flodden: "Charge, Chester, Charge! On, Stanley, on!" were the last words of *Marmion*.

The Stanleys were, of course, great Whig magnates, but they were something more than that, and older, which has survived to the present day; undisputed heads of society in Lancashire, leaders in the activities of the county, with all which that implies. "The head of the Derby family," wrote George III to Lord North, "is the proper person to fill the office of Lord Lieutenant of the county of Lancaster."

Edward Stanley became MP for the "close" (i.e. rotten) borough of Stockbridge before he was twenty-one. The borough was bought for him from a Tory peer, who had in turn bought it from a West Indian planter. In 1826, he moved to the family borough of Preston, where he presented himself to the electors as "an old constitutional Whig", one who wore the traditional Whig uniform of blue and buff. In the interval he had travelled widely in North America, a change from the Grand Tour favoured by young noblemen. He married (1825) Emma Caroline Wilbraham, by whom, in due course, he had two sons and a daughter.

---

*Bulwer Lytton picked up the phrase and improved it:

> "The brilliant chief, irregularly great,
> Frank, haughty, rash, the Rupert of Debate."

47 Edward Stanley, 14th Earl of Derby, by F. R. Say.

In Parliament, there was doubt about the depth and seriousness of the convictions of this handsome young aristocrat. As a Whig, he was in favour of electoral reform, provided it was not too abrupt or too extreme. When he read the text of the first Reform Bill, he dissolved in incredulous mirth, but he made a brilliant speech in defence of the bill not long after. The question remained, did he take politics seriously enough, or did his surface glitter cover a basic flippancy.

When Disraeli was made Chancellor of the Exchequer, he protested his ignorance of finance. Derby brushed the objection aside: "You know as much as Mr Canning. *They* give you the figures." It was not the sort of remark likely to commend Stanley to the grave gentlemen of an intensely economic era.

He was a Whig, a tepid reformer, a Conservative and, it was said, "a protectionist in the country, neutral in a small town and a Free Trader in the cities". At a time when the old political loyalties were dissolving and new parties were coming into being, Derby's changing and hesitant opinions were a reflection of the transformation which was coming over the political scene.

But one feature of his character could not be denied, and was of enormous value to his party: his power as a speaker, especially in the rough conditions of Parliamentary debate. He was, as Macaulay said, "clever, keen, neat, clear". Sometimes he was too rash: his tongue ran ahead of his caution. Greville thought him boisterous and undignified. Like many fine orators, he was intensely nervous before speaking: "My throat and lips are as dry as those of a man going to be hanged." But all this vanished the moment he rose to his feet.

He was three times Prime Minister, in 1852, 1858–59 and 1866–68, yet it would be folly to pretend that politics filled all of his life. Often he left the House of Lords after a late sitting and caught the night mail train to the North, so that he could see his horses gallop.

Stanley's experience as a minister began when Lord Grey made him Chief Secretary for Ireland: there he fell out with O'Connell, who called him "snappish, impertinent, High Church Stanley". At that time, Stanley was moving from the Whigs towards Conservatism, and he resigned in 1834 when he found that most of his colleagues did not share his view that the Irish Church Establishment should be preserved. "Johnny has upset the coach,"* he remarked when Lord John Russell spoke in favour of alienating some of the Irish Church properties to secular use.

He left the Whigs and remained out of office until 1841, when he was Secretary for War and the Colonies in Peel's Cabinet, so that his second term of office as a Cabinet minister was in a Conservative government. However, when it was apparent that Peel wished to go further than he in the direction of Free Trade, Stanley arranged that he should be called up to the House of Lords in one of his father's baronies.

On Peel's declaration for a total repeal of the Corn Laws, Stanley left the government, with Disraeli and Bentinck, and formed a Protectionist party, Protection being "necessary for the maintenance of the landed interest and the colonial system". In 1852, Lord John Russell's government fell and the Queen asked Lord Derby (he had now become, by his grandfather's death, an earl) to form a government. This he did but, after a general election, the balance of power in the

---

* Lord Lytton quoted the remark in the *New Timon*.

Commons was held by the Peelites and Derby, after a few months in office, was defeated. Lord Aberdeen succeeded him.

To the Crimean War, which followed almost at once, Derby was opposed, but did not attack the government on general grounds of policy and, when Lord Aberdeen resigned, failed to form a government to succeed him. He told the Queen that Palmerston was too old, blind and deaf to be capable of conducting the war, but Palmerston came in and brought the war to a respectable, if not a brilliant, end.

Derby's party and, above all, Disraeli, thought that this was a splendid opportunity missed; already they had noted with disapproval his tendency to retreat to the country or to Newmarket, to shoot or race, in moments of political crisis. Now he told Lord Malmesbury that he had never been eager for office and that, until Palmerston's government made some gross blunder, there was no chance of defeating it. Meanwhile he would be shooting. Palmerston made a gross blunder with a Conspiracy to Murder Bill, as a consequence of which, he—of all people—was accused of truckling to the French and was defeated in the House. He resigned (1858), and Derby formed a Conservative administration. He did not expect it to have a long life and in that respect he was right. He was defeated on a modest franchise bill which proposed to give the vote to different categories of professional men and to others with various amounts of investments. In the general election that followed, he won a few more seats than he had held before, but he did not have an overall majority. Palmerston took his place.

It was clear that Derby did not have a following numerous enough to support a government. He devoted himself to translating Homer and, faithful to the traditions of the Stanley family, giving leadership to the relief committee organized to deal with the cotton famine in Lancashire in 1862. After Palmerston's death in 1865, he became Prime Minister for the third time.

By this time, he was an old man suffering agonies from gout and Disraeli was the real power in the government. Yet it was Derby rather than Disraeli who was the pioneer of the measure which gives the administration its place in history—the second Reform Bill.

Stanley had been prominent in passing the first Reform Bill, now he was enthusiastic for the second, which, although a "leap in the dark", would probably "dish the Whigs". And so a bill was passed, stronger than Gladstone's bill, which Disraeli, along with a group of Whig malcontents, had defeated the year before. Six months after the bill received the royal assent, Derby resigned and Disraeli, until then the Chancellor of the Exchequer, became Prime Minister. The gifted amateur was succeeded by a professional of genius. For Derby, politics was only a part of the duty which a great nobleman owed to the state. There were other interests, racing for example. He was a member not only of the Cabinet but of the Jockey Club as well.

His off-hand manner was sometimes mistaken—by Disraeli for example—for indolence. As the years passed, he became stouter and his stylish way of dressing became more careless. His tongue was still sharp and his gift of phrase as lively as ever; but his temper had mellowed. The haughty young aristocrat had become more placid.

A year and a half after his resignation, Derby died, on 13 October, 1869.

XXVII

❧ GEORGE HAMILTON GORDON, ❧
4th Earl of Aberdeen

1852–55

It would be hard to name a British Prime Minister who apparently had less effect on the course of events than George Gordon, fourth Earl of Aberdeen. He is chiefly remembered because he headed the government which declared and waged the Crimean War; he himself was opposed to that war.

These two facts sufficiently explain why Aberdeen does not have an illustrious place in the roll of Prime Ministers. But they encourage a tendency to undervalue his character and ability. He was driven from power in 1855, after the House of Commons passed by 305 votes to 148 a motion for a Select Committee on the condition of the army in the Crimea. But Aberdeen could claim that responsibility for Britain's military shortcomings, admittedly appalling, should justly be distributed among all the appropriate ministers since the last shot was fired at Waterloo.

However, it is no better defence to say that he had embarked on a war for which the country was unprepared than that he had no liking for the war anyway. If he were to argue that the nation wanted the war, as it did in 1854, his position is no better. He emerges all the more clearly as a weak Prime Minister, who allowed himself to be forced into a policy which he believed to be wrong and which he should have known would be disastrous. It was a sad end to the political career of a man who was completely honest and not without ability.

Aberdeen (born in Edinburgh on 28 January, 1784) belonged to a branch of the old and adventurous Aberdeenshire family of Gordon. He was sent to Harrow, against his grandfather's wishes. ("I recommend that my grandson be partly educated in Scotland that he do not despise his own country.") The old man had to be bullied into paying the boy's school fees. At Harrow he had a pillow fight with an obstreperous boy named Harry Temple, whom he later knew as Lord Palmerston; Cambridge followed. By that time he had inherited the Aberdeen title. His cousin, Lord Byron, came to Harrow four years after him.

Having had the good sense as a boy to choose William Pitt as one of his guardians, he travelled abroad as the great man's protégé; and met Napoleon at Malmaison. In 1805, he married Lady Catherine Hamilton, daughter of the Marquis of Abercorn. Aberdeen, now of age, visited his estates in the North. He was appalled by their bleak and dismal appearance and resolved to plant, drain and put up better farm buildings. This he did over the years.

He became a representative Scottish peer in 1806 and he was a Knight of the Thistle two years later. In 1812, his wife died; they had been married for seven years and had three children. He wore mourning for her until his own death, fifty years later; it did not prevent him from falling in love again. However, his mind was distracted to other topics when Castlereagh arranged that he should go as ambassador to Vienna with the duty of persuading Austria to break with Napoleon. He arrived in Stralsund to find that Austria and France were already at war. He made his way to Prague through terrible scenes of war, which made an indelible impression on him: "The horrible thing is the wounded of all nations. It haunts one night and day." After the battle of Leipzig, when he was in the entourage of the Austrian emperor, the horrors were worse.

Aberdeen never forgot what he had seen; it filled him with a detestation of war. When Waterloo was fought, in which his brother Alex was killed, and the war came to an end, he settled down to manage his estates in Aberdeenshire and later estimated that he had planted fourteen million trees. He had told his wife, "I shall make this really a fine place," and kept his promise. He had, too, an interest in classical art and archaeology and for thirty-two years was President of the Society of Antiquaries. He founded the Athenian Society and, not surprisingly, he was an enthusiast for the liberation of Greece.

By this time, he had married again, Harriet, Viscountess Hamilton, a widow with three children, the sister-in-law of his late wife. He did not conceal from her the fact that she could not take the place in his heart that his first wife, Catherine, had held. Harriet was never completely reconciled to this. She bore him five children.

48 George Gordon, 4th Earl of Aberdeen, by J. Partridge.

In 1828, he returned to politics as Chancellor of the Duchy of Lancaster in Wellington's government. It was a tribute to his breadth of view because at the time Catholic Emancipation was a vital issue and Aberdeen was a Scots Presbyterian. A contemporary spoke of his "sound and cultivated understanding, impenetrable discretion and polite but somewhat grave manner". In other words, he was considered a dull man. In truth, he was an unhappy one; one of his children was dying—the last survivor of the three daughters of his first marriage. In appearance he was uninspiring: "more of a scarecrow than ever," said Lady Lyttelton, "and as stiff as timber".

Wellington gave him the Foreign Office (1828) and he became Secretary for War and Colonies in Peel's first government. Then, when Peel won the election of 1841, he returned to the Foreign Office. As Foreign Secretary, during two terms of office, he helped to bring into being an independent Greece and he settled some difficult border disputes between Canada and the United States.

When Peel died in 1850, Aberdeen became the acknowledged leader of the group of Free Trade Conservatives known as the Peelites, and after the short-lived ministries of Lord John Russell and Lord Derby, he took office in 1852 as head of a coalition government of Peelites, Whigs and Radicals. The Queen greeted it with enthusiasm; it was "the realization of the country's and our own most ardent wishes". The intellectual calibre of the new Cabinet was impressive. Gladstone, Palmerston and Lord John Russell were members. But what seemed at first to be the government's strength was soon seen to be its weakness: strong personalities meant strong opinions and fierce ambitions. Aberdeen had not the authority to dominate his colleagues and bend them to his will.

This would have been less important in quiet times, but instead, a crisis, long smouldering in the East of Europe, now burst into flames. The Tsar and the French Emperor Napoleon III respectively claimed the right to protect the Orthodox and the Catholic subjects of the Sultan of Turkey. They were divided on another question: which religious order was to oversee the Holy Places in Palestine? What if the Russians, having quarrelled with the Turks, were to march on Constantinople? No prospect was more alarming to the Foreign Office.

Aberdeen was intensely hostile to the Turks but Palmerston, at that time Home Secretary, wanted to keep the Russians out of the Mediterranean. And public opinion agreed with Palmerston. After a long struggle in Cabinet, the British navy was sent to the Dardanelles. The Russians responded by invading Turkish provinces lying south of the Danube in what is now Rumania. In October, 1853, Turkey declared war on Russia, to the general delight of the British public, including Alfred Tennyson and Karl Marx.

> "May God protect the Turks
> And massacre the Russians"

sang a street ballad of the time.

While Aberdeen wondered what he should do, the Russian navy destroyed a Turkish squadron. A British declaration of war against Russia followed in March, 1854. Manipulated by Palmerston, Aberdeen was swept into a war of which he profoundly disapproved. The war soon justified all his dislike of it. By January, 1855, it was so unpopular, because of the mismanagement which it had revealed, that a motion demanding an enquiry into the conduct of the war was carried in the Commons by a large majority. Bulwer Lytton said, "Dismiss your government and save your army." Aberdeen resigned in 1855.

Disraeli wrote, "The country was governed for two years by all its ablest men, who by the end of that term had succeeded by their coalesced genius in reducing that country to a state of desolation and despair." The Queen gave Aberdeen the Garter. It was the end of his political career.

His failure as Prime Minister was essentially one of character. He lacked the moral fibre to stand against Palmerston and his troublesome and disloyal colleague, Lord John Russell, who was still smarting under his dismissal from the premiership in 1852. When to Russell's unending attempts to assert himself was added Lord Palmerston's avowal of a belligerent foreign policy, Aberdeen was faced with a task beyond his capacity. He is all the more blameworthy in that he was well acquainted with the problems of the Near East. He failed, not from ignorance, but from weakness.

At his house in Aberdeenshire he lived in the state traditional to a Scottish feudal magnate. He was known even to his children as "His Lordship". Every Saturday at noon, he sat at the gate to discuss problems with his tenants and arbitrate on disputes. He and the Countess of Sutherland were the last members of the nobility to observe this old custom.

Every Sunday there was a procession of coaches carrying Lord Aberdeen and other worshippers to the parish church where, at the end of the service, he and the minister exchanged deep bows. His gloom was partly caused by the guilt he felt over the Crimean War: "My conscience has never been quite at ease in consequence of not having done enough to prevent it." He refused to rebuild a parish church which had fallen into ruin. Later, his family found a quotation from First Chronicles which explained this: "The word of the Lord came to me saying, Thou shalt not build an house unto my name because thou has shed much blood upon the earth in my sight."

Six years after his resignation, he died at Argyll House, St James's, on 14 December, 1860, aged seventy-six.

XXVIII

❧ HENRY JOHN TEMPLE, 3rd Viscount Palmerston ❧
1855–58; 1859–65

"If I were not a Frenchman, I should wish to be an Englishman," said the Frenchman. "If I were not an Englishman," said the Englishman, "I should wish to be an Englishman."

Which British Prime Minister said that? When the answer is given, it is seen to be almost self-evident. Palmerston! Palmerston, of course.

Henry John Temple, third Viscount Palmerston, was born on 20 October, 1784, of a landowning family settled in Ireland since the seventeenth century. Much is, as is usual in these cases, heard of his "Irish" charm. Charm he had, and exploited, but why it should be thought of as Irish is not so easy to understand, as the boy was English in his birthplace (Romsey, Hampshire), English on his father's and mother's side, and was brought up and educated in England. He went to Harrow, which he thoroughly enjoyed, and, after that, to Edinburgh, where he attended the lectures on political economy of Professor Dugald Stewart, a disciple of Adam Smith.

Thus, owing to the French Revolution, of which as a child of eight he had caught an alarming glimpse, in Paris, young Temple was brought in touch with the vigorous intellectual discipline of the Scots university in its finest days. Later, he took the habit of hard work to St John's, Cambridge. After several unsuccessful attempts, he entered the House of Commons in 1807 as member for Newport, Isle of Wight. One condition made by the proprietor of the borough was that Palmerston should never set foot in it. This condition he kept without any difficulty.

He was very soon a Junior Lord of the Admiralty and by his maiden speech, defending Canning's decision to bombard Copenhagen and prevent the Danish fleet from falling into Napoleon's clutches, earned his right to promotion. He was offered the Chancellorship of the Exchequer and accepted the post of Secretary at War, concerned with the finances of the army.

Behind him was the influence of his guardian, Lord Malmesbury. Before him was a promising career on a comfortable salary (£2,480 a year) and the glittering social life of Regency London. He was a good-looking young man, fond of the society of pretty women; very soon he had been the lover of three of the seven leading hostesses of Almack's, ladies who had the power to veto the entry of anyone to that inner sanctum of fashionable London. Lady Jersey, Princess Lieven, the intriguing wife of the Russian ambassador, and Lady Cowper—one after another they succumbed to the handsome young man who had nothing beyond his Whitehall salary but the rents from some desolate acres in County Sligo.

49 Princess Lieven, an important political
hostess during the years when her husband was
Russian ambassador in London, 1812-34,
by Sir Thomas Lawrence.

50 Sara Sophia, Countess of Jersey, by E. T. Parris,
engraved by H. T. Ryall. The Countess
was a leader of London social life during
the reign of George IV.

For various reasons, Lady Cowper was the most important of the trio of conquests—she was the sister of Lord Melbourne, intelligent as well as beautiful, and eventually Palmerston married her. Before that, however, it is probable that he was the father of one of her children. For obvious reasons, *The Times* took to calling him "Lord Cupid".

But, in spite of an active social life, which included racing as well as dalliance, Palmerston was assiduous in his work as Secretary at War at the Horse Guards. Yet he took no prominent part in politics outside his departmental duties, although in 1811 he changed his constituency at Newport for the more prestigious Cambridge University seat, which in 1826 he held against Tory attempts to defeat him. He regarded this Tory intervention as particularly discreditable because, if anything, he himself was a Tory.

Canning, who had become Prime Minister, died in August, 1827, and Goderich, his successor, offered Palmerston the Chancellorship. However, it was denied him, owing to the King's dislike. Palmerston gives an account of his interview with the King. "George assured me how much esteem and regard he felt for me and how happy he would have been to have had my services at the Exchequer if he had not the good fortune of obtaining those of Mr Herries, unquestionably the fittest man in England for the office. I bowed, entirely acquiesced, and thanked His Majesty for the gracious and flattering manner in which he had spoken to me.''

In 1828, when the Duke of Wellington had become Prime Minister, Palmerston resigned his place in the War Office on the question of Parliamentary Reform; he was becoming a Whig, but a Whig who had no liking for Radicals. In consequence, when Lord Grey formed a government he made Palmerston his Foreign Secretary, a post for which he had been angling for some time and for which his old friend, Princess Lieven, warmly recommended him. In the Foreign Office he proved a hard task-master, a disciplinarian exacting a high standard of efficiency from his clerks, and becoming very unpopular as a result. His manners to foreign ambassadors were notably brusque and corresponded to the harshness and vigour of his policy. At the back of his mind was always the British navy; he did not let others forget it: "Diplomats and protocols are very good things but there are no better peace-keepers than well-appointed three-deckers." This was just the sort of thing the British public wanted to hear.

His first important stroke of policy was to recognize the independence of Belgium, which had risen in revolt against the Dutch, while preventing the French from taking over the country. After eighteen months of negotiations, he succeeded in achieving all he had set out to do. When Parliament passed the Reform Bill in 1832, Palmerston, who personally thought the bill went too far in the democratic direction, found that the European autocracies had become more hostile to Britain. Accordingly, his policy swung to the left.

Melbourne, who had followed Grey as Prime Minister, was dismissed by William IV. As Palmerston said, "We are all out, neck and crop . . . This attempt to re-install the Tories cannot possibly last; the country will not stand it. I shall now go down to Broadlands and get some hunting."

He was back in the Foreign Office in five months, to the disgust of his overworked officials. He had, however, lost his seat in Parliament, which proved to be only a temporary setback. He paid the MP for Tiverton £2,000 to resign his place and was returned unopposed for the constituency. He devoted himself during the next few years to protecting British interests in the Iberian Peninsula, Turkey and the Middle East. His methods were a mixture of subtlety, bluff and bullying. They were, on the whole, successful.

Business did not fill his whole life just then. In 1839, aged fifty-five, he married his mistress, the dowager Countess Cowper, aged fifty-two. He was a vigorous, hard-working, hard-playing man: she, a shrewd and charming hostess. They lived very happily and—when allowance is made for the wayward temperament they shared—reasonably faithful to one another.

However, Palmerston had not put aside all his old habits. In the same year that he married, he made a determined attempt on the virtue of one of the Queen's Ladies-in-waiting at Windsor. The Queen was shocked; Prince Albert more so. More important were Palmerston's obstreperous policies, which disturbed the Queen and alarmed Lord John Russell, the Prime Minister.

He was dismissed on the pretext that, without telling the Queen, he had approved

51 Emily, Countess Cowper, whom
Palmerston married in 1839, by
Sir Thomas Lawrence.

Louis Napoleon's *coup d'état* in 1851. He took his revenge by bringing about the defeat of Russell's government a few weeks later.

By that time, the Don Pacifico affair had, once and for all, epitomized Palmerston's conception of foreign policy. Don Pacifico was a Portuguese Jew, who, by being born in Gibraltar, was a British subject. During the Easter of 1847, an Athenian mob attacked his house and manhandled his family. The house was set on fire. Pacifico claimed damages from the Greek government, who disclaimed responsibility for the misdeeds of the rioters. Pacifico appealed to Palmerston, who ordered the fleet to Athens and presented a demand for payment to the Greek government. They, in due course, paid Pacifico £6,400 damages. Palmerston defended his action in the Commons in a speech which lasted four and a half hours.

"As the Roman, in days of old, held himself free from indignity when he could say *Civis Romanus sum*; so also a British subject, in whatever land he may be, shall feel confident that the watchful eye and the strong arm of England will protect him against injustice and wrong."

The speech was a triumph. Palmerston had spoken for the Englishman of that age.

Early in 1852, Palmerston was brought down by the Prince Consort; Lord John Russell followed him and Lord Derby became Prime Minister while Disraeli was given the Treasury. Before the end of the year, the Conservatives defeated the Whigs in a general election and Palmerston was in Lord Aberdeen's government as Home Secretary. The Queen's misgivings over the appointment were many, but, as things turned out, Palmerston's record at the office was not too deplorable.

But the war in the Crimea and its disastrous course now distracted public attention from matters of domestic reform.

When Aberdeen's government fell, after a Commons vote of no confidence, Palmerston, aged seventy, took over as Prime Minister (1855). "The aged charlatan," said John Bright, "has at length attained the great object of his long and unscrupulous ambition." It was true that Palmerston's articles in the newspapers had helped to push the government into a war which it could not wage and that a hint of recklessness in his make-up fostered the idea that he could win the war.

"If any man had asked me to say what was one of the most improbable events, I should have said my being Prime Minister. Aberdeen was there, Derby was head of one great party, John Russell of the other and yet, in about ten days' time, they all gave way like straws before the wind. So here am I writing from Downing Street."

The "old painted pantaloon, very deaf, very blind and with false teeth" (Disraeli) took over the control of policy and out of a mismanaged war brought a tolerable peace: Russia agreed to demilitarize the Black Sea.

The cannon boomed in London and the Queen put aside her distrust of the Prime Minister far enough to give him the Garter.

In Asia, Palmerston's policy was active and, on the whole, successful: the Persians were defeated in battle; the Chinese humbled; the British electorate showed its approval by depriving Bright and Cobden of their seats in Parliament. "P's popularity is wonderful," said Lord Shaftesbury. When the Indian Mutiny broke out in 1857, Palmerston met the crisis with coolness and humanity. A crisis of a different kind brought him down.

An Italian named Orsini threw a bomb at Napoleon III; it was then found that he had links with Italian refugees in London and that explosives for the bomb had been made in England. Palmerston brought in a Conspiracy to Murder Bill (see page 122). He was defeated in the House and resigned. He was out of power for a year, 1858–59. When he took office again, in June, 1859, he was a man of seventy-five, but vigorous enough to ride on a grey horse to Downing Street from his house in

52 **The attempted assassination of Emperor Napoleon III by Orsini, 14 January, 1858. Explosives for the bomb had been made in Britain, which prompted Palmerston to introduce his Conspiracy to Murder Bill.**

53 Henry Temple, 3rd Viscount Palmerston, by F. Cruikshank.

Piccadilly and sit up half the night at his place in the Commons, and, if necessary, eat and sleep on the premises.

In his seventy-ninth year he was cited as co-respondent in a divorce case and won the case. His policies showed that his outlook was essentially unchanged; he tried to prevent the French from building the Suez Canal; he opposed death duties on land and the extension of the franchise to the working classes. On this last issue, Gladstone, his Chancellor of the Exchequer, sent him so many letters of resignation that he was afraid, he said, that they would set fire to the chimney at Broadlands. He favoured the South in the American Civil War, although he was cautious not to give recognition to the Confederacy.

Over the Schleswig-Holstein question, he threatened Prussia with war, but Bismarck called his bluff. He took the setback coolly. "There is nothing I can do against 200,000 soldiers," he told his Foreign Secretary. "Palmerston likes to drive the wheel close to the edge," said Cobden, "and show how dexterously he can avoid falling over the precipice."

In October, 1865, this sprightly, hard-living survivor of the Regency caught a chill while out driving and died, two days before he would have been eighty-one. He had sometimes alarmed his colleagues and endeared himself to the public, who shared his opinion that politics is a kind of sport rather than a science.

54 Broadlands, Romsey, Hampshire, home of Viscount Palmerston and later of Lord Louis Mountbatten.

XXIX

BENJAMIN DISRAELI, Earl of Beaconsfield

1868; 1874–80

"The old Jew," cried Bismarck with enthusiasm, "*that* is the man!"

By that time Benjamin Disraeli, with his hair and beard dyed black, could not conceal the fact that he was seventy-four years of age, although his heart was still young enough for love. "There is no greater misfortune," he complained, "than to have a heart which will not grow old." Lady Bradford, Lady Chesterfield, nay, Queen Victoria herself—at least three ladies were aware of the Prime Minister's romantic disposition.

He had arrived in Berlin to attend a congress of the powers following a Russo-Turkish war which had brought the Tsar's army dangerously near Constantinople. Although he was an old man, suffering from asthma and Bright's Disease, he was the delegate who attracted most attention. In addition to his other qualities, he had the charm, as Princess Radziwill said, "which only those possess who have complete confidence in themselves". And that, unquestionably, Disraeli possessed. His charm was exercised, above all, on women, whom all his life he adored; but Bismarck, too, succumbed to it. The two men, so different in their origins and upbringing, shared wit and realism. They understood one another perfectly and each took pleasure in the other's company.

Disraeli had one particular cause to feel pleased with life just then. He found that almost all the women in Berlin were reading his novels. The circulating libraries, unable to meet the demand, bought up all the Tauchnitz editions of his works, while the booksellers sent to London for more copies. He, who was at that moment the first statesman of Europe, had once been known as a successful young novelist.

Benjamin Disraeli started his career with many cards stacked against him. He was born in London on 21 December, 1804, a Jew, son of Isaac D'Israeli, a distinguished author belonging to a Sephardic family which had been driven from Spain by the Inquisition and settled in Italy before reaching England. Isaac D'Israeli looked on all religion with scepticism.

His son was converted to the Church of England when he was twelve; he did not go to any of the "right" schools, attending a Unitarian school in London; his hair fell in glistening curls, his clothes were altogether too flamboyant. If, as it soon appeared, he was in love with England and English life, he was the kind of suitor most likely to be scornfully rejected. If, through some romantic aspiration, he became a Conservative, nothing was so improbable as his arrival at the leadership of the Conservative party. But the improbable happened. What was the explanation?

The young Jew from the well-to-do home in Bloomsbury was a man of exuberant genius. The genius was, however, not translated immediately into success. In the meantime, he acquired a mistress and helped to start a newspaper, *The Representative*, which failed and cost John Murray, its publisher, £26,000. Disraeli gambled heavily on the Stock Exchange in South American mines and ran up debts which haunted him through most of his life. As a result, he suffered a nervous breakdown, "My old enemy", he called it. When he recovered, he went on a tour of the Near East, astonishing his fellow-passengers by the extravagance of his costume: "The people made way for me as I passed. It was like the opening of the Red Sea." He hurried home on the news that a favourite sister had died.

The family had moved from Bloomsbury to Bradenham in Buckinghamshire and about this time he wrote a novel, *Vivian Grey*, published anonymously as the work of a "man of fashion" and containing a cruel portrait of Murray, the publisher. For this book he received £200. It was followed by two other novels, *The Young Duke* and *Contarini Fleming*.

He moved house to the West End and began to dally with Radical politics, having decided "Toryism is dead and I cannot condescend to be a Whig." In 1832, he stood for High Wycombe as a Radical and was at the bottom of the poll. But politics did not fill the whole of his life at this time. He enjoyed London society, where he quickly attracted attention. His talk was lively, his clothes conspicuous. At Bulwer Lytton's he appeared wearing green velvet trousers, a canary yellow waistcoat, lace at his wrists and silver buckles on his shoes. He attracted women as they attracted him. He had a passionate love affair with Henrietta, wife of Sir Francis Sykes, who had become the lover of Clara Bolton, formerly Disraeli's mistress! The affair with Henrietta lasted for four years.

Having fought and lost High Wycombe three times as a Radical, Disraeli lost it a fourth time as a Tory. In the interval, he had met Lord Lyndhurst, who had influenced him towards Conservatism. The indulgent old statesman, Lord Melbourne, asked him what he meant to be. "Prime Minister," he replied. Melbourne shook his head sadly. "No chance at all. Nobody can compete with Stanley." Years later, when Disraeli had been elected leader of the Conservative party, Melbourne exclaimed, "By God, the fellow will do it yet!"

In 1837, Disraeli became Conservative MP for Maidstone. He was on the way up. Two years later, he married a rich widow, Mrs Wyndham Lewis, who was twelve years older than he and living comfortably in Park Lane. "She is an excellent creature," he said, "but she can never remember which came first, the Greeks or the Romans." She brought him not only love but something which can be almost as precious to an ambitious man: "She believed in me when men despised me."

In the forties, he helped to found "Young England", a grouping of Conservatives, idealistic, romantic, with a fair infusion of naïveté. The group appealed to one part of his mind, for the source of his political faith was patriotic rather than partisan, the patriotism which is often the strongest in the adopted son. "I am neither Whig nor Tory. My politics are described by one word, England."

At this time, Disraeli wrote two novels which became instantly famous, *Coningsby* and *Sybil*. The first took the public by storm; it went through three quick editions and America bought 50,000 copies. In it he wrote, "A sound Conservative government? I understand: Tory men and Whig measures." In *Sybil*, "I was told that the Privileged and the People formed Two Nations." Both novels were in fact political manifestoes. They were not great as fiction but as novels of ideas, as displays of dialectic, they were superb. Disraeli's wit was at its most coruscating then; it was not equalled until Wilde wrote half a century later, and, in fact, Disraeli was far more prolific of wit than Wilde. In a third novel, *Tancred*, Disraeli identified himself with the people from which he came. Jesus, he believed, was a Jew, who had not wished to found a new religion but to complete an old one.

From now on, Disraeli's life lay more in politics than in novel-writing. His first speech in Parliament, delivered by a young man with a flashy waistcoat who spoke in affected phrases, was a sensational failure. "Though I sit down now," he shouted, "the time will come when you will hear me." He recovered from that setback; his speeches were attracting notice. But when Peel, his leader, became Prime Minister, there was no office for Disraeli. He waited, nursing his resentment and toning down his oratorical style: "The British people, being subject to fogs, require grave statesmen."

In the autumn of 1845, when the proposed repeal of the Corn Laws brought about a political crisis, Disraeli and his wife, Mary Anne, were in Paris and showed no hurry to return. However, they arrived in time. His attacks on Peel in the Corn Laws debate are a superb example of the power that rhetoric of the highest quality can exert in a democratic assembly. His case against Peel was, in essence, that he had been elected as a Conservative and had become a Liberal. Its effect was, said a newspaper, "perfectly unparalleled". It brought Peel down.

In this crisis, Disraeli was actuated not by a passionate belief in agricultural protection (very soon he was admitting that protection was "dead and damned"), but by personal animosity against Peel, who had kept him from office. However, although Peel was driven out, the Corn Laws were repealed and, in consequence, the Conservative party suffered an electoral blow from which it did not quickly recover. In 1848, Disraeli's ally and backer, Lord George Bentinck, died, at a moment when Disraeli was hoping that he would provide enough money to enable him to buy the 750-acre Hughenden estate in Buckinghamshire. But the money was supplied by Bentinck's brothers, so that Disraeli became at last a landed gentleman. This was an important qualification in those days for anyone aspiring to lead the Conservative party.

For Disraeli to achieve this position, he would have to overcome more than one obstacle; for instance, the memory that once, during his attack on Peel, he had called a Conservative government "an organized hypocrisy". There are circumstances in which a gift for brilliant phrase can become an inconvenience.

When, at last, the Conservatives came into power, Disraeli was Chancellor of the Exchequer (1852) in Lord Derby's administration. His first Budget was defeated by a temporary coalition of Whigs, Peelites and Radicals led by Gladstone; the government was forced to resign. From this time dates the historic and dramatic rivalry of Disraeli and Gladstone, who were divided from one another not only by political views but by personal antipathy.

In Opposition, faced with Palmerston as Prime Minister, Disraeli built up the strength of his party during ten years. On Palmerston's death in 1865, he commented, "tempestuous times ahead!" When a Reform Bill introduced by Gladstone was defeated, Derby and Disraeli, as Prime Minister and Chancellor of the Exchequer respectively, came back and produced a Reform Bill of their own which, in fact, did not materially differ from Gladstone's, but was passed into law thanks largely to Disraeli's Parliamentary skill. He had "dished the Whigs".

In 1868, Derby having resigned owing to ill-health, Benjamin Disraeli was now acknowledged, grudgingly by some, enthusiastically by others, to be the ablest man in his party, and became Prime Minister. "I have climbed to the top of the greasy pole," he said. The Queen, who had long since overcome her dislike of the politician who defeated Peel, was gracious; the House of Commons rang with cheers. But he led a government which had a minority in the House; its life was likely to be brief, its legislative programme unenterprising. He clashed with Gladstone, who demanded that the Irish Church be disestablished; Disraeli, as a loyal Anglican, a convert who was under the necessity of being more demonstrative than others in his loyalty, thought this would lead to the disestablishment of the Church of England. In the general election of 1868, the Liberals won a decisive victory, ending twenty years of minority governments. The Queen offered the defeated Prime Minister a peerage, which he declined, asking, however, that his wife, Mary Anne, be made a peeress.

After twenty years, Disraeli went back to his early love and wrote a novel, *Lothar*. It had an enormous popular success but was not approved by all his party. Disraeli was thought by some members to lack vigour in his opposition to the Liberals, but his analysis of politics led him to the opinion that the Liberals were defeating themselves. He said that the ministers reminded him of "one of those marine landscapes not very unusual on the coasts of South America. You behold a range of exhausted volcanoes."

In 1872, Disraeli's wife died, leaving a letter: "Do not live alone, dearest." He was overwhelmed by the loss. "I am totally unable to meet the catastrophe," he said. For a time he lived miserably in a London hotel: "Hotel life in the evening is a cave of despair."

But in politics, which were becoming particularly interesting just then, he found something which occupied his mind. Gladstone's government was floundering and, when he tried to save it by calling a snap election in 1874, he was heavily defeated. For the first time, Disraeli headed a government with a clear majority in the House of Commons. He said, "Power! It has come to me too late."

It had not come too late. He stayed in power for six years, during which he enacted a series of measures which improved social conditions in Britain and increased Britain's prestige abroad. In addition, with the help of a Rothschild, he bought the Khedive's shares in the Suez Canal Company.

"You have it, Madam," he told the Queen. "The French tried too much, offering loans at a usurious rate. The Khedive, in despair, offered Your Majesty's government to purchase his shares outright . . . Four million sterling, and almost immediately. There was only one firm that could do it—Rothschilds. They behaved admirably."

Disraeli had sent his secretary to Lord Rothschild, who listened, peeled a muscatel grape and put it in his mouth. "What security?" he asked.

"The British government."

55 The dining room at Hughendon Manor, Buckinghamshire, Disraeli's home.

"You shall have it."

Financially, it was a magnificent deal; politically, its success was enormous.

In 1876, by a stroke of policy which brought down on him a torrent of criticism, he declared that the Queen would be Empress of India. It was one of those flamboyant gestures which appealed to the public and pleased the Queen. She was irritated by the opposition of Gladstone in *The Times*. With the "widow at Windsor" his relations grew ever more warm; he knew exactly the mixture of respect and flattery which would win the heart of a lonely, spoilt and imperious woman. He described to Lord Esher his technique in dealing with her: "I never deny. I never contradict. I sometimes forget." The Queen was not his only sentimental interest: he was in love with Lady Bradford; he proposed marriage to her widowed sister, Lady Chesterfield, who rejected him. He suffered from the humiliations of one whose heart stays obstinately younger than his body. But, without the society of women, Disraeli, whether as a young man or an old, would not have been the romantic, effusive person that he was.

In the mid-seventies, an international crisis blew up, of a kind which he was designed by nature to deal with. The Ottoman Empire, the "Sick Man of Europe", was faced with a revolt in its Balkan provinces which Russia, as self-chosen protector of Christian minorities, was quick to exploit. Disraeli asserted Britain's right to be consulted. Gladstone intervened with a pamphlet denouncing Turkish atrocities in Bulgaria. It was entitled *The Bulgarian Horror and the Question of the East*, and 200,000 copies were quickly sold. The British public was roused to a pitch of righteous indignation by this tale of rape and massacre against Christian people; in this state of opinion it was difficult for Disraeli and his government to conduct the cool foreign policy which he would have liked. He was determined that Russia should not be able to use the Bulgarian atrocities as an excuse for invading Turkey and seizing Constantinople.

In the early days of 1877 it seemed that war was at hand—and Disraeli, by this time a man in failing health, found that the strain was more than he could bear. He retired to the House of Lords as Earl of Beaconsfield. When a fellow-peer suggested that he would miss the excitement of the Commons, he replied, "I am dead: dead, but in the Elysian fields."

His most spectacular triumph lay ahead of him, at the Congress of Berlin. Russia and Turkey had fought and, it seemed, Russia was about to capture Constantinople when an armistice was reached. Liberal feeling in Britain, as expressed by Gladstone, was hostile to Turkey; Disraeli—and the Queen—were against the Russians. In the Cabinet, said Disraeli, there were twelve men—and seven different policies on the Eastern Question. Two men in particular were opposed to Disraeli: Lord Carnarvon, who resigned, believing that the Prime Minister was hell-bent on war with Russia; and Lord Stanley, the Foreign Secretary, son of the man who had preceded Disraeli as Conservative Prime Minister. Stanley, who stayed in office, would not allow the fleet to be sent to the Dardanelles and saw to it that the Russian ambassador knew about the split in the British Cabinet.

Disraeli behaved with an equal defiance of the conventions. By-passing the Foreign Office, he made contact with Constantinople and the Tsar's government. Then, when the Russians were still a few miles from the city, he ordered the British fleet to sail for the Bosphorus while a force of Indian troops went to Malta. Stanley resigned and drifted towards Gladstone. His place at the Foreign Office was taken by Lord Salisbury, who had, at one time, been deeply suspicious of Disraeli. Salisbury found the final days of Stanley's career in the ministry highly curious: "The issues of war and peace trembling in the balance. [Stanley] between overwork, alcohol and responsibility, in a condition of utter moral frustration."

The danger of war was acute. By the Peace of San Stefano, Russia took most of the Balkan Peninsula from Turkey, which, it seemed, was destined to become a Russian satellite. In these circumstances, the Congress of Berlin was convoked.

It was a remarkable assembly of notables. In addition to Disraeli and Bismarck, there was the Russian Chancellor, Gorchakov, so old and weak that he had to be carried upstairs; Waddington, the French Foreign Minister, who had once rowed in the Oxford-Cambridge Boat Race; and Andrassy, a Hungarian, who represented Austria. Disraeli was dissuaded from addressing the company in his execrable French by his private secretary, who urged him not to deprive the Congress of the pleasure of hearing "the greatest master of English prose in his own tongue".

Disraeli's aim was to halt Russian expansion in the Balkans without going to war. In this he had some success, thanks to a mixture of luck and bluff. Although Salisbury did most of the hard work of negotiation, Disraeli brought off one or two bold diplomatic strokes, e.g. ordering a special train to take him home and taking care that news of this reached—and alarmed—the Russians. "Before I went to bed, I had the satisfaction of knowing that St Petersburg had surrendered." In the end, Turkey was given a better frontier than the Russians had been willing to concede and Britain was ceded Cyprus by Turkey so that she would have a base if there was any future trouble in the East Mediterranean. This was a coup which particularly aroused Bismarck's admiration. In one respect, the Junker and Disraeli were in agreement:

56 The Congress of Berlin, 1878, showing Disraeli and Bismarck. From a painting by Anton von Werner.

neither had much sympathy with Balkan nationalists—"cattle thieves", as Bismarck called them.

When the Congress ended, Disraeli claimed that he had brought back "peace with honour". He was received by vast enthusiastic crowds in London and by something less than enthusiasm on the Liberal benches—"a series of congratulatory regrets", as he put it. He and Salisbury were given the Garter. Gladstone denounced the acquisition of Cyprus as insane. Disraeli retorted by calling Gladstone "a sophistical rhetorician, inebriated with the exuberance of his own verbosity". As a witty parody of the thing that it denounced, the phrase is still remembered.

The popular acclaim which the Berlin triumph had brought did not last long. There was a military disaster in Afghanistan and another one in Zululand. The Greeks were fractious, grumbling that they had been unfairly treated at Berlin. More serious than any of this, economic depression struck Britain in 1879. The situation was one that Gladstone could exploit. In March, 1880, Disraeli went to the country in a general election. Gladstone won a landslide victory. While the Queen was left to deal with Gladstone, whom she detested, Disraeli turned to finishing his novel, *Endymion*, for which he was paid a £10,000 advance, the highest sum paid for a novel up to that time.

By this time his health was getting worse. He was using more rouge to conceal the pallor of his cheeks. Gout and bronchitis afflicted him. He feared cold weather. In the early spring of 1881, he had taken the lease of a house in Curzon Street and there, in the icy winds of that time, he caught a chill. He sat up in bed correcting the proofs in Hansard of his last speech in the House: "I will not go down to posterity talking bad grammar." He died on 19 April, 1881, and was buried at Hughenden where his wife lay.

Of all the men who have reached the political summit in Britain, he is the most unexpected and the most fascinating. His political career was a literary triumph. His novels, which were in fact political tracts, spread his ideas over the reading public; his speeches were distilled essences of irony and wit in which surprising turns of phrase delighted the sleepiest members of the House of Commons. The humdrum levels of Parliamentary abuse were lit with flashes of brilliance: "Her Majesty's ministers live in a blaze of apology." His letters to the Queen interested and amused her; he took trouble over them and they played a part in his success. He used his talent for words as a political instrument. But Disraeli's was not only a triumph of style. Character, tenacity and grit were present, and their origin could not be doubted.

To a young Jewish friend he said: "You and I belong to a race which can do everything but fail."

XXX

❧ WILLIAM EWART GLADSTONE ❧

1868–74; 1880–85; 1886; 1892–94

The casting director of the high political drama of the nineteenth century, looking for the perfect foil for Disraeli, found him in a man of commanding presence and eagle glance, an intensely religious High Anglican with a tormented Calvinist sense of sin, a magnetic orator and a master of finance, one who would be swept by emotion into the espousal of crusades, one who believed that politics was a field for the play of moral forces. He was William Ewart Gladstone, Scots by blood, English by birth and education. Half the tension of the public conflict of the time springs from the profound antipathy of these two men.

Gladstone was born in Liverpool on 29 December, 1809, the youngest son of John (later Sir John) Gladstone, a merchant who had come from Lanark to prosper in the shipping business of the Mersey port. Some of the money was made in the slave trade. Growing very rich, the Gladstones moved house to an estate in the Highlands and William took the conventional road to political success, Eton and Christ Church. His first thought, like Walpole before him, was of a career in the Church, but before he left the University he had decided that in politics he could find a cause almost as worthy. President of the Union, with a double first, he was one of those whom watchful party talent-spotters are likely to recruit. At twenty-three, Gladstone was MP for Newark, a seat in the Duke of Newcastle's pocket. He was, of course, a Tory.

He was a Junior Lord of the Treasury and, soon afterwards, Under-Secretary for the Colonies in the Peel government (1835). Four years later, he married Catherine Glynne, daughter of a baronet and cousin of the Pitts and the Grenvilles, the Whig upper crust. Marriage eased, but did not solve, one of his gravest personal problems: he was obsessed by sexual desire, which drove him to use the scourge in the hope of taming his nature and also—which was hardly judicious—to seek the company of young London prostitutes in the hope of leading them to a better way of life. His wife knew about his "peculiar night work", as she called it, although it may be doubted whether she knew it all Some of his contemporaries took a robuster view of this missionary activity, which continued until he was over eighty. Children, eight in all, arrived at regular intervals to the serious, prayerful young politician and his wife.

When Peel came back to power, he made Gladstone Vice-President (1841), then President (1845) of the Board of Trade: his talent for finance was already apparent. On a minor church matter, he resigned, but later returned to office as Secretary for the Colonies. When Peel was defeated in 1846, a general election quickly followed, in which Gladstone came back to Parliament as member for Oxford University. He was, by that time, a Free Trade Conservative, member of a small group called the Peelites, who, after the general election of 1852, held the balance of power in the House of Commons.

When Lord Aberdeen patched together a coalition ministry, Gladstone was Chancellor of the Exchequer (1853) and moved from his London house in Carlton Gardens to 11 Downing Street. His first Budget was presented in a speech which was thought to be masterly; the Queen was delighted. Gladstone's recipe was: "Get your figures up thoroughly and then give them up as if the *whole world* was interested in them." He proposed to abolish the income tax gradually over a period of seven years from seven pence to three pence and then to nil. It was, in his opinion, a thoroughly immoral tax, tempting statesmen to extravagance and taxpayers to fraud.

Three weeks later, the Chancellor was involved in one of those incidents to which his social work made him prone: an attempt at blackmail by a man who was sentenced to imprisonment. Gladstone acknowledged that his accosting of prostitutes was "certainly not within the rules of worldly prudence". He continued his work at an increased tempo.

In 1854, when the Crimean War was coming, the Prime Minister, Lord Aberdeen, wanted to resign until Gladstone talked him out of it, arguing that Britain would not be fighting *for* the anti-Christian Turks but *against* the expansionist Russians. It was a good example of Gladstonian sophistry. In a matter of months, however, he decided that the war was no longer a just one and resigned when Palmerston succeeded Aberdeen as Prime Minister. The government, said Gladstone, had fallen with such a whack "that they could hear their heads thump as they struck the ground".

There were a few years in Opposition, when he devoted himself to the study of Homer, on which he produced a book (in three volumes). In it he argued that the doctrine of the Trinity was foreshadowed in the *Iliad*. Then came a spell as High Commissioner for the Ionian Islands (then a British protectorate); the post appealed to him because he would meet Greek Orthodox prelates, who might help him to realize one of his dreams, the reunion of the Christian churches. From the point of view of religion, the mission was not a success; politically, it was a disaster. Gladstone opposed the union of Corfu with mainland Greece, which made him very unpopular there and at home. He returned, a failure, apparently at the end of his career but, as Lord Aberdeen said, "Ah, he is terrible on the rebound!"

His financial policy had a Free Trade foundation and he was in process of becoming a convert to the idea of Parliamentary Reform, helped by the fact that the moral fervour of his oratory had a powerful effect on mass audiences. His growing Liberalism cost him his Oxford University seat in the election of 1865.

In 1859, the various Liberal sects had united under Palmerston and Lord John Russell, "those two dreadful old men", as the Queen called them; Gladstone voted for the Conservative government but, when it was defeated, took office as Chancellor of the Exchequer under Palmerston, who was giving support to the Italian *Risorgimento*, of which Gladstone approved. It need not be said that his decision to return to the government roused some mockery.

His Budget speech lasted four hours (helped by raw egg beaten up with sherry) and was regarded as a notable feat of finance as well as endurance. But in the Cabinet he was constantly at odds with his colleagues. Palmerston deluged the Queen with minutes about his unreasonable behaviour and said, in talking about defence, that if he had to choose between losing Portsmouth, Plymouth and Mr Gladstone, he would reluctantly choose the latter.

By 1866, Gladstone had reduced income tax (which had been tenpence) to fourpence. It seemed that, while the rich were growing richer, the poor were not so poor. Karl Marx, disappointed prophet of doom, groaned that prolonged prosperity had demoralized the workers. Gladstone, cast out by Oxford, found a new platform among the working people of Lancashire, to whom he announced, "At last, my friends, I am come among you. And I am come unmuzzled." He had broken, finally, with the Conservatives and had become a demagogue, reaching the minds and hearts of a vast population, who were just coming into political maturity. "A man ponderous, copious, of evident faculty, but all gone irrevocably into House of Commons shape." Thus, pessimistically, wrote Carlyle, whose contempt for the House of Commons was unbounded. Carlyle thought that Gladstone was "the representative of the multitudinous cants of the age". He preferred Disraeli.

When Palmerston died, Lord Russell, who took his place, devoted himself to the passing of a new Reform Bill. On this issue, the government was defeated and Lord Derby and Disraeli came into power. Gladstone, on holiday in Italy, found on his return that Disraeli had concocted a Reform Bill which Gladstone called "a gigantic engine of fraud". Before it was finally passed, the Conservative proposals contained many amendments; but the effect was that a million additional men could vote, as compared with the 400,000 who would have been enfranchised by Russell's bill. Disraeli had scored a remarkable Parliamentary victory and Gladstone, searching round for a way to improve Liberal fortunes, began to think that in Ireland he had found the cause he needed. He would disestablish the Irish Church. In 1868, a general election produced a huge Liberal majority; the Queen sent for Gladstone, who wrote in his diary, "I ascend a steepening path, with a burden ever gathering weight. The Almighty seems to sustain and spare me for some purpose of His own." He believed that his special mission was to pacify Ireland, a task which should take a year or two. His ignorance of Irish realities was exceptional.

Meanwhile, he had trouble with the Queen, who, after the death of the Prince Consort, had more or less retired from public life but would not allow the Prince of Wales to take over any of her public functions. Gladstone had been warned that he must be tactful in dealing with Her Majesty but tact, especially where it conflicted with the duty which the Almighty had laid on him, was something Gladstone could not display.

"The Royalty question", as he called it, bulked large in his mind: "The Queen is invisible and the Prince of Wales is not respected!" The Queen's antipathy to him hardened into something approaching hatred. The Liberal government drifted into unpopularity and, in a general election, the Conservatives won an overall majority. Deeply depressed, Gladstone contemplated withdrawal from politics so that he could devote himself to religion. He wrote a pamphlet attacking the Pope over the Infallibility Decree which had just been promulgated. The pamphlet had an enormous sale.

On a different subject, and even more inflammatory, was his pamphlet on the

Turkish massacres in Bulgaria. On this issue, he came into direct conflict with Disraeli, who was, above all, anxious to prevent Russia from obtaining an entry to the Mediterranean. Gladstone presented it as a moral question and was so carried away by his feelings that he described the Tsar as "a Christian gentleman". He regarded foreign affairs as, essentially, a sphere for moral exercises. Sidney Herbert besought him to remember that the British were flesh and blood, not a congress of moral philosophers.

In his crusading zeal, Gladstone risked destroying the unity of his party. "Gladstone and Dizzy seem to cap one another in folly and imprudence," said Sir William Harcourt, "and I don't know which has made the greatest ass of himself." Gladstone was not helped by the military success of his friends, the Russians, who invaded the Balkans and, as it seemed, were about to capture Constantinople.

Gladstone denounced the arrangements reached at the Congress of Berlin as immoral and, by the general election of 1880, was returned to power. In the previous year he had been the hero of what was the most spectacular and stirring incident in the popular politics of the nineteenth century, the Midlothian Campaign. It consisted of a series of five mass meetings, and several smaller ones, in Edinburgh, Glasgow and other Scottish towns. It had rather the atmosphere of a religious revival than a political demonstration. The moral tone was exalted, the emotional fervour intense. The organizing talent behind it was Lord Rosebery's; a good deal of the money it absorbed was his as well. The general theme was the need to defend human dignity; the particular enemy was Disraeli, and his selfish, unworthy policies: "The battle to be fought is a battle of Justice, Humanity, Freedom, Law . . . the great simplicities seem to demand captial letters . . . I should regard myself as morally forced into this work as a great and high election of God."

57 **Gladstone addressing the Scottish crowds during the Midlothian Campaign, 1879.**

The great mass meetings (20,000 men in the Waverley Market, Edinburgh), the torchlight processions, the extraordinary enthusiasm—all this was evoked by an orator speaking, not about taxes or wages, but about moral issues—and foreign ones at that. It was as if Scotland was hearing far-off echoes of the voice of John Knox. What was the most remarkable feature of it was that very few of his vast audience had a vote. When the by-election was held in Midlothian, fewer than 3,000 men, Liberal or Conservative, were entitled to vote.

When, in April, 1880, it was clear that the Liberals had won a decisive victory at the polls, Gladstone was not surprised: "To God the praise." Much to her disgust, the Queen asked him to form a government. She did not at all relish a renewal of close personal contact with a man popularly known as "the People's William".

58 Lord Randolph Churchill, leader of the "Fourth Party", which assailed Gladstone in the House of Commons.

"VICE VERSA"—THE OLD CHANCELLOR OF THE EXCHEQUER AND THE NEW

The new government soon ran into trouble. In Afghanistan and South Africa there were military setbacks; Ireland grew steadily more menacing. Gladstone, the prophet of peace, the friend of nationalism, bombarded Alexandria and invaded Egypt. He was annoyed that an engagement at Hawarden prevented him from hearing the victory salute for Tel-el-Kabir.

In the Commons he was assailed with pitiless ingenuity by the "Fourth Party", led by Lord Randolph Churchill. Gladstone's favourite exercise of cutting down trees was the subject of one of Churchill's most brilliant flights of humour: "For the purposes of recreation he has selected the felling of trees, and we may usefully remark that his amusements, like his politics, are constantly destructive. The forest laments in order that Mr Gladstone may perspire." And so on from one absurdity to another still more absurd.*

Graver was the rising tide of revolt in Ireland. Parnell, leader of the Land League, the most dangerous subversive organization, was arrested and the League was banned. Then the Chief Secretary for Ireland, Lord Frederick Cavendish, husband of Gladstone's sister-in-law, was murdered in Phoenix Park, Dublin.

59 Charles Stewart Parnell, Irish Nationalist leader.

But the most serious trouble of all came from the Sudan, where a religious rising under a fanatic called the Mahdi massacred an Egyptian army with an English commander. Lord Salisbury, the Conservative leader, was suffering from the gibes of Lord Randolph Churchill at that time. He said: "Randolph and the Mahdi have occupied my thoughts about equally. The Mahdi pretends to be half-mad but is very sane; Randolph occupies exactly the converse position." Gladstone's government sent out General Gordon, who got himself cut off in Khartoum and, as Queen Victoria feared would happen, was murdered by fanatical tribesmen. It was, no

---

*Churchill *Speeches*. I, p. 113, where connoisseurs will find the whole passage worth reading.

doubt, Gordon's own fault; that was not, however, how his fellow-countrymen regarded it. Nor was it how the Queen regarded it. People in the streets thought that Gladstone was, in effect, Gordon's murderer and the Queen agreed with them.

Taking advantage of Britain's involvement in the Sudan, Russian troops crossed the Afghan frontier; Gladstone announced that the threat would be met by all available forces, whereupon the Russians climbed down and Gladstone wrote to his wife, "Praise to the Most High." But his government's days were numbered, and on 8 June, 1885, it was defeated by the Conservatives, with whom the Irish Nationalists voted. Lord Salisbury formed a government, which remained in office until a general election could be held.

At this point, Gladstone became a convert to Home Rule for Ireland, but, while he was making up his mind on this issue, a general election produced an embarrassing result: the Conservatives, with the Irish Nationalists, had the same number of seats as the Liberals. When Salisbury announced that the legislative union with Ireland would be preserved and a new Irish Coercion Bill would be introduced, Gladstone, with the Irish Nationalists, turned the government out. He took office again in January, 1886; but his party was split in two and, three months later, Joseph Chamberlain, the most strident of its younger members, left it, having heard an outline of the Home Rule Bill which the aged Prime Minister was about to introduce.

In his three-and-a-half-hour speech, Gladstone said, among other things, that Ulster "should have its wishes considered to the utmost practical extent". It was uncertain what that meant but quite certain that Gladstone had not allowed for the strength of feeling in Ulster. Lord Randolph Churchill invented the cry, "Ulster will fight; Ulster will be right." The Prime Minister had plunged ahead recklessly, without considering the state of mind in his own party. John Bright, for example, the keeper of the Liberal conscience, thought that Gladstone was strangely blind on Ulster, and strangely credulous of the Irish Nationalists' good faith. The Home Rule Bill was defeated by Liberal votes.

Lord Randolph said that the Liberal party had been "shivered into fragments to gratify the ambitions of an old man in a hurry". A general election confirmed that view. Lord Salisbury became Prime Minister. After that, it seemed for a time that events were flowing Gladstone's way when the O'Shea divorce led to the fall of Parnell and a split in the Irish Nationalist party. Moreover, from the election of 1892, Gladstone emerged victorious, with a majority in the House of forty-five. The Queen was in the painful necessity of selecting as her Prime Minister, for the fourth time, "a deluded, excited man of eighty-two".

He, for his part, was often exhausted but able to see the Home Rule Bill through its Second Reading, speaking again and again in the House, an extraordinary feat for a man of his age. The Lords threw the bill out. In 1894, quarrelling with his Cabinet over the naval estimates, he resigned on grounds of ill-health; the Queen did not consult him about his successor. Her dislike of Gladstone persisted to the end.

He died four years later, busy, until his health broke down, with agitation against the Turks over the Armenian massacre, with controversy with the Vatican over Anglican orders and with preparing a new edition of the works of Bishop Butler. The Queen was annoyed that the Prince of Wales and the Duke of York were pall-bearers at the funeral. So passed the most dynamic leader that British Liberalism has ever had.

XXXI

ROBERT ARTHUR TALBOT GASCOYNE-CECIL,
3rd Marquis of Salisbury

1885; 1886–92; 1895–1902

The British have no objection at all if their noblemen are eccentric: if, for example, they do not go to the races but stay at home and read books; if they have a highly individual taste in clothes—the height of dandyism, perhaps, or, better still, if they look like one of their own gardeners. Such foibles are easily forgiven to the man of title. A young lord who pottered about in the laboratory, who wrote (for money) serious articles on foreign policy, who disliked society and went to church first thing every morning was obviously a "character", a "card", he had already one foot in the door of public esteem. Such a man was Lord Robert Arthur Talbot Gascoyne-Cecil, later Viscount Cranborne, later still, third Marquis of Salisbury.

Since the great statesmen of the Elizabethan era, the Cecils had lived, magnificent but undistinguished, at Hatfield, where Lord Robert Gascoyne-Cecil was born on 3 February, 1830 to the second Marquis and his wife, Frances Mary Gascoyne. At fifteen, the boy was taken away from Eton, where he was abominably bullied, and, in due course, went to Christ Church—fourth class honours in mathematics. He spent two years in Australia and, on his return, was elected MP for Stamford. Very soon, he was recognized as one who owned an unusually caustic tongue. In 1857, he married Georgina Alderson, daughter of a judge. As his father did not think the marriage was good enough for young Cecil, they lived rather unfashionably, but very happily, in Fitzroy Square, while he supplemented his income by writing articles on foreign policy for the *Quarterly* and *Saturday Reviews*. At that time, the Liberals were in office; his articles criticizing them attracted notice in political circles.

He was of independent and, on the whole, reactionary opinions. He voted against the admission of Jews to Parliament and against the abolition of religious tests for entering universities. On the other hand, he thought the London Board of Guardians was too harsh to the poor. He protested when Gladstone tried to apply the income tax to endowed charities. He wrote powerful and deeply studied articles on foreign policy; he argued, for instance, that to challenge Prussia on the question of Schleswig-Holstein and then back down, to ask the Danes to abandon strong positions and then fail to help them—that such a policy was a crime against honour and loyalty.

He joined Lord Derby's ministry as Secretary of State for India (1866), but resigned in 1867 over the proposed Reform Bill. A year later he inherited his father's title and seat in the Lords and, in 1874, he was Secretary for India in Disraeli's government, although he had said, "The prospect of having to serve with this man again is like a nightmare." It was a remarkable turn in events, however, which he justified, later on, in a memorable statement, "It is the duty of every Englishman, and of every English party, to accept a political defeat cordially, and to lend their best endeavours to secure the success, or to neutralize the evil, of the principles to which they have been forced to succumb."

Very soon, too, he succumbed to Disraeli's charm, as Disraeli did to his ability. In the meantime, he had set up a laboratory for himself at Hatfield where, among other

60 Hatfield House, Hertfordshire, home of the Marquis of Salisbury.

interests, he devoted himself to photography. "He is never happy," said Lord Randolph Churchill, "out of that damned laboratory at Hatfield." He was made Chancellor of the University of Oxford and responded, in Latin, to the deputation which came to confer the honour on him. At this time, he wrote an article in the *Quarterly* vehemently pleading for Britain to prevent the transfer of Alsace and Lorraine to Germany after the Franco-Prussian war: "a ceded territory would be a constant memorial of humiliation." He heartily supported the Prime Minister when he made the Queen Empress of India. At this time, Turkish atrocities grew as Turkey's power dwindled; Salisbury was sent as High Commissioner to Constantinople, where he was distrusted by the British community and became friendly with the Russian ambassador. He had an audience with the Sultan, who, among other foibles, refused to read anything written in black ink and, owing to his dread of fire, would not allow a candle to be lighted in the whole of his palace. If Salisbury had ever thought he could bring an international settlement back from Constantinople, he was soon disillusioned.

He returned to find that the Cabinet greeted him with enthusiasm: he had not done too badly in a task which they knew was almost impossible. At this time, Russian armies were marching southwards in the Caucasus and the Balkans. By the spring of 1878, they were on the outskirts of Constantinople. The Sultan appealed to Britain to mediate. Disraeli sent a British fleet to keep an eye on the Russian army; the elephant and the whale, as Bismarck called them, were within striking distance of one another. The House of Commons voted £6,000,000 for military preparations; Lord Derby resigned as Foreign Secretary and Salisbury succeeded him.

Almost the first thing he did was to compose a circular letter to the five great European powers, suggesting a basic agreed settlement of all the disputes comprising the "Eastern Question": Russia could not be the sole architect of a peace; any treaty between Russia and Turkey must be a European treaty. The circular, sent out before Salisbury was officially installed as Foreign Secretary, was a decisive document. He was Disraeli's right-hand man at the Berlin Congress, was bored by the official festivities ("that tiresome Princess asking me to lunch at Potsdam") and made the journey to Dresden for the pleasure of worshipping in an Anglican church. On their return in triumph together, Salisbury was, like his chief, given the Garter, which he accepted reluctantly. He insisted, however, that the most enjoyable event during the stay in Berlin had been the opportunity it gave him to discuss electro-magnetism with Herman Helmholz, the physicist. As for the outcome of the negotiations, he said, "Europe may now rest for a couple of months, watching the interesting process of a Tsar recovering his temper."

When Disraeli died in 1881, Salisbury succeeded him as Conservative leader in the Lords and, when Gladstone was defeated four years later, the Queen sent for him to form a government. He was at Hatfield when the summons came from Balmoral, engaged on some experiment in his laboratory, and he left for London in time to catch the night train to Scotland. He was willing, but not eager, to take the job: never, in any of his premierships, did he live in 10 Downing Street. He worked either at the Foreign Office, at Hatfield, or at his London house in Arlington Street. The Queen he regarded with the devotion he owed to the sovereign and the respect he had for a woman of long and wide experience of men and affairs.

He was determined to continue to be Foreign Secretary as well as Prime Minister. His ministry did not last for many months. At the end of it, he returned to the laboratory at Hatfield and resumed his interrupted experiment. But soon he was Prime Minister once more, in 1886, and resumed his old place at the Foreign Office.

During the next six years, Salisbury, a cautious imperialist, acquired three colonies in Africa and, in addition, Borneo. He exchanged Heligoland for Zanzibar and, as a result of arduous negotiations with the Portuguese, obtained for Britain the territories which came to be called Rhodesia; their capital was named Salisbury. He lost the election of 1892; although there were a few more Conservative MPs than Liberals, the Irish Nationalists tipped the scales in favour of Gladstone. Salisbury retired to a chalet near Dieppe which he loved, and to his ancestral mansion at Hatfield; there he could sleep, ride on his bicycle, meditate, and prepare speeches on scientific subjects; he was President of the British Association in 1894.

He made a resounding attack on Gladstone's Home Rule Bill, which was duly thrown out by the House of Lords; the Liberals were routed in the general election of 1895. Queen Victoria was delighted to have Salisbury back as her Prime Minister instead of "that dreadful old man", Gladstone. Salisbury now had a majority in Parliament. He had a dynamic Colonial Secretary in Joseph Chamberlain; his nephew, Arthur Balfour, was Leader of the House of Commons. He himself was, once more, Foreign Secretary, responsible, as it turned out, for guiding policy through one crisis after another, e.g. the Venezuela crisis with the United States, the Fashoda incident with France.

He invented the Concert of Europe, a diplomatic instrument intended to protect the interests of Christian communities under Turkish misrule. They were much in need of protection, as was shown by a massacre of thousands of Armenians in Constantinople while the Turkish police looked on. But Lord Salisbury had "no belief in a policy of scold"—what could he do? He did nothing. His down-to-earth realistic policy naturally involved concessions as well as gains. Thus, he was forced to allow the Russians to establish a naval base at Port Arthur. This his colleagues, quite reasonably, regarded as a disaster. But at that moment Kitchener was on his way to Khartoum and Fashoda; there was a grave danger of war with France. "I can't afford to quarrel with Russia now," he explained.

By 1899, Salisbury's mind was slowing up, although his wit remained as sharp as ever. "I think I must take up bridge," he said, "so that I can meet the Duke of Devonshire" (who was one of his ministers). His eyesight also seems to have been failing. When King Edward VII handed him a signed photograph, he peered at it and said, "Poor old Buller."

He was a bearded, portly old gentleman with a bad memory whose authority over his Cabinet and in the country was as great as ever. He allowed Chamberlain a wide measure of freedom in conducting British policy in South Africa. When war came that year—"Joe's war", as he called it—Britain's military unreadiness was revealed and necessitated a complete change in the command of the army in the field. Salisbury remained loyal to his lieutenants all through the war and the hate-campaign against Britain which broke out on the Continent. In November, 1900, the old gentlemen handed over the Foreign Office to Lord Lansdowne.

When, about then, the Labour party was foreshadowed, he was sympathetic to some of its aims; he favoured trade unions and the right to strike; he had opposed compulsory education but, since it became law, insisted that it should be free; better poor laws and the encouragement of municipal enterprises—to all that he was sympathetic. But he disliked the emergence of a new, separate party, and he hated the theory of Socialism, which worked towards replacing the family unit with a state bureaucracy.

In the "Khaki Election" of September, 1900, Chamberlain, not Salisbury, was the central figure on the Conservative side. The government won with an overall majority of 134. Salisbury remained in office, although he was sinking into the weakness of old age. One reason that he did so was that the Queen, whom he regarded as a friend, was likewise nearing the end of her reign. He retired before King Edward was crowned and went for a last holiday on the Continent. He died at Hatfield on 22 August, 1903, aged seventy-three, having to the last attended early morning service in the chapel. He was buried in Hatfield churchyard beside his wife.

He had been Prime Minister for thirteen years, ten months; more important, for it was his real mission in life, he had been Foreign Secretary during eleven and a half years, with one short break. After the sparkle of Disraeli and the swoop of Gladstone's mind, there is something at once anonymous and inscrutable about this aristocrat. Christian dogma excepted, he suspected doctrine. He disliked demagogues and distrusted experts. "If you believe the doctors," he said, "nothing is wholesome; if you believe the theologians, nothing is innocent; if you believe the soldiers, nothing is safe. They all require to have their strong wine diluted by a very large admixture of insipid common sense." What he brought to politics—what, indeed, accounted for his domination of his party and his time—was a respect for character. The shallow, the meretricious, the "too clever by half" aroused his deepest antipathy. His severest judgment was spoken of the Kaiser: "he is *false*."

**61 Robert Gascoyne-Cecil,
3rd Marquis of Salisbury, by Spy.**

XXXII

❧ARCHIBALD PHILIP PRIMROSE, 5th Earl of Rosebery ❧

1894–95

"Are you not glad Ladas has not won the Leger?" asked Lady Salisbury. Her delight was easily explained. Ladas, who had been beaten by a 50–1 outsider, was owned by Lord Rosebery, one of "the two Rs", as she called him (the other being Lord Randolph Churchill), who badgered Lord Salisbury in Parliament. Lady Salisbury was not one of those women who thought that party feelings should not intrude on private life. She preferred Randolph to Rosebery: "he has heart . . . the other is entirely inhuman." It was a mistake which some people made.

If Archibald Primrose, fifth Earl of Rosebery, did not win the Derby in that year, his horses did win the Derby thrice later, thus fulfilling one of his three reputed ambitions; the others, also achieved, were to marry an heiress and to become Prime Minister. The remark is attributed to him but he always denied it; however, he did carry off the three prizes.

He was born in London on 7 May, 1847, in Charles Street, Berkeley Square, son of Lord Dalmeny; and after being educated at Eton and Christ Church, succeeded his grandfather in the earldom (1868). Ten years later, he married Hannah, daughter of Baron Mayer de Rothschild.

His mother, who had married again and was Duchess of Cleveland by this time, found her son's marriage hard to bear; her house had, for years, "stood out against an infusion of Jewish society". She was not present at the wedding, which was a double event, a Jewish ceremony in Mount Street and an Anglican one in Christ Church, Down Street, Mayfair, when Disraeli gave the bride away and the Prince of Wales signed the register. The marriage was opposed in the Jewish press, which spoke of it with "the most poignant grief". Hannah Rosebery remained faithful to her religion and, at the end of the Day of Atonement, her husband would take to her bedroom the tray of food with which she ended her fast. The Roseberys had two sons and two daughters.

As a boy, Dalmeny was handsome and aloof, "not remarkable for scholarship", as his Eton tutor thought, "plenty of cool assurance; one of those who like the palm without the dust." At Oxford, he was one of a small aristocratic clique which avoided the company of less fortunate undergraduates. He was mad about racing to the point where the College gave him the choice of selling his horse, which was entered for the Derby, or leaving the University, where he was expected to take a first. Dalmeny kept the horse, which finished last.

62 Mentmore Towers, Buckinghamshire, home of Lord Rosebery.

At that stage, he was a thoroughly arrogant, insolent, unpleasant young man. He inherited the title with an income of £30,000, which was augmented by £100,000 when he married a Rothschild.* He was—and he remains—an enigmatic figure: a haughty Scottish patrician with great houses at Dalmeny, Mentmore and Epsom, to say nothing of a house in Berkeley Square and a villa in Naples; a devotee of the turf, who owned a famous stud and gambled heavily, in one night at Newmarket winning £1,300 at baccarat; later giving up this extravagance for the pleasures of collecting; at the same time, a serious student and, when he became engrossed in politics, one who found his sympathies increasingly with the Liberals.

His first spectacular intervention in public life occurred when he master-minded Gladstone's Midlothian Campaign in 1879; it was a remarkable feat of political showmanship but it was not followed by political advancement. One minor consequence of it was that Rosebery was black-balled for the Travellers' Club in London.

Gladstone offered him a minor post in his government, which he, at first, refused. Coolness between the two men increased until Rosebery resigned in 1883 as Under-Secretary at the Home Office on Gladstone's failure to create a separate Scottish Department with himself as Secretary for Scotland. At that time, the northern kingdom was administered by the Lord Advocate, a Law Officer. But Gladstone was absorbed in the woes of Ireland and thought that Rosebery was behaving very foolishly to press the case for Scotland. It was true, however, that Scotland felt that she was neglected and Rosebery was her spokesman. His resignation was a serious setback to his political career.

---

*Hannah's fortune amounted to £2,000,000, including the ownership of Mentmore.

He left for Australia and was captured by the notion of a "sane Imperialism", as distinct from "wildcat Imperialism". "There is no need for any nation, however great, to leave the Empire," he declared in a speech he delivered in Adelaide. "For the Empire is a Commonwealth of Nations."

When Gladstone's government ran into deep trouble over the murder of General Gordon in Khartoum, Rosebery entered it as First Commissioner of Works in 1884; it was an impetuous gesture of chivalry but it did not save Gladstone's government. A general election, held in the autumn of 1885, produced a House of Commons in which the Irish Nationalist members held the balance. A Tory government was followed by another short-lived Gladstone administration in which Rosebery served as Foreign Secretary. He could no longer complain that he was overlooked.

The Home Rule Bill, Gladstone's favourite child, was rejected by the House of Lords and the Liberals were then defeated in a general election. Rosebery, who had stayed faithful to Gladstone when other men had deserted him, now emerged as "the man of the future", in a phrase of Gladstone's.

When the London County Council came into existence he was elected (1889) as a member for the City and, by a large majority, became the first chairman of the Council. He worked hard at the job and did it well, emerging as a social reformer whose fame extended far beyond the bounds of the metropolis. In Scotland, he had a unique position, founded on a series of speeches delivered to great audiences and touching on Scottish pride and imagination. While he lived there was no need to ask who was "the uncrowned King" of Scotland.

He lived like a prince, whether in his great houses in England, Scotland, Italy, or, even, in the little old Scots castle called Barnbougle on the Dalmeny estate where he would go to escape to his books from the tedium of guests or the bustle of politics. His personality remained impenetrable even to his few intimate friends. The Whig

63 Archibald Primrose,
   5th Earl of Rosebery,
   by H. Furniss.

grandee who loved books, racing and lively conversation over the dinner table was also deeply, almost morbidly, religious. "Behind all his external urbanity and humour lay this haunting sense of transience . . . at heart, he was the Calvinist of seventeenth century Scotland."* As time passed and insomnia afflicted him increasingly—after every speech he had a sleepless night—the feeling grew that he had lost his way in politics, that perhaps politics was not his proper vocation, and, finally, when his wife died in 1890, gloom took an ever stronger grip on his nature.

The Queen was horrified by the speeches he was making at this time: "radical, almost communistic. Poor Lady Rosebery is not there to keep him back." She dreaded that he might be in the next Cabinet, not knowing that it was his fixed resolve at this time to leave public life after the election which was due to be held and, in fact, came about in July, 1892. It left the Liberals dependent on the Irish Nationalist vote in the Commons.

Rosebery, who had been yachting with his children off the west coast of Scotland, was pestered to join the Liberal government about to be formed, and he retired to Paris for a weekend "to clear the cobwebs of his brain". The Queen was urged by the Prince of Wales to send for Rosebery but would have no part "in the formation of this iniquitous government".

After days of anguished indecision, Rosebery agreed to be Foreign Secretary in the new Gladstone ministry; he was, as Campbell-Bannerman thought, "in wretched health"; he had no one to look after his children, as he told the Queen. After taking office, his health improved. One of his first acts was to raise the Washington Legation to the rank of an Embassy; but he refused to appoint Labouchère to it. Labouchère, who had angled for the post, replied by making Rosebery the target of a stream of abuse in his weekly, *Truth*.†

On the question of whether Britain should keep control of Uganda or not, the new Foreign Secretary soon found himself in trouble with his colleagues and, in particular, with Gladstone. Rosebery thought that Britain should annex the territory but accepted a delay of three months as a compromise. Gladstone was annoyed by Rosebery's tendency to conduct foreign policy independently of himself or the Cabinet.

On Egypt, where the Khedive had dismissed a pro-British Prime Minister, he carried the day over his critics, insisting on maintaining British influence by sending a British battalion to Port Said. "He is absolute at the Foreign Office," said Sir Reginald Brett. "He informs his colleagues of very little and does as he pleases. If it offends them, he retires." As Rosebery's policy was in its general tendency imperialist, the relations between him and Gladstone grew worse. Another point of difference between the two men was that Rosebery was deeply distrustful of French policy, which Gladstone was not. But he recognized that there were limits to what Britain could and should do. France was, in his opinion, behaving badly in Siam (Thailand) but that was not Britain's affair. "We cannot afford to be the Knight Errant of the world, careering about to redress grievances and help the weak."

The Prime Minister was at this time feeling the burdens of his great age—above

---

* John Buchan.
† Henry Labouchère, a radical politician and owner of the weekly, *Truth*.

all, deafness and excitability. The question of the succession to the premiership loomed. (In fact, Gladstone was within a year of retirement.) The Home Rule Bill—third of the series—had been thrown out by the Lords and it was now apparent to everyone that in its absence there was no Liberal policy. As the Cabinet disintegrated, Rosebery's star was in the ascendant, especially when he settled an obstinate coal strike.

There followed a struggle for Gladstone's throne between him and Sir William Harcourt, whose son, Louis ("Loulou"), carried on a busy, independent campaign to undermine Rosebery's position. He did so in vain, for the reason that influential Liberal ministers—Asquith and Grey, for example—were opposed to Harcourt. There remained, however, a difficulty: Rosebery was a peer. Would a Prime Minister in the House of Lords need to have the consent of the government's leader in the Commons for foreign policy decisions and government appointments? Harcourt sought to force this condition on Rosebery—who was not ready to concede it. In the end, Harcourt relented and agreed to be Chancellor of the Exchequer and Leader of the Commons; Lord Kimberley was Foreign Secretary, on condition that he should communicate as freely with Harcourt as with Rosebery.

On 2 March, 1894, Rosebery agreed to form a Cabinet. His position was not an enviable one: a government dependent on the vote of Irish members, who were playing a game of their own; a divided party, and resentful, defeated ministerial rivals, the Harcourts, thirsting for revenge. Small wonder that Rosebery's insomnia troubled him more than ever! It was a modest consolation that his horse, Ladas II, won the Derby, although this, too, helped to deepen the image of him as a lightweight Prime Minister. He formed the impression, correctly, that his colleagues were not giving him whole-hearted support against the onslaught in the Commons.

64 Sir William Harcourt, by F. Carruthers Gould.

Harcourt's Budget of 1895 proposed to introduce estate duties; it was a popular innovation but it caused a furious quarrel between him and Rosebery. There were also sharp disagreements on foreign policy. The depression which these events produced in him was acute. By-elections were going against the government and when, in June, the government was defeated on a trivial issue, Rosebery and his weary Cabinet resigned. Their party was resoundingly beaten by the Conservatives in the election that followed. "It can hardly fail to do good," Rosebery thought. The Rosebery-Harcourt partnership had been "a fraud upon the public". Thus ended, at the age of forty-seven, his career in government. "There are two supreme pleasures in life," he said later. "One is ideal, the other, real. The ideal is when a man receives the seals of office from his sovereign. The real pleasure comes when he hands them back."

A year later, he gave up the Liberal leadership and five years followed during which his health revived and his popularity in the country rose. He stood aloof from party politics to the irritation of those, like Asquith, who were necessarily absorbed in it and to the reawakened anticipation of those who thought he might still step forward and seize the reins of Liberal leadership.

While the South African war was dragging on, he spoke as a Liberal imperialist, supported by men like Asquith and Sir Edward Grey, but at odds with the mass of the Liberal party in Parliament. Campbell-Bannerman, the party leader, looked with jealousy on Rosebery's occasional appearances from the shadows to excite and disturb the party faithful. But these interventions, as time passed, grew less frequent, and the Liberal rank and file, still ready to admire him, became reconciled to the fact that they must look elsewhere for their leader. As he withdrew into ever deeper seclusion, events in the public sphere, at home or in Europe, did not give him encouragement. When the *Entente* with France was made in 1904, his verdict was, "It will lead you straight to war." To this sombre view, he remained faithful; five years later, at the first Imperial Press Conference, he held the delegates spellbound with a picture of the international scene as he saw it: "This calm before the storm is terrifying; there never was in history so overwhelming preparation for war."

By the time the war came, the war he believed was inevitable, he was already out of the political mainstream; his most faithful admirers no longer thought of him as a possible leader. His favourite son, Neil Primrose, was killed in Palestine in 1917. It was, after his wife's death, the bitterest blow in his life. A few days before the end of the war, he was laid low by a stroke, from which he made only a partial recovery, although he lingered on for years. He died at The Durdans on 21 May, 1929.

He was a remarkable man, who touched life at many points: a great aristocrat, a scholar, a millionaire, a collector of discrimination, especially a collector of books. (In his library at Barnbougle were to be found Napoleon's travelling library, Charles I's copy of Laud's Liturgy, Mary Queen of Scots' Bible. On the walls at Barnbougle hung Gilbert Stuart's portrait of Washington, authenticated by artist and subject. Night after night, he would escape from his magnificent surroundings to the tiny bedroom at the top of his little castle, with its view over the grey firth.) He was a writer of distinction, a magnificent orator. Only Bossuet has surpassed his funeral rhetoric. This, for example, on Lord Randolph Churchill: "the chief mourner at his own protracted funeral, a public pageant of gloomy years." In character, petulant and fastidious, wrapped in himself; his "moody grandiloquence"* was not to everyone's taste; committed to politics and unable to endure the party dogfight; a Prime Minister and, in the end, a failure, gloomily aware that somewhere along the line he had taken the wrong turning. He wrote, when the battle was over and the dust had long settled:

"The secret of my life, which seems to me sufficiently obvious, is that I always detested politics. I had been landed in them accidentally by the Midlothian election, which was nothing but a chivalrous adventure. When I found myself in this evil-smelling bog, I was always trying to extricate myself. That is the secret of what people used to call my lost opportunities."

Such is the explanation, or the apologia, of the strangest and, perhaps, the most tragic of all the British Prime Ministers. Is the explanation true? Did the apologia convince the man to whom it was addressed, himself? What is certain is that there was more to uncover.

65 Archibald Primrose, 5th Earl of Rosebery.

---

* Lord Balcarres.

XXXIII

❧ ARTHUR JAMES BALFOUR ❧

1902–05

"Never forget, Arthur," said Lord Rosebery, earnestly addressing Mr Balfour, who had just succeeded Lord Salisbury as Prime Minister, and now waited for the wise words of the elder statesman. "The garden belongs to No. 10 and has nothing to do with No. 11." It was characteristic of Rosebery that he should have mentioned this infinitely unimportant question of privilege, and it was most unlikely that Balfour's mind at such a moment was prepared to deal with it. Although they had the same background in breeding and education, the two men were different in temperament. And Balfour, the younger, was more sinewy and realistic.

He was a Scottish patrician, born 25 July, 1848, son of a rich laird, James Maitland Balfour, and, by his mother, Lady Blanche Gascoyne-Cecil, a nephew of the formidable Conservative Prime Minister, Lord Salisbury. Balfour's property, 10,000 acres in extent, was on the south shore of the Firth of Forth, a few miles east of Rosebery's. Like Rosebery, he went to Eton; after that to Cambridge, where he studied Philosophy and Science. His languid, drooping appearance combined with his aesthetic interests (porcelain, music, serious conversation) to give him a reputation as one who was effeminate, "decadent", as it was called then. On the other hand, Balfour was an enthusiastic player of real tennis and, later, golf. In fact, there was a general misunderstanding of "Pretty Fanny", as he was nicknamed; time was soon to show that there was steel in that willowy frame.

He was attracted by the charming May Lyttelton and may have fallen in love with her, as she seems to have done with him. When the girl died of typhoid fever in 1875, he walked for hours in the London streets, and asked that a ring which had belonged to his mother should be placed in her coffin. All through his life he spent the anniversary of May's death with her sister, Lavinia Talbot, and her husband. Although he had, in later years, friendships with women, one of which was certainly passionate, he never showed the slightest desire to marry.

He was one of an unusual family. His brother Eustace was a considerable architect, who drank himself to death; his brother Frank, whom Balfour regarded as the most brilliant of the family, was an FRS and a world authority on embryology. He was killed mountaineering in 1882. Another brother forged a cheque and was banished to Australia.

Son of an MP (who died when the boy was six, leaving Arthur the bulk of a fortune of £4,000,000), it was natural that Balfour should become a Member of Parliament;

66 Arthur James Balfour.

as a nephew of Salisbury's, it was natural that his constituency should be Hertford. He was twenty-six when he was elected, in 1874. He was in no hurry to speak in Parliament and, when he did speak, he was, at first, ineffectual. He accompanied his uncle Salisbury to the Congress of Berlin where he met Bismarck, who asked if he was a descendant of the Balfour of Burleigh in *Old Mortality*. (He was not.)

He was one—the least active—of the four young Conservative MPs called the "Fourth Party", who badgered the government under Lord Randolph Churchill's leadership. As a contemporary said, "he was a good comrade to the Fourth Party without ceasing to maintain his succession to more permanent honours."

While politics flagged, he consoled himself with the pleasures of London society, in which he found decorative people, male and female, and sparkling talk. At that time, London was the brilliant intellectual centre which it remained until the Second World War. He became his uncle Salisbury's private secretary; he published, in the following year, *A Defence of Philosophic Doubt*. The title seemed to convey the essence of the man: evasive, sceptical—a dilettante. However, there was more in Balfour than doubt. "He always seemed to me to have a heart of stone" [Neville Chamberlain]. "Amid the labyrinthine intrigues of Renaissance Italy, he would not have required to study Machiavelli" [Winston Churchill]. The first comment was unjust; the second, not.

In 1887, when he had sat in Parliament for thirteen years, his uncle made him Chief Secretary for Ireland, a country then passing through one of its periodic phases of disorder. The Irish Nationalists were amused at the thought of this drawing-room ornament trying to cope with their native brand of terrorism. Very soon, however, they were complaining about the doings of "Bloody Balfour". He dealt severely— and effectively—with crime; he offered measures of economic improvement. He was without fear. Until then, few had heard of him; from now on, his name was made.

What made Irish government so difficult, he thought, "was English sentimentality". He evolved a policy mixing coercion and benevolence. For years, it seemed that he had killed Irish nationalism. When his work in Ireland was over, he went off to the Bayreuth Festival.

In the House of Commons he developed into a fearsome and stylish debater. He looked on the trends in contemporary politics with an indulgent disbelief; "democracy", that is, universal suffrage, was bringing into existence a kind of man who was a politician and nothing else, a professional who would inevitably look on politics as a way to advance his professional interests. The House of Lords was an assembly with a declining prestige (as was the House of Commons) and was, therefore, less capable than it should be of slowing down "the temporary surge of the moment". To abolish the House of Lords would, no doubt, be easy enough, but to replace it with a more respected, and, therefore, more effective, body was apparently beyond the wit of man. (Eighty years later the same could be said.)

Thinking like this, Balfour was unlikely to make a strong appeal to the masses, who had just been given the vote and meant to use it for purposes that seemed to them attractive and were certainly selfish. The tyranny of the majority was at hand with, as he believed, a form of despotism as its end-product.

Such philosophic musings as these meant nothing to an electorate which, in the latter years of the Salisbury government, was dazzled by the hectic imperialist vision of Joseph Chamberlain or by the quasi-Socialist schemes of the Radicals, who were steadily encroaching on the left of the Liberal Opposition. It was likely, then, that Balfour would be increasingly out of touch with his own party and with the country as a whole. But, in the meantime, he served Salisbury as his lieutenant in the Commons, in government and, from 1892 to 1895, in Opposition.

He still kept his interest in science, even in its most "far-out" manifestations; thus, in 1895, although not a "believer", he became President of the Society for Psychical Research. It was one of those features of his life which politicians found hard to understand.

When Salisbury came into power with a large majority in 1895, Balfour, who had just published a philosophical book, *The Foundations of Belief*, was Leader in the Commons; he was soon thought to be too lackadaisical for the post; he was in difficulties over an Education Bill, which was threatened by sectarian quarrels, and then over relations with Germany on colonial problems. Chamberlain, the Colonial Secretary, believed that a German alliance was possible; Salisbury had a profound distrust of the Kaiser. When war broke out with the Boers in 1899, Salisbury's health was already declining; when he retired in 1902, Balfour succeeded him. By that time, Edward VII was on the throne.

With the new King, Balfour's relations were brittle. Edward was mentally lazy and kept frivolous company. Trouble arose in the government over Chamberlain's fervent espousal of Protection by tariffs and Balfour's more pragmatic approach to the subject. It was given actuality by the fact that Britain had now outlived the head start in trade which she had held since the Industrial Revolution. A group of Free Trade Tories emerged to give complexity to politics, as the Liberal Unionists had done a decade before.

At this time, Balfour's supreme achievement was the creation of the Committee of Imperial Defence under himself as Prime Minister. He was, therefore, responsible for co-ordinating the defence of the whole Empire. It was as a consequence of this concern for defence that he remained in office longer than was necessary, in order to ensure that the army was equipped with a new gun, the eighteen-pounder.

In 1905, he had led the House of Commons for ten years, during which time Joseph Chamberlain forced the issue of Imperial Preference to the forefront. Balfour's views on this subject were equivocal and his leadership hesitant. "He nailed his colours to the fence," said Harry Cust, who was one of the "Souls".* The discontent in the Tory party grew. Balfour recognized that it was time for him to go. He resigned in December of that year and, in the election that followed, the Conservative government was destroyed; after nearly twenty years of Conservative domination, it was not surprising.

What was most significant was that fifty-three Labour members were now in the House of Commons. Austen Chamberlain thought, "it will end in the break-up of the Liberal party." The immediate result for Balfour was that he lost his Manchester seat. But his chief interest at the time was in the Zionist question: he had met Dr Weizmann, at that time a demonstrator in Manchester University, and Weizmann had converted him to the idea of a National Home for the Jews in Palestine. It was, he

---

*A coterie of well-to-do young intellectuals who met regularly for serious talk and love-making.

said, "a great cause, and I understand it". At the same time, he thought that the influx of Jews into Britain must be checked.

When Campbell-Bannerman, the Liberal Prime Minister, died in 1908, Asquith succeeded. One of his first acts was to call Balfour into the discussions at the Committee of Imperial Defence. He became a full member of the Committee in 1914. But during the years between, he played a secondary role in the party struggle, although he had returned to the House of Commons in 1906 as a member for the City of London. He had no strong convictions about Tariff Reform, which, in his defeated party, became an ever more important cause.

Without it, what was the party's platform to be? His second-in-command, Bonar Law, could not be relied on to be loyal; and the cry BMG (Balfour must go) grew in stridency.

By 1909 (Campbell-Bannerman had died and Asquith had succeeded him in 1908), when Lloyd George introduced his Budget, the movement of opinion in the country had changed. The Liberals were losing by-elections. The Budget was aimed at recovering lost popularity by increasing the taxes of the well-to-do, especially the landowners. Under Balfour, the Conservatives opposed it tooth and nail. It passed the Commons; would it pass the Lords? The Lords rejected it. A general election followed which left the two parties equally balanced, so that power was left with

67 Scene at the National Liberal Club as news of Balfour's defeat is heard, January, 1906.

Labour and the Irish Nationalists. In May, 1910, a new factor was brought into the situation when the King died.

The chief question now concerned the powers of the House of Lords. A second general election, held in 1910, confirmed the decision—or non-decision—of the first. The Lords were now faced with a Liberal threat to create enough new peers to ensure the passage of a Parliament Bill, limiting the power of the Second Chamber. Balfour believed that the bill should be accepted. Sick of the struggle, he resigned the party leadership in November, 1911. His place was taken by Bonar Law, who was no friend of Balfour's. It ought to have been the end of his life in politics but, instead, a new and, in a way, more splendid career, lay ahead. Not as leader of his party, not, certainly, as Prime Minister, but as a major statesman in the new political groupings made necessary by the war, which he had foreseen.

As it came nearer, various questions which had seemed of vital importance were hurriedly put on the shelf. Thus, Irish Home Rule legislation was indefinitely postponed in July, 1914. A year later, Balfour was First Lord of the Admiralty in a coalition government; he was responsible for the evacuation of Gallipoli and, as it turned out, for the first communiqué on the Battle of Jutland. This gave a candid account of events as they were known to the Admiralty at the time; in reality, the facts were not so bad and Balfour was held to have created a great deal of needless despondency. In the crisis that arose over the leadership of the coalition, he thought that Asquith should quit in favour of Lloyd George, as Lloyd George thought that *he* should quit the Admiralty. In December, 1916, Balfour became Foreign Secretary, in Lloyd George's government.

Four months later he was on his way to Washington, which was now the capital of a country engaged in the war as Britain's ally. President Woodrow Wilson had been prepared for his coming by a description sent by the American ambassador in London, Walter H. Page. According to Page, Balfour was "a sort of high-toned Scotch democrat. I have studied him with increasing charm and interest." His American mission was counted as a great success and, from this time onward, he settled down very comfortably and usefully to the role of elder statesman, for which, by temperament and ability, he was well suited.

He was made an earl (1922) and given the Garter in the same year. His authorship of the Balfour Declaration (November, 1917), proposing that the Jews should have a National Home in Palestine, was his most momentous contribution to world politics. It made him a hero among the Zionists, who were at that time (it was before the Nazi persecution) only a portion of world Jewry. It was a strange development for Balfour, but it was explained partly by his friendship with Dr Chaim Weizmann, the Zionist leader, and partly by Balfour's own upbringing by his formidable mother in the Scottish Church and the Evangelical wing of the Church of England.

His attitude to the Jews was, as his biographer Kenneth Young says,* ambivalent. Seeing in the Jews a highly gifted race, he was, at the same time, "uncertain and uncomfortable about their place in a Gentile society". He denounced anti-Semitism and restricted immigration. He came to believe that the Jews must have a National Home; Weizmann convinced him that only Palestine would do.

---

*Young. *A. J. Balfour*, pp. 257–8.

The result was the Declaration. What did it mean by "National Home"? Balfour explained to the Cabinet: some form of British, American or other protectorate under which full facilities would be given to the Jews to work out their own salvation; it did not necessarily mean "the early establishment of an independent Jewish state".

When he died on 19 March, 1930, aged eighty-two, he was worried about money, for he had made a disastrous investment in a project to use peat as industrial fuel. His fear of poverty was exaggerated but the library he had built up at Whittinghame had to be sold. He died as a philosopher should: "I do not think, so far as I can judge in the absence of actual experience, that I am at all afraid of dying." He was a theist, but a theist who believed in a personal God.

68 Arthur James Balfour. Caricature by Powys Evans, c. 1926.

XXXIV

❧ SIR HENRY CAMPBELL-BANNERMAN ❧

1905–08

At last! A Prime Minister who was educated at a day school, and a Scottish day school at that! Henry Campbell, born in Glasgow in 1836, was sent to Glasgow High School in 1845 by his father, a self-made business man, head of a firm of warehousemen and wholesale drapers, a Tory, later a Knight and Lord Provost of the City. Sent abroad as a boy, Henry Campbell toured Europe with his brother and returned speaking fluent French and Viennese German. He went to Glasgow University and from there to Trinity, Cambridge, where his academic achievements were not spectacular. Later, he entered the family business as a partner; he impressed the other members of the firm by his laziness.

In 1860, he married Charlotte Bruce, daughter of a general. Every year, the couple, who remained childless, spent their holidays abroad, often at Marienbad.

In 1868, he stood as a radical Liberal for Stirling Burghs; "the son of a staunch Tory", as he said in a speech during the election, one who "in fair weather and in foul, has stuck to his party and his principles, so his son in like manner will stick to his". He was member for Stirling for forty years. When a rich uncle, James Bannerman, left him an estate it was on the condition that he added Bannerman to his surname. He sighed, as a Campbell, and obeyed, as a man of good sense.

In politics, which, in his good-natured, unpretentious way, he enjoyed, he became Financial Secretary at the War Office, Parliamentary Secretary to the Admiralty and, in 1884, Chief Secretary for Ireland. When he took the last office, a friend reminded him that a Scotsman was even more unpopular than an Englishman with the Irish Nationalists; his secretary presented him with a revolver. His wife, Charlotte, persuaded him to accept the job.

Ireland was at that time affected by a wave of nationalism sweeping over Europe. What was to be done? Coercion or conciliation? Parnell said, "It is a great mistake to suppose that Ireland cannot be governed by coercion but . . . under your English party system, neither party can be trusted to make the policy continuous." The *United Irishman* in New York called daily for more murders and offered ten thousand dollars for the body of the Prince of Wales, dead or alive. In the House, Campbell-Bannerman met the daily onslaught of the Irish members with cheerful imperturbability; he and his wife were less concerned about assassination than about the drains in the Chief Secretary's Lodge in Dublin. After seven months, the Liberal government was beaten; but "CB" was now an MP who had immensely improved

69 Sir Henry Campbell-Bannerman.

his reputation. He was a convinced Home Ruler—for Scotland and England, as well as Ireland. After quitting the Chief Secretaryship, he never visited Ireland; he went regularly to Paris, which he loved, and to Marienbad. His favourite home was his house, Belmont, near Meigle in Angus. He slipped easily into Scots dialect.

In 1885, he was back at the War Office, where he managed one of the most ticklish of problems, the ousting of Queen Victoria's cousin, the old Duke of Cambridge, from his post as Commander-in-Chief of the army, without losing the Queen's affection or the Duke's goodwill. It was a triumph for his diplomacy. This episode was no sooner over than the Liberal government (Rosebery's) fell, on a motion to reduce Campbell-Bannerman's salary in disapproval of the failure to provide the army with enough cordite. The Liberal Whips were negligent and the government was beaten by seven votes.

At a time when it seemed that the Liberals were likely to be out of office for a long time, Campbell-Bannerman had hopes of the Speakership, which he and his wife would have liked. But Rosebery and Harcourt thought that the Liberals could not spare him and he went into the wilderness on the fall of the Rosebery government. When the South African war broke out he had become leader of the Opposition with his party split into those who supported the war (like Asquith and Grey) and those who opposed it (e.g. Lloyd George). Himself taking a middle course, he fought hard to keep the party together.

Then, in the summer of 1901, in a speech at the Holborn Restaurant, he denounced acts like the putting of Boer women and children into concentration camps as "methods of barbarism". Uproar followed. By that time, it was clear that Chamberlain's belief that the Boers would not fight was mistaken and that the generals' estimate of Boer fighting power was too optimistic. The mass of Liberals—the "grass roots"—were with Campbell-Bannerman. But at this time a struggle for power broke out in the upper echelons of the party.

Rosebery delivered a speech at Chesterfield which attacked the government on moderate lines. Sir Edward Grey and Haldane hoped to oust Campbell-Bannerman from the party leadership and bring in Asquith in his place. Campbell-Bannerman went to see Rosebery at his house in Berkeley Square to find out what he meant to do. Rosebery, who was divided from the Liberal party on the Irish Home Rule issue, would only take an active part in government if "the country" called him, a nebulous condition which in fact meant that he was out of politics for good.

Campbell-Bannerman now had to fight for his political life against a hostile trio: Asquith (the most formidable of the three); Haldane, a tireless intriguer; and Sir Edward Grey, who felt sentimentally attached to Rosebery. These three had agreed, with a mixture of conceit and naïveté, that Campbell-Bannerman was not up to the job. He could be Prime Minister only if he went to the House of Lords so that Asquith would be leader of the Commons. Summoned from Scotland, Campbell-Bannerman's wife, Charlotte, by this time a very sick woman,* announced that he must resist. This he did, with some cunning, so that the three conspirators came into his government without any unacceptable conditions. His only setback was that Grey, whose outlook on policy he disliked, came in as Foreign Secretary. Balfour

---

* She was a diabetic and insulin had not yet been discovered.

resigned on 4 December, 1905; Campbell-Bannerman took office the next day; in the general election in January, 1906, the Liberals were returned with a majority of 88 over all the parties combined and of 222 over the Conservatives.

Campbell-Bannerman had enjoyed his fight with the three Liberal "conspirators"; now he basked in the sunshine of an overwhelming victory at the polls. He did not offer a post to Rosebery, now a sulking shadow of once-mighty promise, but he promised that Rosebery's son, Lord Dalmeny, should second the Address to the Throne.

"If you accept," said Rosebery, "you are no son of mine." It was the end of Dalmeny's hopes of a career in politics.

Campbell-Bannerman was now head of a government which was, even more than other governments, made up of mutually hostile elements—imperialists and pro-Boers, near-Socialists and those who believed in laissez-faire–peace-at-any-price men and men who gave the all-clear to military conversations with the French. But he controlled his team with extraordinary ease. The fears that Asquith and others had held of his inadequacy were blown away: however, there was a letter from the doctor at Marienbad which warned him that, at his age and with his state of health, he was taking on more than he should. It would be wiser to go to the House of Lords. His burden became heavier when in August, 1906, his wife died at Marienbad.

On the question of military preparations, the Liberal Cabinet was in a position of some difficulty. It contained isolationists and pacifists, but it was embarked on an important transformation of Britain's military power; Haldane was organizing the Territorial Army and what was to become the British Expeditionary Force; at the same time Campbell-Bannerman kept the military talks with the French secret from colleagues like Morley, whom they would be likely to alarm. When do staff talks become a commitment to fight? It is not an easy question to answer. Did Campbell-Bannerman see how Britain was gradually being committed? It is uncertain, although it seems that he did.

Campbell-Bannerman did not serve for many months after his wife's death. The doctor at Marienbad had been right. His heart failed and he died in 10 Downing Street on 22 April, 1908, three weeks after he had sent his resignation to the King.

He came to the premiership at a time when Britain had had two Scottish Prime Ministers: after the langour and condescension of Balfour and the magnificence of Rosebery, this product of the business world of Glasgow was a Scotsman of a more prosaic kind. But, of the three, it was he who was the most successful in the rough trade of politics. His achievements were not small. He made the settlement in South Africa and he forged the electoral alliance with Ramsay MacDonald that won for his party the victory of 1906. He was Prime Minister for only two years, when he was already an old man, so that he did not for long enjoy the triumph he had won. In consequence, there has been a readiness to underrate him. But, as time goes on, less and less so.

70 Sir Henry Campbell-Bannerman arrives at Windsor station for the Kaiser's state visit, November, 1907.

XXXV

❧ HERBERT HENRY ASQUITH ❧

1908–16

Poor, industrious, equipped with a powerful, if not too sensitive, intellect; ambitious; of stalwart character: the man possessed of these qualities is, surely, the type-hero of a success story. Taken together, they are a fair description of the young Herbert Henry Asquith (born 12 September, 1852), at the time he came down from Yorkshire. His father, a small employer in the woollen business and a Nonconformist, died when the boy was of school age; his mother was an invalid; young Asquith, aged twelve, went to live with an uncle in London and attended the City of London School. From there, he proceeded with a scholarship to Balliol, which was, then as later, a great nursery of statesmen and administrators. There, Asquith's record was one of steady brilliance; most of the great prizes were his. His future as a don was assured.

But the Bar called, and in 1875, aged twenty-three, he left Oxford for London. When he was still a struggling, almost briefless, barrister, with occasional earnings from journalism, he married the daughter of a Manchester doctor, named Helen Melland, who had a modest income of her own. They had four sons and a daughter, children who, as it turned out, were exceptionally gifted. Meanwhile, an opportunity came to go into politics. Through a lawyer friend, a Scot named R. B. Haldane, Asquith was adopted as Liberal candidate for East Fife in 1886, a year before he married. He won the seat.

His fees at the Bar remained modest until his cross-examination of the manager of *The Times* in the case of the Piggott forgeries. This was a forensic triumph and after it his income soared to £5,000 a year. In 1891 came a shattering blow: his wife died while they were on holiday in Arran and he was left a widower with five little children. Three years later, he married Margot Tennant, daughter of Sir Charles Tennant, Bart, an intense, forthright and sociable person, who encouraged him to enjoy the fashionable world of which she was an ornament. His part in Parliament was growing more important. In 1892, he moved an amendment of no confidence in the government which was carried. Lord Salisbury thereupon resigned and Gladstone came into office, making Asquith his Home Secretary.

To have reached the Cabinet in 1892, six years after his entry to Parliament, was a remarkable achievement which he justified by his performance in office. He was, in the opinion of one good judge, "the best Home Secretary of the century"*, and a

---

* Sir Philip Magnus.

71 Herbert Henry Asquith, by A. Cluysenaar.

powerful if not a thrilling debater. When Gladstone was followed by Rosebery, Asquith remained at the Home Office during the fifteen months that elapsed before Salisbury came back into power after an election in 1895 in which the confusion about the Liberal leadership was punished by a disastrous defeat. Asquith held East Fife with an increased majority. He was the man of the future so far as the Liberal party was concerned.

He lived in London in some style, with a house in Cavendish Square in which were fourteen servants, plus two in the stables; for a politician out of office it was quite a burden. Small wonder that Asquith broke with established custom and went back to the Bar, where his practice brought him between £5,000 and £10,000 a year.

72 **Margot Asquith (**neé **Tennant).**

The South African war was approaching and the Liberal party was split three ways, as has been told. By the time the war ended in 1902, there were, however, signs that Liberal unity was returning.

When, in 1903, Joseph Chamberlain spoke out in favour of Imperial Preference, including a tax on food imports, Asquith saw the signs of impending Liberal victory in a new general election. He, Sir Edward Grey and Haldane made a compact that, after the election victory, which they took for granted, the party leader, Campbell-Bannerman, would be Prime Minister but would take a peerage and that Asquith should lead in the Commons. When the time came, however, Campbell-Bannerman would not budge and the "compact" trio, as we have seen, meekly took office in his government. A Liberal landslide followed. Asquith was Chancellor of the Exchequer (1905) and heir to Campbell-Bannerman's throne.

He introduced, during his term of office, three Budgets, of which the second contained the revolutionary idea of a difference between earned and unearned income. At this time a constitutional quarrel between the two Houses of Parliament broke out. Campbell-Bannerman's health broke down irretrievably in 1908; in April he resigned and the King sent for Asquith, who at once became Prime Minister. He and his family moved house to 10 Downing Street, which his wife, Margot, thought "an inconvenient house with three poor staircases". David Lloyd George was the new Chancellor of the Exchequer.

Asquith ran into trouble in his Cabinet: ministers as powerful as Winston Churchill and Lloyd George agreed in urging that an Admiralty demand for six new capital ships was unjustified. They were members of a group in the government known as the "Economists". Asquith proposed, as a compromise, that there should be four new ships at once and four more when the need for them was proved (as it was five months later). Lloyd George's first Budget (1909) was furiously attacked as "inquisitorial, tyrannical and Socialistic" (Rosebery), and was clearly about to be rejected by the Lords, who were being encouraged to do so by the Conservative leader, Balfour. Asquith prepared to create enough new peers to reverse the rejection of the Budget. In January, 1910, a general election showed that the independent Liberal majority had vanished; the balance of power was held by forty Labour members and seventy Irish Nationalists (who disliked the Budget's increase in the whisky duty). While the crisis was still unresolved, King Edward died. The new King proposed a conference of party leaders to discuss the constitutional crisis. They met, eight in number—"the Holy Eight", as they were called. "It is just like a Cabinet but much more united," said Balfour. It did not solve the problem. The constitutional dispute went on in the new reign and a second general election at the end of the year almost exactly repeated the verdict of its predecessor. The House of Lords gave in; there was no need to use the barely reputable expedient of a mass creation of peers.

Novel, and far more dangerous, problems lay ahead: industrial upheavals at the docks and in the coal mines and Suffragette agitation, led by Mrs Pankhurst, coinciding with a darkening of the sky over Europe. It was the time of the Agadir crisis. Churchill and Lloyd George, who had been "Economists" a few years before, were now passionate for "preparation".

Before the crisis in Europe reached its climax, however, another crisis nearer home shook the constitutional fabric in Britain. An Irish Home Rule Bill (the third in the series) was passed by the Commons in January, 1913 and rejected by the Lords. It was necessary that this bill be re-submitted to Parliament in 1914. One question that arose was, should Ulster be excluded from the Dublin Parliament and, if so, to what extent? Asquith needed the votes of the Irish Nationalists if he was to stay in power and the Nationalists were opposed to any separation of Ulster from a Dublin government. The King, who was intensely worried by the danger of bloodshed, proposed an all-party conference, from which an agreed settlement might emerge.

And Asquith, seeking a compromise, saw Bonar Law, the Conservative leader. They discussed which Ulster countries should be excluded from "Home Rule" Ireland. Later, Asquith suggested to the Ulster Unionist leader, Sir Edward Carson, that Ulster might have a special right of veto over certain powers of a Dublin Parliament to legislate for Ulster. Then he persuaded Redmond, the Irish Nationalist leader, to consent to a three-year exclusion of Ulster from the Irish Parliament.

All these events were eclipsed by what is known as the "Curragh Mutiny", in which fifty-eight cavalry officers resigned, rather than be sent to "coerce" Ulster. There was no intention to order them to do anything of the kind. In order to steady the situation, Asquith took over the War Office. In the last days of July, 1914, a conference at Buckingham Palace tried, and failed, to solve the Irish problem. Then the onrush of war in Europe swept the Irish problem into the wings. Asquith agreed with Bonar Law that it must wait until the greater conflict was over. Whether he thought that, after an interval, the pieces would all be found on the board where he had left them, no one can tell.

73 Mrs Pankhurst being arrested near Buckingham Palace, 21 May, 1914.

74 Neutrality League announcement in the *Manchester Guardian*, 4 August, 1914.
→

NEUTRALITY LEAGUE ANNOUNCEMENT No. 2.

BRITONS, DO YOUR DUTY

and keep your Country out of
A WICKED and STUPID WAR.

Small but powerful cliques are trying to rush you into it; you must

DESTROY THE PLOT TO-DAY

or it will be too late.

Ask yourselves : WHY SHOULD WE GO TO WAR?

THE WAR PARTY say: We must maintain the Balance of Power, because if Germany were to annex Holland or Belgium she would be so powerful as to threaten us; or because we are bound by treaty to fight for the neutrality of Belgium; or because we are bound by our agreements with France to fight for her.

All these reasons are false. THE WAR PARTY DOES NOT TELL THE TRUTH

The facts are these :

1. If we took sides with Russia and France, the balance of power would be upset as it has never been before. It would make the military Russian Empire of 160,000,000 the dominant Power of Europe. You know the kind of country Russia is.

2. **We are not bound to join in a general European war to defend the neutrality of Belgium.** Our treaties expressly stipulate that our obligations under them **shall not compel us to take part in a general European war** in order to fulfil them. And if we are to fight for the neutrality of Belgium, we must be prepared to fight France as well as Germany.

3. The Prime Minister and Sir Edward Grey have both emphatically and solemnly declared in the House of Commons that we have no undertaking whatever, written or spoken, to go to war for France. We discharged our obligations in the Morocco affair. The *Entente Cordiale* was a pact of peace and not an alliance for war.

4. If Germany did attempt to annex any part of Belgium, Holland, or Normandy—and there is no reason to suppose that she would attempt such a thing——she would be weaker than she is now, for she would have to use all her forces for holding her conquests down. She would have so many difficulties like those arising out of Alsace that she would have to leave other nations alone as much as possible. But we do not know in the least that she would do these things. It would be monstrous to drag this country into war on so vague a suspicion.

It is your Duty to Save your Country from this Disaster.

ACT TO-DAY OR IT MAY BE TOO LATE

Write your member that you will try and turn him out at the next election if he does not use his influence with the Government on the side of peace.

Get your local notables to hold meetings of protest against England taking part in the war.

Make your Trade Union, your I.L.P., or B.S.P. branch pass strong resolutions.

Persuade your Clergyman or Minister to urge the need for standing clear.

Send letters to your newspapers.

There are a thousand things you can do if you really love your country.

Distribute the Leaflets of the NEUTRALITY LEAGUE.

WE WANT THOUSANDS OF HELPERS!   WRITE OR CALL AT OUR TEMPORARY OFFICES:

D. ROBERTSON, Salisbury Hotel, Salisbury Square, Fleet Street.   GEORGE BENSON, 8, York Street, Manchester

When the war came, Asquith, although he did not realize it, was nearly at the end of his career at the head of British politics. Without hesitation, he led Britain into the fight, accepted the resignations of old friends like Lord Morley and John Burns, and appointed Lord Kitchener as War Minister. He could look back—but it is unlikely that he did—on leadership of a government which had laid the foundations of the Welfare State—Old Age Pensions, Unemployment Insurance, Employment Exchanges, Health Insurance. He had presided over the constitutional battle with the House of Lords. This ended in half a victory—the claws of the Lords were clipped but the need for a reformed Second Chamber remained unsatisfied. Even so, the record of accomplishment was extraordinary and remained unmatched until Attlee's administration after the Second World War. In its last phase—for so it proved to be—the old Liberal Britain displayed a vigour and a steadiness of purpose worthy of the party of Gladstone. And Asquith was at its head, in complete control of the strangely assorted, variously talented team: think of Lloyd George, Churchill, Haldane and Grey, to mention no others. To have commanded such an army with hardly a whisper of mutiny gives the measure of Asquith as he was in 1914. He drank too much and in Tory circles was known as "PJ" (Perrier Jouet). But Bonar Law, who had no personal reason to like him, said, "Asquith, when drunk, can make a better speech than any of the rest of us when sober."

The war was another story.

War called for a quite different kind of government, one with a single purpose to which all policies must be ruthlessly subordinated; and for ministers who were executives first and politicians afterwards. A wartime Prime Minister needs dynamism as well as wisdom. He will be condemned not for the loss of an election, but for the loss of a battle. Military failure at the Dardanelles led, in the end, to the

75 Sir Edward Grey addressing the House of Commons immediately before the declaration of war, August, 1914.

Liberal government being superseded by a coalition. It may be said that the Dardanelles was Churchill's campaign. Maybe. But Asquith was the Prime Minister, in effect, the Commander-in-Chief, responsible for the appointment and, therefore, for the mistakes of one of his generals. It makes it all the worse that Asquith did not trust Churchill's judgment.

Generals who had lost a battle in France blamed it on a shortage of ammunition for the guns; later on, at Passchendaele, it was seen that too many shells could be an equal cause of military disaster. But, meanwhile, the press blamed the ministers and, above all, Asquith. There was this amount of truth in the press campaign, which reached surprising depths of malice, that Asquith was getting old, he was sometimes tired and he was drinking—although never, it was said, to the length of affecting his judgment. The fact was one on which his enemies seized avidly. He could not put enough fury into the waging of war and had no taste for the political in-fighting in which, for instance, Lloyd George revelled. He had not enough respect for the abilities and character of the Conservative leader, Bonar Law. There were worse troubles ahead: the issue of conscription, on which Asquith exaggerated the amount of public dislike for the measure, and a rebellion in Ireland in Easter week, 1916. At that time, the Chief Secretary for Ireland was Augustine Birrell, an old friend of Asquith's. This did not make things easier for the Prime Minister.

A personal grief made these things harder to bear. For years Asquith had carried on a constant and loving correspondence with an attractive, intelligent young woman, Venetia Stanley. He poured out the secrets of his heart—and, incidentally, of the state. Now, suddenly, without warning, she announced her impending marriage to Edwin Montagu, one of Asquith's most loyal political supporters, whom she had previously rejected. Love by letter is, notoriously, a strain on at least one of the parties. Miss Stanley found it unbearable. The blow fell at a moment when Asquith was filled with dejection. He had given in to a Tory demand that Haldane should not be a minister in the projected coalition government. This betrayal of an old friend had, he thought, something contemptible in it, like Charles I's sacrifice of Strafford.

The war dragged on, with mounting and dreadful casualties (including Asquith's son, Raymond, killed in the first hours of the Somme battle) and bitter quarrels in Cabinet. Lord Lansdowne, a member of the Cabinet, wrote a memorandum, at Asquith's suggestion, in which he argued the case for opening negotiations with the Germans. "We are slowly but surely killing off the best of the male population of these islands . . . " The pessimism was extreme. The memorandum was circulated to the Cabinet on 17 November, 1916. It was soon leaked to the press, where it was used as fresh material to attack the Prime Minister's conduct of the war, although, in fact, Asquith did not agree with it. A violent press campaign coincided with political intrigues in which Lloyd George, Bonar Law and Sir Max Aitken took part—and which Asquith either could not or would not counter. Lloyd George now delivered an ultimatum: either the War Committee would be reconstituted with three members and himself as its chairman, or he would resign. After confused and acrimonious talks, Asquith resigned in December, 1916. He had been Prime Minister for eight years.

The chief offices in the government which Lloyd George, a Radical, headed, were held by Conservatives. "The change of government," says Lord Blake, "was the death knell of the old Liberal Party." For Asquith, the bitterest blow was that his friend, Balfour, had joined the enemy. This he never understood, said Mrs Asquith.

In the general election of 1918, Asquith lost his seat in East Fife, but won Paisley in 1920, only to lose it four years later. He became Earl of Oxford and Asquith in 1925. The Garter followed a few months later. These were the consolation prizes given to one whose sad fate was to preside over the declining fortunes of his once great party. He died on 15 February, 1928.

In the early months of the war, he had amused himself by writing a little fantasy, in which he imagined himself being addressed by a judge in the other world: "The really great men of the world are the geniuses and the saints. You belonged to neither category. Your intellectual equipment left you far short of the one; your spiritual limitations and your endowment of the 'Old Adam' left you still shorter of the other . . ." His private judgment on his Cabinet colleagues is revealing. Lloyd George and Winston Churchill were placed high and equal; but above them he put Lord Crewe, Sir Edward Grey and Reginald McKenna. Like other men, Asquith was capable of serious errors of appraisal; he tended to like men who resembled himself.

XXXVI

❧ DAVID LLOYD GEORGE ❧

1916–22

Nobody can have any doubt what was the chief motive force in David Lloyd George's life, least of all his first wife, Margaret Owen. In the year he married her he told her in a letter, "My supreme idea is to get on. To this ideal I shall sacrifice everything—except, I trust, honesty . . . My love for you is sincere and strong. But I must not forget that I have a purpose in life. And however painful the sacrifice I may have to make to attain this ambition, I must not flinch." So there it was, plump and plain.

Margaret was warned about the kind of man she was marrying, except that she could hardly be expected to foresee the day, thirty years later, when he would write: "You must make allowances for the waywardness and the wildness of a man of my type." There were several amorous adventures. Defending himself to his wife, he said: "What if I were a drunk as well? What about Asquith and Birkenhead?" Being a kindly, homely Welsh woman, Margaret put up with what she did not like and could not cure. She never found it possible to like London: as much as possible she lived at Criccieth. Her husband was born in Manchester on 17 July, 1863, and brought up at Llanystumdwy, near Criccieth. After starting his career as a solicitor's clerk, he became the Radical MP for Caernarvon Burghs at the age of twenty-seven; he was a Welsh Nationalist, the sworn foe of the aristocracy and the Anglican Communion. When the South African war came, he was fiercely against it and suffered the abuse and persecution meted out to pro-Boers. By that time the family was living in Wandsworth.

By the time of the Liberal landslide victory in 1905, Lloyd George had become famous as the most infectious of left-wing speakers. He was made President of the Board of Trade in 1905 and, three years later, Chancellor of the Exchequer in Asquith's government. To this period belongs the outpouring of social legislation which laid the foundation of the Welfare State. There was the Old Age Pension, Asquith's idea but carried through by Lloyd George. Above all, there was the National Insurance Act. All this occurred at a time when the Liberal government was divided between those wanting Free Trade and little government and those pressing for social reforms. Lloyd George became the leader of the latter group. In the course of controversy, he picked on the House of Lords as a convenient and vulnerable target. In that chamber, the social legislation of the Liberals was being systematically frustrated. "It is," he declared, "Mr Balfour's poodle. It fetches and carries for him. It bites anybody he sets it on to." What is remarkable as a tribute to Lloyd George's audacity and coolness at this stage of his career is that, although he was being blackmailed by women for non-political reasons, he was not diverted from the party battle. That battle was hotting up.

His 1909 Budget, introducing what were then regarded as dangerous increases in taxation, and, above all, taxes on landed property, was the occasion of a great turmoil. The climax was reached in a speech delivered by Lloyd George in the "Edinburgh Castle", a popular hall in Limehouse. It was a magnificent display of inflammatory rhetoric aimed at the great landowners. Among other effects, it threw King Edward VII into a great state of agitation during Cowes Week. "I have never known him so irritated," reported Asquith, "or more difficult to appease." The case which Lloyd George developed against the big landlords, whom he personified as "the dukes" ("Oh those dukes—how they harass us"), was simply that their income had increased enormously by no exertion or skill of their own but as a consequence of the general increase in wealth. "You have got a system in this country whereby landlords take advantage of the fact that they have got control of the land to let it for a number of years . . . and at the end the whole of it passes away to the pockets of men who never spent a penny upon it." The Dukes of Westminster and Northumberland were singled out for attack by name as representatives of a class which did not discharge the duties of their stewardship. No country, however rich, could afford to have such a class quartered upon its revenue. It was a sustained attack, at once humorous and violent. No wonder it alarmed the King and infuriated the dukes.

76 *The new Guy Fawkes plot; or, the best advertised conspiracy in the world.* **Lloyd George vs. The House of Lords.**

When Lloyd George wrote to the King defending himself, the King replied that a minister should not have the same freedom of expression as a private MP. However, he agreed that Lloyd George had shown patience and good temper during the Budget debates. Lloyd George continued his attack on the great landlords, skilfully identified with the House of Lords—"five hundred men, ordinary men, chosen accidentally from among the unemployed". His attack on the landlords as a class was becoming an attack on the House of Lords as an institution—"Who is to govern this country," he asked at a meeting in Newcastle Drill Hall, "the people or the peers?" However, when the votes were counted in the general election of January, 1910, the Liberal majority had been reduced to two. The government could only rule with Irish Nationalist support. For this setback, the right wing of the party blamed Lloyd George's oratory.

The King's death interrupted intense controversy about how the powers and veto of the House of Lords should be dealt with. There was another general election which had the same result as the first. Lloyd George, about this time, was urging on others, like F. E. Smith, Churchill and Balfour, a plan for a coalition.

He was not wedded to the traditional methods of Parliamentary government; he was not enamoured of the party system. It took some time for him to be convinced that his novel ideas could not be realized. In July, 1911, Lloyd George made his début in the international arena. At the annual bankers' dinner at the Mansion House, he said that if peace could only be preserved by Britain surrendering her position in the world, then the price would be too high. Coming at a moment when Germany was thought to be about to establish a naval base on the coast of Morocco, the speech of one whom many suspected of being a pacifist made a sensation.

Those two years before the outbreak of war were the apogee of Lloyd George's life as a social reformer. Taking up the plan for a Welfare State, which Asquith had prepared, he passed the Old Age Pension Act and founded, along with Winston Churchill, the system of Unemployment Insurance by which the existing sixty-one unemployment bureaux were taken over by the State and another 350 added. The most ambitious of his projects of social reform was, however, the National Health Insurance Bill, an immensely complex measure on which he and his advisers worked from the beginning of 1910. There was already a voluntary system of insurance but, as he explained to the House of Commons, "it is no use shirking the fact that a proportion of workmen with good wages spend them in other ways" (i.e. beer and betting), so that less than half of them had any provision for sickness. The new scheme must therefore be compulsory. In spite of this innovation, the proposals were welcomed by the Tory Opposition—and encountered strong opposition from the doctors, who disliked the system of contract practice which it enforced on them. Lloyd George met the doctors and made important improvements in his bill. He believed, rightly as it turned out, that most doctors wished the scheme to succeed. His conduct of the Committee stages of the bill was a masterpiece of Parliamentary tactics. To win the support of Labour, which he needed, he invented a catchphrase which became notorious. "For fourpence a week, the workman gets nine-pennyworth." The trouble was that most of the workmen who had the vote had already provided for their health insurance and did not like to be asked to contribute to a system which would benefit the less prudent. However, within a year, and after remarkable exertions by its author, the bill became law. Britain had joined Germany and Norway as a land of State insurance. Lloyd George was recognized as the greatest man in the House of Commons.

About the same time he was involved in a scandal which needed all his verve and audacity to surmount. He was accused, with other Liberal politicians, of having traded in shares of the Marconi company at a time when it was negotiating a wireless licence with the government. He denied the charge and it was found that his shares had been in the *Canadian* Marconi company. This prevarication did great damage to his reputation; a lesser man might have been ruined. In fact, although his armour was dented, it was not pierced. But the public was warned: this was not a man of austere principles.

When the European crisis of 1914 came, Lloyd George was, at first, uncertain what he should do. It was as if the actual face of war, so close, so terrible, re-awoke in him all the horror of war that lay not far below the surface of the Welsh Nonconformist boy he had been. Two years later, in 1916, when Asquith was failing to provide the leadership and energy which the nation needed in a struggle more titanic, bitter and prolonged than anybody had imagined, Lloyd George became Prime Minister at fifty-three, accepted as the one politician who could give the national effort the demonic energy that it demanded. What he could not do—it was not reasonable that he should—was to devise military solutions for a novel kind of warfare. He distrusted the generals and had not the power to replace them.

What he could do, and did, was to streamline the higher direction of the war by setting up a small War Cabinet and a Cabinet Secretariat. He organized the defeat of the U-boat campaign, which, had it not been beaten, would have brought Britain to her knees. The entry of the United States made it certain that German resistance would crumble. When it did, the end came swiftly.

But, before that, there was a great military crisis on the Western Front when, on 21 March, 1918, the Germans pierced the British line where it was weakest. This was, in the opinion of Lord Beaverbrook, a good judge, Lloyd George's greatest hour: "Our line of defence had been broken, our troops were in retreat, the Russian armies out of the war, and the American armies had not yet come into it . . . It was at that moment that Lloyd George penetrated the gloom of doubt and indecision. He would talk only of counter-attack."*

The military crisis had a Parliamentary side-effect: the "Maurice Debate". This took place in 1918 on General Maurice's statement that Lloyd George, then the Prime Minister, had kept troops in Britain which could have strengthened the army in France, almost overwhelmed by the German onslaught, and had given a false account of the manpower situation to Parliament. The truth was that Lloyd George had been sent corrected manpower figures by the War Office and the box containing the figures was put in the fire by Lloyd George's secretary, J. T. Davies. Lloyd George's triumph in the debate was complete. Moreover, the division lists at the end of the debate became an important political test because, in the general election which followed the Armistice, any Liberal MP who had voted against Lloyd George in it was opposed by a pro-Lloyd George candidate. Lloyd George won what

---

* Lord Beaverbrook. *Men and Power*, p. 35.

appeared to be a great electoral victory—478 Coalition MPs as against 229 Opposition. Ironically, it ensured that the victor was a prisoner of the Conservative party, which, apart from Lloyd George's close associates, distrusted him more and more.

Their main complaint—there were many: he was, they thought, not reliable; not honest; still a Radical at heart—concerned "honours", which was a dubious ground for any politician to be self-righteous about. Honours. There was always an ill-defined No-Man's-Land between what could be tolerated and what was going "one over the odds". It was more or less a question of discretion, of not giving an honour to somebody who plainly was not "all right". Of avoiding too blatant a connection between cash paid and goods delivered. Now, as the war came to an end, there sprang up something that resembled a market in honours; there were agents, a tariff, commissions exacted and paid. And the people who were honoured! It was said that the royal nose was sometimes held between his fingers as he signed the warrants. But the Prime Minister insisted, and the Prime Minister was all-powerful. Of course, it could not last. Lloyd George became too careless. And, for all his prestige, he was vulnerable in one respect: he had no party.

Meanwhile, it was said that he was tucking money away—whose money? what money?—into a trust fund which he alone controlled. One day there would be a revolt. As it turned out, the break when it came occurred over an issue of foreign policy—Lloyd George backed the Greeks against the Turks in Asia Minor and the Greek army was, to everyone's surprise, destroyed. The Christian population of Smyrna was massacred. Shades of Gladstone! It seemed that Britain was about to launch a crusade. And then Bonar Law, the Conservative, who had meekly followed Lloyd George during the war and then quietly resigned, spoke out: Britain could not alone be the policeman of the world. And a minor minister named Stanley Baldwin, who had watched with dismay spreading across the political scene a miasma of what he regarded as corruption, staged a palace revolution. After a Conservative party meeting in the Carlton Club, Lloyd George was forced to resign. He and his Conservative henchmen, such as Austen Chamberlain and Birkenhead, thought he would soon be back in power. He was never back in power. Against him there was an unspoken, unwritten ban, as implacable as that by which Walpole had excluded Bolingbroke from public life after the failure of his mad Jacobite intrigues. The Conservative party, dominated by Baldwin, would not have him. Labour, under MacDonald, would not have him. Half the Liberal party would never forgive him for ousting Asquith in 1916. The coalition was dead, unmourned.

Lloyd George lived for another twenty-three years. He had plenty to contribute—ideas, eloquence, organization, money—during a period of desperate social and economic stresses—but he could never fight his way back to the centre of the arena. There could scarcely be a more dramatic instance of the punishment which the gods mete out to *hubris*. Lloyd George fell for the same reason as other ministers have fallen, a belief that he was indispensable.

But before closing the record of his ministry, two achievements should be mentioned: (1) the treaty with the Irish Nationalists which established the Free State and Northern Ireland and might have solved the whole Irish question had there only been more patience and flexibility on one side of the Border and the other. The tenacity and the skill which he showed in his negotiations with the Irish leaders had been beyond praise; (2) the extensive social legislation, dealing with Unemployment Insurance, Education and Housing. It was an era of dangerous strikes, which Lloyd George dealt with cunningly, fending off a social upheaval which at one time seemed to be inevitable.

After 1922, these problems passed into other hands. His personal life, although continuing to be adventurous, had two main poles: his wife, Margaret, to whom he remained sincerely attached, and Frances Stevenson, an attractive young woman who had come into his household to coach his daughter, Megan, and who became his secretary and, as was to be expected, his mistress. She fell passionately in love with him and bore him a daughter. When Margaret died, he married Miss Stevenson. He was created an earl in March, 1945, and died on the 26th of that month.

In the long misfortune of his later days which followed so brilliant a noon, one fact must be noted: he never lost his buoyancy, his high spirits, his irrepressible humour or his self-assurance. When Churchill met him during World War II, at a time when Lloyd George was in the shadows and Churchill was the dominant figure in Britain, he reported, "We were immediately on the same terms as of old, master and servant. He was the master." In the critical days of 1940, Churchill exerted himself to persuade Lloyd George to go as ambassador to Washington. It might have been dangerous to have him in England, which could at any moment be invaded. Lloyd George declined the offer.

77 Arthur James Balfour and David Lloyd George at a garden party, 1922.

XXXVII

❧ ANDREW BONAR LAW ❧

1922–23

The first British Prime Minister from Canada, Andrew Bonar Law, was born on 16 September, 1858, in the Free Church manse of Kingston, New Brunswick, his father being the Rev. James Law, an Ulster-Scot, his mother, Elizabeth Annie Kidston. He was, therefore, of Scottish blood on both sides, the Kidstons being a wealthy Glasgow family of merchant bankers. When the child was two, his mother died and her sister, Miss Janet Kidston, came out from Glasgow to look after the family. This she did until James Law married again in 1870. Janet Kidston proposed that she should take Bonar back to Scotland where she and her Kidston relations would bring him up. Thus, aged twelve, the boy left New Brunswick.

In 1874, he was at Glasgow High School, from which, at sixteen, he went to be a clerk in the Kidstons' office. He lived in Helensburgh and travelled up to Glasgow every day. He learnt public speaking in the Glasgow Parliamentary Debating Society, in which he sat as a Conservative member (the Kidstons being Conservatives) in its mock Parliament. He was an exceptionally good chess player and a teetotaller. When Kidstons' were taken over by the Clydesdale Bank, Bonar became a partner in the iron merchant's business of William Jacks and Company. In 1891, he married Annie Robley, the daughter of a Glasgow shipbroker. They had six children.

Towards the end of the century he was reasonably well off, enough to go into politics: he won the Blackfriars Division of Glasgow in the so-called "Khaki Election" of 1900 and for some years afterwards divided his life between Helensburgh and a rented house in London. It was the era of imperialism and Joseph Chamberlain, and Bonar Law was a Conservative imperialist whose maiden speech in the House was a reply to an attack by Lloyd George on the harshness of the British army to the Boers. He quickly decided that he had arrived in politics too late (he was forty-three), and that he disliked London society. But his knowledge of the world of business had already been noted when Balfour formed his government in 1902, and Bonar Law became Parliamentary Secretary to the Board of Trade. He had been in politics for only eighteen months, which indicates that his training in the Glasgow Parliament was not to be despised. He made a speech in the Brussels Sugar Convention which won admiration from Joseph Chamberlain. At that moment, the great man was moving towards Imperial Preference and the great debate in the Conservative Cabinet between Free Traders and Protectionists was about to break out.

When Chamberlain was out of the country on a visit to South Africa, the Conservative Free Traders won a tactical victory, which Chamberlain countered by a public avowal of his faith in Imperial Preference. However, when the country spoke its mind in the general election of January, 1906, the Liberals won by an overwhelming majority. Bonar Law lost his seat in Glasgow but another and safer one was found for him in Dulwich a few months later; he was already too valuable a spokesman for the Tory party on the tariff issue to be long out of Parliament, all the more so after Joseph Chamberlain was incapacitated by a stroke. Bonar Law settled permanently in London.

In the same year he suffered a heavy personal blow when his wife died; his sister, Mary, came to look after his home. He found escape from his grief in the furious political battle that followed Lloyd George's Budget. In the January, 1910, general election he increased his majority at Dulwich but, as a leading Tariff Reformer, went to fight a seat in Free Trade Manchester, which he lost. At the same time Max Aitken, a Canadian, who had become Law's closest friend and was to play an important part in his career, won the contest at Ashton-under-Lyne.

In a few weeks Bonar Law was back in the House as MP for Bootle. On Balfour's resignation he became leader of the Conservative party, partly as a result of the astute work of Max Aitken. However, to maintain party unity, he agreed to modify the party line on tariffs. Imperial Preference was shelved. On the Irish question he was

78 Max Aitken, later Lord Beaverbrook, by Low.

even more bitterly involved as one whose origins were in Presbyterian Ulster. On the question of an Ulster Rising, he said (April, 1912), "Do Hon. Members believe that any Prime Minister could give orders to shoot down men whose only crime is that they refuse to be driven out of our community? . . . The thing is impossible." Bonar Law was passionately involved in the Ulster cause, which, in due course, led to the Curragh Mutiny. His speeches had been vituperative before, because of the need to give a new and harder edge to Conservative leadership; now their violence sprang from conviction. But privately Bonar Law was not so uncompromising: he thought that Ulster could be left as she was, with Home Rule for the rest of Ireland. This, however, was to be the last resort.

When the chances of an Irish compromise seemed to have vanished, Bonar Law's mind turned to more dangerous tactics. The Army Act might be amended so as to exclude the use of the army in Ulster. The idea was considered and dropped. But, in the meantime, officers in a cavalry brigade stationed at the Curragh announced that if ordered to Ulster they would prefer dismissal. While the government tried to wriggle out of the position they were put in, events were made much worse by the landing at Larne of 35,000 rifles bought in Germany and intended for the Ulster Volunteers. Bonar Law exploited to the full the conflict of loyalties in the army, believing that the government, above all Winston Churchill, had embarked on a plot to coerce Ulster. His conduct during these events had little of the canny common sense for which he was noted: the ancient passions of the Ulster-Scot had boiled to the surface. In the end the question of Ulster and of Ireland was thrust into the background with the coming of the World War. Bonar Law suggested, and Asquith accepted, that the matter should be postponed. Later, after the outbreak of war, Asquith made the Irish Home Rule Bill an Act of Parliament, its operation to be postponed to the end of the war. Bonar Law regarded this as a breach of faith.

The situation was made more embarrassing by the fact that with the war going on, and going badly, the Opposition could have driven the government from office. But that would have appeared as unpatriotic in wartime.

Bonar Law's fire was concentrated on Churchill, First Lord of the Admiralty, whom he had long distrusted, and to whose personal magnetism he was immune. The antagonism between the two men came to a head over the Dardanelles expedition, which Churchill championed against the opinion of his own First Sea Lord, Lord Fisher. When the expedition was clearly falling short of the hopes of its supporters, Bonar Law forced Asquith to get rid of Churchill from the Admiralty and form a coalition government. He became Colonial Secretary, a post of the second rank, although carrying with it a seat in the Cabinet; Balfour was First Lord of the Admiralty. While the question of evacuating the Dardanelles dragged on, Bonar Law, by a threat of resignation, brought the matter to a head. The Dardanelles were evacuated without any of the tragic consequences that were feared.

Meanwhile he was aware of the growing unpopularity of Asquith's government, at least in high Service circles. The situation changed when Lord Kitchener was drowned in the sinking of the *Hampshire* while on his way to Russia. Asquith offered the post of War Minister to Bonar Law, who had previously discussed the problem with Lloyd George and told the Prime Minister that he thought the latter was the most suitable man for the post. More important was the opinion, which he shared

79 Andrew Bonar Law.

with others, that the Prime Minister was too tired a man to carry on the supreme direction of the war. However, he thought that Lloyd George was too unscrupulous to be his successor. Finally, however, he agreed to press for a small War Council, of which Lloyd George would be chairman. To this Asquith agreed after intricate discussions. But, after reflection, Asquith resigned and Lloyd George became Prime Minister, with Bonar Law as Chancellor of the Exchequer and Lloyd George's closest counsellor during the war. When it ended, a general election was held, in December, 1918, in which Asquithian Liberals were cast for the role of Opposition: and the coalition government won 478 seats. Bonar Law was returned for Glasgow Central.

He was now Lord Privy Seal and Leader of the House. In that capacity, he dealt firmly with labour disturbances in the country but in 1920, at a time when the government was losing popularity, his health began to fail. Threatened with a breakdown, he retired from public life in May, 1921, although his influence with Lloyd George had some effect on the treaty with Ireland which excluded Ulster from the Irish Free State. The disagreement between Lloyd George and the right-wing Conservatives widened: especially on what was thought to be too easy an attitude towards Ireland. This was particularly so after the murder of Field-Marshall Sir Henry Wilson (Chief of the Imperial General Staff) by Irish terrorists. The final occasion of the downfall of the government was, however, the Middle East, where it seemed, in 1922, that Lloyd George was on the verge of war with Turkey. A meeting of Conservative MPs and peers was held at the Carlton Club. Bonar Law, supported by the Beaverbrook and Rothermere newspapers, emerged from retirement to speak in favour of the Conservative party ending the coalition, a course which the meeting approved by 187 votes to 87. Lloyd George gave the King his resignation that afternoon.

The King sent for Bonar Law, who was not, at that moment, leader of the party. This, however, was made good on 23 October at a party meeting in the Hotel Cecil. Bonar Law kissed hands as Prime Minister; a general election was to be held on 15 November. Conservative ministers in the coalition—apparently the élite of the party—announced that they would have no part in the new government. But if they thought to strike an early and fatal blow to Bonar Law and his supporters, they were disappointed. Like many politicians before and after, they underrated the magnetism of office. A "government of the second eleven" was formed. It proved to be strong enough. The Bonar Law government won the election with 344 seats against 138 Labour and 117 Liberals, evenly divided between the followers of Asquith and Lloyd George. Bonar Law now found himself engaged in a confused mass of international problems, of which a settlement of the American Debt was the most urgent.

His view was that payment to the United States should be counterbalanced by a similar payment to Britain from her European allies. He sent Stanley Baldwin, the Chancellor of the Exchequer, to Washington to negotiate a settlement on these lines, with the proviso that any agreement Baldwin reached would be referred to the Cabinet. Baldwin returned with a settlement involving an annual interest payment of £34 millions, rising to £40 millions. The agreement was one which the Cabinet could only repudiate at the risk of destroying the government. It was a *fait accompli*.

Bonar Law proposed to reject it. He said, "I would be the most cursed Prime Minister that ever held office in England if I accepted these terms." His trusted friend, Beaverbrook, was among those who urged him to stay in office. This, in the end, he did.

But his premiership lasted only six months. Immediately after the general election, the first symptoms of some trouble in his throat appeared: by April, his voice had weakened almost to the point of inaudibility. A month later, Lord Horder diagnosed cancer. Bonar Law tendered his resignation on 20 May, 1923. He died on 30 October, at his home in Onslow Gardens, and was buried in Westminster Abbey.

"It is fitting," said Asquith, "that we should have buried the Unknown Prime Minister by the side of the Unknown Soldier."

XXXVIII

❧ STANLEY BALDWIN ❧

1923–24; 1924–29; 1935–37

The letter in *The Times* on 24 June, 1919, said that the writer was giving one-fifth of his fortune to the nation "as a thank-offering in the firm conviction that never again shall we have such a chance of giving our country that kind of help". The amount was substantial, £120,000. The donor signed himself simply "FST". It was not until four years later that these initials were elucidated: Financial Secretary of the Treasury. The writer thought that £1,000 million might be raised by others following his example; as it turned out, however, only £500,000 was subscribed.

The post of Financial Secretary was held at that time by Stanley Baldwin, an ironmaster aged 52 (born 3 August, 1867), educated at Harrow and Trinity College, Cambridge, and elected MP for Bewdley in 1908, his father's old seat.

In 1892, he had married Lucy Ridsdale; they had two sons and four daughters. He was a student of economics and a pragmatic Protectionist. His career in politics was anything but spectacular until, in 1916, Bonar Law, Chancellor of the Exchequer in Lloyd George's coalition government, picked him as private secretary and then made him joint Financial Secretary to the Treasury. In the immediate post-war years, when he was President of the Board of Trade, he became increasingly opposed to Lloyd George's conduct of the government, which, in his opinion, tended towards a corruption of public life through the sale of honours. He thought that the party system itself was disintegrating as the Prime Minister attached to himself politicians of exceptional ability, to the detriment of their party loyalty. As a protest against the tendency, he resigned from the Cabinet in 1922 and led a revolt of junior ministers which culminated in a Carlton Club meeting which Bonar Law attended.

Baldwin told that meeting: "The Prime Minister is a dynamic force and it is from that very fact that our troubles arise . . . If the present association is continued, you will see the process go on inevitably until the old Conservative party is lost in ruins." The upshot was the destruction of the coalition and the emergence of a Conservative government with Bonar Law as Prime Minister and Baldwin as Chancellor of the Exchequer. As the leading force in this revolt, the daring of which may be obscured by its success, Baldwin emerged as an important new factor in British politics.

Lloyd George, with that inclination to underrate a contemporary which is one of the weaknesses of brilliant men, had said that Bonar Law was "honest to the verge of simplicity". Honest, Bonar Law was, but not simple. When Baldwin heard the remark he said, "By God, that is what we have been looking for!" He was himself anything but a simple man. His stocky exterior of old-fashioned ironmaster hid a

complex and sensitive personality. He loved Bach and sang bass *decani* in the choir of his local church. He loved watching cricket. He escaped sometimes from his wife's Low Church beliefs to vestments and incense. He read widely and intensely. His taste was conventional but deeply felt. He disliked Epstein's sculpture, as he showed quite clearly when he unveiled "Rima" in Hyde Park. He was the cousin of Rudyard Kipling and Philip Burne-Jones. But in 1922 it was his politics and not his views on art that interested the public, which had scarcely heard his name until then.

"In many ways," said the *Scotsman*, "Mr Baldwin resembles Walter Bagehot. Banking is in his blood, economic theory his study and a pleasant outlook on life his habitual cultivation."

At the Treasury it was Baldwin's duty to deal with the problem of the American Debt. He went to Washington and brought back in 1923 an agreement which involved Britain in payments for sixty-two years. Bonar Law exploded with rage when he learnt the terms, and was even more furious when Baldwin, by a few ill-judged remarks to the press, made it difficult to amend the settlement. Some months later, it was apparent that Bonar Law was a dying man. Who would follow him? Lord Curzon came to London, certain that the crown was within his grasp. George V chose Baldwin. The failure of his ministry was confidently and, in some quarters, gleefully awaited.

He was left to form a government among the debris of the explosion which had destroyed Lloyd George's coalition only a year before. Tom Jones, a Welshman who had been Lloyd George's confidant, said of him: "Nothing like Bonar Law's brain, much slower and always eager to consult one or two others before coming to a decision, but stands by his decision once taken." One useful gift the new Prime Minister had; he had acquired an "image"—pipe, baggy clothes, suburban look, honest, good-natured—"no foreigner ever had that face" (A. B. Walkley). He was a well-to-do businessman, who was uncomfortable in the presence of the aristocracy of London's West End. He looked rather like a successful farmer.

His first task was to push the conception of Protection by tariffs through his Cabinet and, then, go to the country on this issue, as he was bound to do as a result of a pledge given by his predecessor, Bonar Law. He lost the election and Labour took office, although with sixty-six seats fewer than the Tories, the balance being held by the Liberals. But that Labour government did not last long, being swept out of office on an anti-Russian tide. The so-called "Zinoviev Letter" played an important part in this reversal of fortune.

Baldwin's new Cabinet was, it seemed, the most impressive assemblage of Tory talent of the century, including, among others, Churchill, Curzon, Balfour, Birkenhead and two Chamberlains. This galaxy might have proved difficult to handle: Baldwin managed it pretty well. Churchill said: "He is singularly adroit in letting events work for him." Birkenhead: "He takes a leap in the dark; looks round and takes another." In fact, his leadership, although governed by instinct, was cautious. He rode the Cabinet on a loose rein and he was a careful student of the whims of the House of Commons. A Prime Minister cannot play President: "The House can" (A. P. Herbert said) "be beautifully kind or stupidly cruel. It can make the best man look silly, and the greatest man afraid." Baldwin watched it like a hawk: "I *must* stay in the House tonight. It was in a curious and rather ugly mood all yesterday." He never relaxed. A private member's attempt to alter the trade union political levy was defeated by him with a single speech, ending with the call, "Give us peace in our time, O Lord." What followed was not peace but the General Strike of

81 The General Strike of 1926. Disturbance in the New Kent Road.

1926. The settlement of that struggle, in which all were involved but which, in his heart, nobody wanted, was one of Baldwin's outstanding achievements.

What followed seemed later on like a period of exceptional calm. At the time, though, it appeared to be stormy enough. There was trouble with the Americans, who wanted, with a fanatical enthusiasm, to cut down Britain's naval strength. There was trouble inside the Cabinet with those, like Churchill, Chancellor of the Exchequer, who wanted to economize on the building of cruisers. Baldwin, as chairman of the Committee of Imperial Defence, thought that the Prime Minister ought to be aware of the problems of grand strategy. He was soon feeling the physical effects of his long spell in office. He had, too, domestic worries: depression in the steel industry brought his income down so sharply that he was forced to sell his London house; his son, Oliver, was an homosexual. When a general election came in 1929, Baldwin had no answer to the popular appeal of Labour and the Liberals. He was blamed for the Tory defeat. The discontent in the Tory party was given focus by anti-government propaganda. In the newspapers, Lord Beaverbrook raised the cry of Empire Free Trade (i.e. Imperial Preference); Lord Rothermere wanted to resist any political concession to India. In early 1931, there was a by-election in St George's, Westminster. Against the official Tory candidate, Duff Cooper, Lord Rothermere put up an independent. "Gandhi is watching St George's," cried the Rothermere newspapers. Baldwin entered the fight with unusual vigour. What the newspaper proprietors were driving at was power, he said—"power without responsibility, the prerogative of the harlot throughout the ages". It was a memorable phrase which Baldwin owed to his cousin, Rudyard Kipling. Duff Cooper won the election by a substantial majority.

In the great controversy over India, Baldwin was in favour of an advance towards self-rule and Churchill was his chief opponent. "I felt that if George III had been endowed with the tongue of Edmund Burke," Baldwin said after one Churchill oration, "he might have made such a speech." His answer prefigured a speech by another Tory Prime Minister years later: "There is a wind of nationalism and freedom blowing round the world . . . The time has now come . . . "

Meanwhile, the economic sky was darkening and the Labour government, which came into office in 1929, was plainly wilting under the blows of adversity. The crisis came in 1931. Ramsay MacDonald's Labour government collapsed and was followed by a National government in which MacDonald was Prime Minister and Baldwin was Lord President of the Council, sacrificing £3,000 of his salary. "The exchanges are nearly bust today," he told his wife, "and if we save the situation it will only be by the skin of our teeth." When the inevitable general election followed, "the greatest electoral tide in the whole story of British democratic politics"* swept Labour out of office and, almost, out of existence. The Tories and their allies won 556 seats against Labour's fifty-two. There were also four Liberal followers of Lloyd George.

It was four years before Baldwin, although leader of the strongest party in the government, came back on the resignation of MacDonald as Prime Minister. By that time, Chamberlain's economic policy had prevailed; Britain had become a

---

* *The Economist.*

Protectionist country and the main problem facing the government was that of defence. Mussolini was annoying in Italy and, far graver, Hitler was in power in Germany. In the country, pacifism and a muddle-headed advocacy of the illusion of "Collective Security" was a powerful force. Against it the government addressed itself, with greater or less enthusiasm, to the task of educating the public in the need to rearm.

Another troublesome event, which at the time was inflated out of all reason, was the Abdication crisis. Edward VIII wanted to marry Mrs Simpson, who was a married woman. Baldwin's handling of this delicate business was regarded as masterly. It postponed for a year the date of his resignation.

The outstanding event of this period was a talk between Hitler and Sir John Simon in March, 1935, in which the Führer declared that the Luftwaffe had already reached parity with the RAF. If this were true—as it was—then Germany had the capacity swiftly to surpass Britain in the air unless there was a drastic and immediate change in the British air programme and in the organization of production in the country. In short, there was need for rearmament on a scale for which the nation was not prepared.

The situation became more complicated when Mussolini invaded Abyssinia and an outcry arose against the colonial plans of the Fascist dictator. When Sir Samuel Hoare, by that time Foreign Secretary, and Laval agreed that the Italians should partition Abyssinia, public indignation rose. In the general election of 1935, the government lost eighty of the extraordinary haul of seats they had won in 1931. The Conservative party had 432 members in the House, as against Labour's 154. It was a remarkable proof of Baldwin's command over British public opinion. Meanwhile, discussions with the Italians over the future of Abyssinia went on. At this point the Hoare-Laval Pact was made. Baldwin's views at the time were clear and simple. He did not trust Laval an inch. And he told his Foreign Secretary, Sir Samuel Hoare, "Keep us out of war, Sam. We are not ready for it."

This was true enough; the question, however, was, would Britain be ready when the time came for the showdown with Nazi Germany which seemed likely and, as the months passed, inevitable? The first step along the way was the rejection of the Hoare-Laval Pact by the British public. In this matter Baldwin had made one of his most serious misjudgments of the people's mood. Let it be admitted, however, that the public was being exceptionally illogical at that time: willing to "stand up to the dictators" and hoping to bring Mussolini to heel by "sanctions" alone, yet unwilling to be realistic when, as an inevitable consequence, Mussolini and Hitler were driven into alliance. When Hitler invaded the Rhineland in 1936, the British reaction was to say that "he had only gone into his own backyard". Yet, of course, when the Rhineland's unarmed position disappeared, there was no hope, short of a major war, of saving Central and Eastern Europe from the Nazis.

Worse lay ahead: the collapse of the Abyssinian policy—the "midsummer of madness" of sanctions, as Neville Chamberlain called it. Rearmament went on, systematically; the building-up of a huge arms-making machine which was to exist alongside the normal industrial organization of the country. The question was: Was it growing fast enough to match the terrifying machine that Hitler was building? And now a new psychological factor was being added to the widespread semi-pacifism

82 Stanley Baldwin, by R. G. Eves.

which acted as a brake on rearmament. This was a movement to "appease" Germany, which became stronger on the right wing of Britain. In November, 1936, Baldwin made a speech which did his reputation more harm than any other single act of his life: "I want to say a word about the years the locusts have eaten . . . I put before the whole House my views with appalling frankness . . . You will remember the election at Fulham in the autumn of 1933, when a seat which the National government held was lost by about 10,000 votes on no issue but the pacifist . . . My feeling as the leader of a great party was not altogether a comfortable one ... Supposing I had gone to the country and said that Germany was rearming and we must rearm ... I cannot think of anything that would have made the loss of the election from my point of view more certain."

Baldwin had good reason to mention East Fulham, for in that by-election the voters had rejected a Conservative candidate, who called for "a bigger navy, a bigger army and a bigger air force", in favour of a Socialist, who said that evidently his Tory opponent's only solution for the nation's difficulties was to prepare for war. A Tory majority of 14,521 was turned into a Socialist majority of 4,840. It was hard to imagine a clearer indication of what the country wanted of its government.

The echoes of this speech of 1936 pursued Baldwin to his dying day. It could be said—and it *was* said—that he had hidden the facts about rearmament from the people in order to save the government in an important by-election. What he had meant was marginally less discreditable: to have spoken frankly about the arms would have presented the election to the Labour Party, who were *against* rearmament. But the fact remains that, in a democracy, the first duty of a political leader is to tell the people the truth. In Churchill's history of the Second World War, the index mentions this incident: "Baldwin confesses to putting party before country."

When the Abdication crisis came, Baldwin exerted himself to persuade King Edward not to take the course which must end in his loss of the crown; when that failed, he laboured to bring about a smooth and orderly transition to a new reign. "It was like one of the great chess games—and yet only one man could have played it. If it had gone wrong, could anything have saved the monarchy?" The game had been played at a heavy cost: Baldwin, whose health was failing fast, was forced to stay in office for another five months "to see the new King into the saddle". As his doctor, Lord Dawson of Penn, told him: "You will pay for this."

He was old, he was tired, he suffered more and more from asthma; the emotional strain of the Abdication had been severe. The problems of Europe came crowding in on him, more intractable than ever since now the Labour party were denouncing rearmament as a betrayal of "Collective Security" and were voting against the Service Estimates. But very soon another pair of shoulders would carry these burdens. In May, 1937, after the Coronation, Baldwin retired. The Garter followed and an earldom.

He mouldered away in retirement until 1947, having become the target of popular abuse by those who blamed him for Britain's unreadiness in the war. The ornamental iron gates at his house, presented by the Worcester Conservative Association on his retirement, were taken by the Minister of Supply, Beaverbrook, for scrap. It seemed rather an unworthy revenge. In the end, it was Beaverbrook alone whom he could not forgive. He died peacefully on 13 December, 1947, and his ashes were buried beside those of his wife in Worcester Cathedral. Let Winston Churchill have the last words: "He was the most formidable politician I have ever known in public life."

XXXIX

❧ JAMES RAMSAY MACDONALD ❧

1924; 1929–35

Either a martyr or a traitor, either clad in shining white robes or in the habiliments of infamy, such—depending on whether you are on one side or the other of a great ideological divide—is James Ramsay MacDonald. Yet it is possible to depict his life in less extreme terms. To say, for example, that MacDonald was a reasonably successful politician of the Left Centre, who led his party from obscurity to office and would have led it to power if it had been mature enough for power. To argue that he presided over an era of rapid evolution, during which Labour was becoming "a natural party of government", i.e. one half of "the Establishment". If that was betrayal, then it has been the avowed purpose of successors of MacDonald like Attlee, Harold Wilson and Callaghan.

However, there is this to be said for the view that MacDonald "betrayed" his party. He failed to realize, or he forgot, that Labour in the Twenties was more than a party. It was a "cause", a "movement", which existed on a different emotional plane from the world of harsh realities. Those who "held the faith" might be incompetent or muddled or hysterical, but they were "comrades" and to abandon them was an act of desertion. In 1931, MacDonald may have saved Britain from ruin but his colleagues, who became his implacable enemies, saved their cause for the future. MacDonald's failure to understand the nature of his party argues a certain arrogance on his part, some contempt for his followers and perhaps a lack of enthusiasm for "the cause". Arrogance he had, and some reason for it.

He was born in Lossiemouth on 12 October, 1866, the child of a passing love. His mother was Anne Ramsay, a servant girl; his father, John MacDonald, a ploughman from the Black Isle of Ross. At the Free Kirk School, "the machinery was as old as Knox," he said, "the education, the best ever given to the sons and daughters of men." Under the dominie, he became a pupil-teacher, salary £7.10s a year. At eighteen, he set out for Bristol, where a local clergyman was looking for someone to help him with a Young Men's Guild. There, in a British Workmen's Coffee Tavern, MacDonald picked up the germs of Socialism. But Bristol turned out to be a false start. Next year he was in London, addressing envelopes at 10s a week for the Cyclist Touring Club and reading in the Guildhall Library. At that time, his staple food was oatmeal which his mother sent him from Lossiemouth. He was a convert to Labour politics and to Scottish Nationalism and, very soon, a member of the Fabian Society. One Sunday, in Regent's Park, he made his first political speech and, in 1894, joined the Independent Labour Party.

83 James Ramsay MacDonald.

When he fought, and lost, his first election at Southampton as an ILP candidate, he received a letter enclosing money for his expenses. The sender was Margaret Gladstone, whom he met a month later. She was the only child of Dr J. H. Gladstone, FRS, a distinguished chemist. The girl was religious and deeply interested in social work. In midsummer of 1896, they became engaged on the steps of the British Museum, where MacDonald was reading. They were married in the autumn and lived in a flat in Lincoln's Inn Fields. In due course, they had six children, of whom five survived childhood. From then onwards MacDonald was speaking all over the country, his fine presence, fine voice and grave Morayshire accent being assets which could be turned to good use in politics. With his earnings as a lecturer and journalist added to his wife's private income, the MacDonalds found it possible to travel extensively and to keep open house at Lincoln's Inn Fields for friends with similar interests to their own. Sometimes the flat was the scene of a political meeting. The Labour Party was about to be born. Its predecessor was the Labour Parliamentary Committee; MacDonald, its first secretary, salary twenty guineas; office, a small back room in his flat.

During the Boer War, which MacDonald strongly opposed, he had his first taste of unpopularity. It proved that he had moral as well as physical courage. He also showed political shrewdness. It was he who made a secret agreement with the Liberals, by which each party promised not to oppose the other in certain constituencies. This agreement, as it turned out, provided the conditions for Labour's emergence in Parliament as an effective, recognizable ally of the Liberal government of 1906—officially called the Labour Party and with twenty-nine out of its fifty candidates members of Parliament. MacDonald himself was returned as MP for Leicester. Twenty-eight men like him sat in Parliament that year.

His tactics were to insist that his party was Socialist but not Marxist and, still less, Anarchist. Its methods must be Parliamentary and not revolutionary. These principles seem obvious to us now but, in the early years of the century, the Labour movement was still troubled by heady dreams of "the barricades" and "the Revolution". At any moment the long-awaited, oft-predicted, "Crisis of Capitalism" would arrive and the hour of "irreversible" change. (Seventy years later, these delusions still persist in obscure corners of "the movement".)

As was to be expected, MacDonald, as Chairman of the Independent Labour Party (1906), and then as Chairman of the Labour Party (1911), had his work cut out to hold together his unruly and impatient flock. The death of his wife in 1911 left him lonely and sorrowful. He had five young children to bring up and, for a time, no heart for the party struggle or the wearisome squabbles within his own faction.

When war came in 1914, he was against British intervention, which most of his Parliamentary colleagues approved; he was not a "pro-German" and not a pacifist; he believed that a negotiated peace could be made. With anti-war Liberals, he took part in the Union of Democratic Control, which was thought to be harmful to the British war effort. Its general purpose was to assert public control over diplomacy and, as the war dragged on, to negotiate a peace with the Germans. This was a view shared by high Tories, like Lord Lansdowne, but it laid open those who held it to the charge that they were damaging the war effort. MacDonald was the chief victim of the campaign of abuse aimed at the "pacifists". A rogue named Bottomley even printed his birth certificate in an attempt to harm him.

In those days MacDonald needed all his physical and moral courage. His opinions were too complex to be understood in the midst of a life-and-death struggle. When he was asked to address a recruiting meeting at Leicester, his letter of refusal was a masterpiece of flatulence: "We are in [the war]. It will work itself out now. Might and spirit will win and incalculable political and social consequences will follow upon victory. Victory, therefore, must be ours", and so on. Lord Snowden later reprinted it as a prime specimen of MacDonald's gift for "dancing round the mulberry bush". Even more striking specimens were to come. In trying to hold his heterogeneous team together, he was making sounds which would please all of them and could mean almost anything, according to the preference of the hearer. He was the prophet of a vague moral urge, of desire for a better world in which all men could be brothers. But something more definite was wanted.

When the Russian Revolution came in 1917, MacDonald declared that "it was a sort of spring-tide of joy" bursting over Europe. When the second wave of revolution brought the Bolsheviks to power, MacDonald urged that Britain should send an ambassador to Petrograd and should give proper diplomatic status to Litvinoff, who was being vilified as one who had robbed a bank in Tiflis.* On these matters, MacDonald was far out of touch with ordinary opinion in Britain as the war rushed to its climax; it is not surprising, then, that he (along with other "pacifists") lost his seat in the general election of December, 1918. However, the party he had hammered together emerged stronger than the Asquith Liberals. It was becoming recognized as the Opposition.

Out of Parliament, MacDonald attacked the Versailles Treaty. "If I wished for revenge upon the *Entente*, I should encourage it to impose upon Germany an indemnity so great that it could not be paid for many years. That would keep Germany united and resentful . . . " On Russia, his views remained that she should, if possible, be brought back to sanity, i.e. to Parliamentary Socialism; military intervention by the Allies to promote a counter-revolution was a piece of folly. Communism he detested as a "product of Czarism"; above all, he condemned the Bolshevik invasion of the Georgian Republic, "a callous political crime". In conformity with these opinions, he prevented the Independent Labour Party from joining the Communist International.

In the general election of 1922, he was returned as member for Aberavon in a party which by then knew how much it needed him. He was once more Chairman of the Labour Party.

Events were moving fast. Unemployment mounted. Bonar Law died; Stanley Baldwin took his place as Conservative Prime Minister and asked the electorate for the right to bring in tariffs. The electorate said No, and Labour was the larger of the two Opposition parties. In January, 1924, then, MacDonald with his Cabinet went to Buckingham Palace to kiss hands. He was Prime Minister until the Liberal Party decided that the moment had come to join its votes to those of the Tories and turn the first Labour government out. It was, it seemed to him, not the time to introduce a full-blooded Socialist programme.

MacDonald, who was Foreign Secretary as well as Prime Minister, concentrated on high diplomacy, for which he had liking and aptitude. He brought France and

---

*What he had done was to help to dispose of the stolen money. A receiver rather than a thief.

Germany to agree to the Dawes Plan for settling the reparations question; he recognized the Soviet government and made a cautious commercial treaty with the Russians. However, he was not deceived, as some of the more starry-eyed of his followers were, by the notion that governments of the Left, wherever they existed, were drawn together by a community of ideals. When his government decided not to prosecute J. R. Campbell for incitement to mutiny, Tories and Liberals united to bring to an end MacDonald's first term of office as Prime Minister, which had lasted less than a year. Helped to some extent by that dubious document, the so-called "Zinoviev Letter", the Tories won a majority over both the other parties in a general election. The Liberal vote fell ominously. Labour lost seats but increased its poll. Nevertheless, the Independent Labour Party hived off, impatient with MacDonald's slow progress towards the Socialist Utopia.

When the General Strike came in 1926, MacDonald remained true to his belief that neither strikes nor revolutionary violence were the way to Socialism. The nation as a whole must be converted. This high moral line did not appeal to the emotional Left, eager to put its doctrines into practice, no matter what were the opinions of the masses. Unemployment persisted, with a tendency to grow worse. The Liberal Party seemed to be reviving, its organization much improved and with fresh, bold propaganda. The Liberal Yellow Book was followed by a report, "We Can Conquer Unemployment", price sixpence. When voting day came again, however, in 1929, it was Labour who won: 287 seats to 261 Conservative and 59 Liberal.

MacDonald's second premiership began in 1929, with the Liberals still holding the balance in Parliament but less inclined than before to turn Labour out. However, such hopes as MacDonald may have had were blasted before the year was ended. The Great Depression struck the United States and sent tremors of economic alarm across the Atlantic. If this was indeed the expected "Crisis of Capitalism", its first consequences were ironical: a million more British workers were out of a job; the Labour government was shaken and eventually brought down, and, in Europe, German democracy was destroyed and replaced by a sinister totalitarian dictatorship.

In this mounting crisis, it seemed that MacDonald had run out of ideas. Indeed, at that moment the only signs of boldness and novelty of thought came from the Liberals, who, led by Lloyd George and inspired by Keynes, urged that a vast programme of public works was the proper answer to a crisis of deflation. MacDonald had no stomach for anything so large and unorthodox. He took over the fight against unemployment. The crisis deepened, there were two and a half million out of work. The Tories complained of the squandering of public money by the Socialists. A committee of bankers and economists—the May Committee—prescribed higher taxes and more cuts in public spending; above all, a cut of ten per cent in the Dole.

At an all-party meeting in Downing Street, Neville Chamberlain said that the government's proposals for meeting the crisis (which did not include a cut in the Dole) were unacceptable. The Tories meant to turn the government out as soon as Parliament met but the financial crash would come before that. MacDonald said he had decided to resign and proposed to ask the King to consult the party leaders on the next step. His Cabinet, by a majority, accepted the bitter pill of a ten per cent cut in

84 Edith, Marchioness of Londonderry.

the Dole. But the majority was not big enough. MacDonald decided that the government could not go on. He asked his colleagues for their resignations and became head of a "National" government in which he was joined by Baldwin, the Tory leader, as Lord President of the Council and Sir Herbert Samuel, the Liberal, as Home Secretary. His former colleagues in the defunct Labour Cabinet thought he had not been straightforward with them. And he, for his part, was surprised by the fury with which they turned on him. MacDonald, the *bête noire* of the Right twelve years earlier, became, in a night, the most hated man to British Socialists. In their rage, there was a special venom: he was the Lost Leader.

One irony followed another. The government, which had been elected to save the Gold Standard, took Britain off it. It went to the country asking for a "doctor's mandate", i.e. a right to do whatever was necessary, including tariffs, and was given it by a vast majority. MacDonald, with hesitation and reluctance, accepted it, in spite of the warning of his daughter, Ishbel, that the Tories would suck him dry like an orange before throwing him aside. In fact, the Tories knew that if MacDonald did not lead the government, it would lose its national appeal. In the general election, the Conservatives won 471 out of 556 National government seats. It was, perhaps, the greatest misfortune of MacDonald's career: he was Prime Minister of a government which must be steadily and increasingly Tory in policy. Things had not worked out at all as he had hoped. The last phase is thus marked by pathos which became deeper as eyesight faded, memory weakened and power to sustain a thought or keep hold of an argument failed. He became a target for derision from his nominal supporters in Parliament and for hatred by the Opposition. In 1935, he resigned as Prime Minister and lost his seat at Seaham. He became Lord President of the Council and member for the Scottish Universities, a seat he held until 1937. He died on 9 November of that year.

His former Socialist allies accused him of having succumbed to the allurements of aristocratic society. It was true that he was vain of his looks and bearing and that his imagination was kindled by the traditional, the ceremonial, the magnificent. He was, as Bernard Shaw said, a Highlander of the seventeenth century, who had little in common with trade union leaders and party hacks. He had what can only be called a love affair with Edith, Marchioness of Londonderry, to whom he wrote letters (which she kept) calling her "My dearest Ladye" and signing them "Hamish". She signed hers "Circe". It was the last emotional, or at least sentimental, fling of a man who was attractive to women and had for twenty years been a lonely widower.

XL

❧ ARTHUR NEVILLE CHAMBERLAIN ❧

1937–40

Arthur Neville Chamberlain's career, like that of Stanley Baldwin, demonstrates the sad truth that nothing is so dangerous to a politician's reputation as success in pleasing the people. Baldwin did not rearm—or did not rearm quickly enough—which exactly fulfilled the democratic will in 1936; the result was that, in retirement, he was loaded with contempt and abuse. Chamberlain went to Munich to negotiate a settlement of the Czech crisis, as seventy per cent of the British people wanted him to do.* A year later, he and his policy of "Appeasement" were looked on with detestation.

He was hopelessly miscast for the part he had to take—the play, the time, both were wrong. It was not his fault that he looked like a successful undertaker and that on his lips the clarion call to battle sounded like a dirge. He belonged to a type of introvert politician, like Peel, Bonar Law and Attlee, and the hour called for an extrovert. Not only was Chamberlain not that, but he had an instinctive distrust of men who were: thus, he hated Lloyd George and was not at home with Winston Churchill. It would have been far better if he had been able to stick to things he liked and understood: social policy, municipal reform, that sort of thing. As it was . . .

He was the second son of the great Radical imperialist, Joseph Chamberlain, born on 18 March, 1869, in Birmingham and educated at Rugby and then at Mason College, Birmingham. He was articled as a chartered accountant and, after that (1890–97), went to manage for the family a sisal plantation in the West Indies. But the sisal would not grow; and £80,000 of Chamberlain money was lost. He came back to settle down to a business career in Birmingham in the copper brass industry, and, being a member of the leading political family in the city, was drawn into local politics. In 1915, he was Lord Mayor, and, in the following year, was appointed by Lloyd George Director-General of National Service. Lloyd George thought he had failed in the post; Chamberlain thought he was denied power to make a success of it. In the general election of 1918, he became Unionist MP for the Ladywood division of Birmingham; it was not a difficult seat for a Conservative to win; it was not a difficult year. He had married (1911) Anne Vere Cole; they had a son and a daughter.

His political ascent was swift and predictable: Postmaster-General; Paymaster-General; then Minister of Health in 1923. There his success was undeniable. It was

---

* See Mass Observation Survey, September, 1938.

**85 Arthur Neville
Chamberlain.**

an area of affairs which he understood and in which his talent for thorough
administration flourished. But by the time he went to the Exchequer in 1931, issues
of a different magnitude had become predominant. He was Chancellor of the
Exchequer in the National government when, according to the best financial advice

of the time, a policy of stern deflation was called for if Britain were to be rescued from bankruptcy. Chamberlain gave the impression that he was following that policy without due sympathy for the vast human misery that it involved. But the real test of himself and his policy lay ahead. While Baldwin was still Prime Minister, the threat from the totalitarian powers grew and became acute. As Baldwin drifted out of the overall control of affairs, Chamberlain came more and more to take over the reins. He had a harsh and clear-cut vision of the situation. While he had some illusions of his own, they were not the illusions of the Left, for whom, as political thinkers, he had a profound contempt which, being the brusque sort of man he was, he did not trouble to conceal. Above all, he had no patience with the sentimental talk about "Collective Security" which, in his heart, he knew would lead to nothing. His policy was hard-edged and confident and was dominated by three axioms: France was "decadent"; Germany, under Hitler, was united as no other European nation was, and Soviet Russia was an untiring mischief-maker with whom no friendship was possible.

He sent his sister-in-law to Rome to talk to Mussolini; his idea was to prise Mussolini away from Hitler. Early in 1938, when the Foreign Secretary, Anthony Eden, was out of the country, President Roosevelt suggested a world conference on the international situation. It was a short step by the United States into the arena but even the shortest step by the greatest power in the world was important. Chamberlain's reply was that the American plan was interfering with Britain's hope to buy Italy off. Eden came back too late to change the message, and resigned.

Chamberlain's self-assurance, which some thought was conceit, had rid his government of its most popular member. He had also, whether he wished to or not, sent out a signal which Hitler and Mussolini thought they could decipher: here was a British statesman to whom they could talk. The notion meshed exactly with Chamberlain's view of the role he should play. He used the word "Appeasement" to describe his general approach to policy; it implied that Germany had a just grievance as the result of the Versailles treaty and that this should be met by wise concessions. As time went on, the meaning of the word was modified so that what had begun as a plea for justice became a progressive surrender to force. And gradually Chamberlain was regarded by his political opponents in Britain as the accomplice of the totalitarian dictators when they—and, above all, Hitler—pressed forward to reshape the world on a pattern of their own.

The pace of events grew steadily more frantic as Hitler tried to realize his full programme before Britain and France were in a military condition to resist him. Austria was swallowed up by Germany; next it was the turn of Czechoslovakia. Meanwhile, a civil war had broken out in Spain which was going to the advantage of General Franco, whose cause Hitler and Mussolini had espoused. However, it was over Czechoslovakia that Chamberlain's policy ran into an emotional storm. Believing, or at least hoping that he could negotiate with Hitler, he set off on the melancholy visits to Germany which are collectively known as "Munich". He obtained no concessions of any value—Hitler agreed merely to mutilate Czechoslovakia and to postpone for a few months its final dissolution. Worse than that, Chamberlain had bullied the Czechs into accepting Hitler's monstrous terms, so that Britain was morally involved in the murder of a small democracy.

This macabre episode was imprinted indelibly on the public memory by various

86 The appeasement of Hitler's Germany was a political cause espoused by important people in London. Among others, Lord and Lady Astor were regarded as leaders in this movement. Their friends, known as the Cliveden set, included Dr Thomas Jones here seen entering Lady Astor's house in St James's Square, 1 April, 1938.

incidental circumstances: Chamberlain's description of Czechoslovakia as a distant country of which we knew little; the umbrella which he took with him on his journeys and which, from a symbol of peace, became one of sinister mockery; his return to Downing Street waving a piece of paper and announcing that he had brought "peace with honour". The cheering crowd in Downing Street agreed. "No conqueror returning from a victory on the battlefield," said *The Times*, "has come adorned with nobler laurels."

It may be that for a little Chamberlain really believed that he had brought peace. If so, events soon disillusioned him. "This time *he* [Hitler] has made the promise to *me*," he said, confident that the promise would be kept. Instead, Hitler swallowed the remnants of Czechoslovakia and prepared his plans for the destruction of Poland.

"Appeasement" was dead, but it had lived too long. Chamberlain gave a guarantee to Poland which could be carried out only if Russia were drawn in. The facts of geography and military power made it impossible for Britain alone to come to Poland's aid. And Poland would not accept Russian military aid on Russia's terms. In view of what happened later, who can wonder?

Late in August, 1939, came a brutal reminder of political realities: Germany and the Soviet Union made a pact which meant the immediate partition of Poland. A few days later, Chamberlain, his voice quavering with anguish, announced that Britain was at war with Germany. The peace which he thought he could make had eluded him; now he was left with a war which assuredly he did not think he could make. In the years he had been in office, the quality of his Cabinet had fallen. It had, as one observer said, "become a Cabinet of nonentities presided over by one magisterial personality".* When Churchill joined it, there was a feeling that at least one member of the government measured up to the gravity of the situation. But the "phoney war" went on, a period during which people in and out of the government believed that the war could be adequately waged by the blockade of Germany and that "time was on our side". All these delusions were exploded when Hitler seized Denmark and Norway in the spring of 1940. The war had at last begun.

Hitler's Norwegian operation, which had looked difficult to the point of being impossible, was carried out with speed and efficiency. The answer of the Western Allies was inadequate. But for this, for which, if anyone, Churchill, the Minister of Defence, might have been blamed, the odium fell on Chamberlain. Speaking in the House, he mistook one Norwegian port, Larvik, of which everyone had heard, for another, Narvik—which was unfamiliar and far to the north of any point on the coast that the Germans should have reached. Those who had long wanted to get rid of Chamberlain now concentrated their fire. Leo Amery shouted across the floor to Arthur Greenwood, the Labour spokesman, "Speak for England, Arthur!" The government's majority fell from two hundred to eighty. Chamberlain resigned; Churchill came in.

Within months, Chamberlain was dead (19 November, 1940). His term of office as Prime Minister had been short, its close was sad. He had been called upon to deal with a dynamic force, a dictator whose ideas were barely sane but who applied them with astuteness and a total lack of scruple. Chamberlain had tried to meet this danger with good sense and reason. They were not enough.

---

* Colvin. *The Chamberlain Cabinet.*

XLI

❧ SIR WINSTON LEONARD SPENCER CHURCHILL ❧

1940–45; 1951–55

With Winston Churchill, ducal England, after almost a century of absence, stepped back into 10 Downing Street. The journey had been long; forty years had passed since he first entered Parliament as MP for Oldham; he had changed his party twice; his political career had been despaired of; in one great war he had been a minister and a soldier; now, in a second war, he had been called to the supreme position in the state. The hour was grave; his greatest days lay ahead.

He was born in Blenheim Palace, on 30 November, 1874, son of Lord Randolph Churchill and Jennie, daughter of Leonard Jerome of New York. As a boy, his father, the tragic Lord Randolph, thought so little of his ability that he judged the army, in those days a refuge for the less brilliant sons of the upper classes, the right place for Winston. He was sent from Harrow to Sandhurst. While at Sandhurst, he made his first incursion to public life; the bar at the Empire Music Hall had been closed. Winston, shouting "Follow me!" led the mob and forced the way in. After that, he went with a smart cavalry regiment, the 4th Hussars, to India. All the time he was learning to use the English language with power and distinction by reading the best authors. It would not be an exaggeration to say that Winston was self-educated. One thing was quickly proved: the young cavalry subaltern was not going to have a conventional military career; nor was it going to be inactive. His first experience of war was in Cuba where there was a rebellion against the Spaniards. A series of descriptive letters from him appeared in the *Daily Graphic*. While in India, he wrote a novel, *Savrola*. It is exceptionally bad.

By dint of bullying the authorities he had himself sent to Malakand, where the local tribes had risen, arriving to his chagrin after the fighting was over. However, he wrote a book on the campaign, much resented by older officers as a subaltern's hints to generals. More important, by ceaseless wire-pulling he was sent (against Kitchener's determined opposition) as a journalist and soldier to join the army that was about to invade the Sudan and avenge the murder of Gordon. He was going, he said, to write a "big book" on the subject. He took part in the charge of the 21st Lancers at Omdurman. By the time he returned to England he was a successful journalist. He plunged into politics. "He talks and talks," said a fellow-journalist, "and you can hardly tell when he leaves off quoting his idol Macaulay and begins his other, Winston Churchill." His book on the Sudan campaign, *The River War*, was an instant success.

He fought an election at Oldham as a Conservative, lost it and, not long after, signed on as a correspondent for the *Morning Post* to cover the South African war. Soon after reaching the war zone he was captured. Without delay, he escaped and £25 was offered by the Boers for the return of an Englishman who "walks with a forward stoop, reddish brown hair, hardly noticeable moustache, talks through his nose and cannot pronounce the letter 's' properly". Hidden under bales of wool, Churchill reached the Portuguese frontier. He was promised support in the next election by the Liberals. He returned to England to be greeted in Oldham with "See, the Conquering Hero comes". He was elected in October, 1900; he made £10,000 from lectures about his escape.

It did not take him long to impress the House of Commons with his eloquence or with his independence of mind. "Thank God we have a Liberal Party," he declared on Free Trade, a policy which the Conservatives were abandoning. He crossed the floor of the House and, in the next general election, stood as a Free Trade candidate for N.W. Manchester. He won the seat and entered the new Parliament as one of 371 Liberal members. He was appointed Under-Secretary of State for the Colonies (1906). When Asquith followed Campbell-Bannerman as Prime Minister, he made Churchill President of the Board of Trade and a member of the Cabinet (1908). On this promotion he was obliged to fight a by-election in which he was defeated. A vacancy for him was made at Dundee, which he won.

At this time he married Miss Clementine Hozier; in due course, they had one son and three daughters. He depended on his salary as a Cabinet minister and the income which his writing brought him. He formed an alliance with Lloyd George, whose sensational Budget of 1909 was the best hope that the flagging Liberal government had of staying in office. When the Lords rejected the Budget, there was a new election which brought the Liberals to power again, but now with so small a majority that they depended on Irish Nationalist votes. Against the general trend, Churchill held Dundee with an increased majority; became Home Secretary in 1910 and, as such, was a prime target for Suffragette attack. In the same capacity he had to deal with an anarchist outbreak in the East End of London. In an attack on a jeweller's shop by an armed gang led by "Peter the Painter", a Leftist terrorist, a policeman was killed. Police troops and a field gun were brought against a house in Sidney Street. Churchill was present at the incident, which ended when the burning roof fell in on the desperadoes. Needless to say, Churchill was accused of over-dramatizing the affair.

By this time, events in Europe were moving faster and more ominously. Churchill, who had opposed the naval building programme, was now a convinced protagonist of preparation. He was so energetic and effective in the discussion of defence problems that Asquith made him First Lord of the Admiralty in 1911. In a speech at Glasgow he annoyed those who thought of him as a pacifist and, still more, he annoyed the Germans. The German navy was a luxury, he said, ours a necessity. He proposed that Britain and Germany should take a "naval holiday" in 1913; when the Germans refused, he secretly changed the armament of his new battleships from 13.5 inch guns to 15 inch.

As war approached in the summer of 1914, he took decisions to ensure British readiness; after a review at Spithead on 14 July, the fleet was not to disperse for the usual leave; on 29 July, he ordered the fleet to sail to its war stations; on August 1 he called up the naval reservists (a step which the Cabinet had vetoed) on hearing that Germany had declared war on Russia. In the first days of the war he ran into serious trouble: he had sent a naval brigade to prevent Antwerp falling into German hands; it was already too late to do anything of the kind and in the upshot three battalions of the brigade were interned in Holland. The incident did Churchill great harm with the public. Those who were ready to find him too excitable and impetuous were confirmed in their belief. More spectacular testimony was soon provided. With the Western Front frozen, Churchill turned to the notion of a flank attack on the Central Empires through the Dardanelles. The plan had the imaginative quality which appealed to him but, to be successful, it called for an equal degree of imagination in those who executed it. It failed. Conservative ministers took part in a coalition government. Demoted, Churchill became Chancellor of the Duchy of Lancaster in 1915. Among other misfortunes, he had incurred the implacable distrust of the Conservative leader, Bonar Law. When the War Council of the Cabinet was re-formed, Churchill resigned and went to the front as commanding officer of a battalion of the Royal Scots Fusiliers.

When Lloyd George became Prime Minister at the end of 1916, he wanted to make Churchill a minister but this was frustrated by Conservative opposition. In May, 1917, however, Churchill was Minister of Munitions in a re-shaped government. He spent a great deal of time in the ensuing months shuttling between London and a château in France from which he could watch the progress of the war. The Armistice was followed by a general election in which he held his seat at Dundee. He had now a double role—Secretary for War and Minister for Air. But Lloyd George's coalition fell and was succeeded by a Conservative government led by Bonar Law. Churchill lost Dundee and was out of Parliament for two years. He spent the leisure profitably by writing a history of the war in five volumes. He fought West Leicester in 1923 as a Liberal Free Trader and lost; his next contest was for the Abbey division of Westminster in 1924, when he was beaten by forty-three votes. Then, when the Labour government collapsed later that year, he won Epping as a "Constitutionalist" and became Chancellor of the Exchequer in Baldwin's government in 1924, to the displeasure of many Conservatives. The General Strike of 1926 diverted attention from Parliament; Churchill became editor of the *British Gazette*, a government propaganda sheet.

Churchill's definite breach with Baldwin occured over India. "On the release of Mr Gandhi in order that he might become the envoy of Nationalist India to this London conference" on Indian Self Government) "I reached breaking point," says Churchill.* His resignation came in January, 1931. The collapse of credit in the United States had taken place not long before and MacDonald had succeeded Baldwin as Prime Minister. He found himself faced with an unemployment figure of close on three million. Unable to command the political stamina to deal with so grave a crisis, the Socialist government fell and was replaced by a National, or coalition government. In this, Churchill, opposed to Baldwin over India and to Labour on general grounds of policy, had no place. He remained out of office until a still graver

---

*Churchill. *The Second World War*. Vol. I, p. 26.

87 Winston Churchill and Lord Northcliffe at Versailles, 1919.

crisis of a different kind. He busied himself with writing. His *Life of Marlborough* belongs to this time.

In the Abdication crisis, when he was out of the government, he was a champion of King Edward VIII. Generally speaking, he was out of harmony with the public. If he hoped, as some thought, to form a "King's Party", he misjudged the temper of public opinion and, when the Hitler menace rose, he was for a time a voice in the wilderness calling the nation to rouse itself, to open its eyes, to arm, to get ready for

88 Lord Beaverbrook becomes Minister of Aircraft Production in Churchill's government in May, 1940.

89 Sir Winston Churchill (photo by Karsh).

war. This was the last thing that Britain wanted to hear at that time. When the Munich agreement came, he took the unpopular—that is, the pessimistic—line. Within a year he was proved right. Britain was at war and he was First Lord of the Admiralty (1939) in Neville Chamberlain's ill-starred government.

After military failure in the Norwegian campaign, it was clear that there must be a change in the higher direction of the war. Chamberlain resigned on 10 May, 1940. Churchill became Prime Minister. After forty years of the rough and tumble of politics, he had reached the summit. He had done so in an hour of terrible crisis, which before long was to be still graver. France fell; the whole of Western Europe was under Hitler's heel; the British Expeditionary Force was brought back from

Dunkirk, stripped of its guns and equipment. From that moment onwards, Churchill's story is that of the war. His speeches were in the classical mould of defiant oratory. There had been nothing remotely like them since the days of Chatham. They played a vital part in rousing the nation to the extremity of its need and to the greatness of its destiny. The speeches were, of course, only a minor item in the gigantic task he had undertaken of saving a lost war. His strategy was at once cautious and impatient—cautious because he realized the long-term weakness of Britain as a nation with a low birth-rate, and impatient because the British people needed something to show for the remarkable, if belated, effort they were making. For that reason, he was inclined to support offensives when Britain was in a condition to conduct nothing but the most cautious defensive action. He was not a great strategic thinker, for strategy demands a coolness of judgment which he did not possess. But his intuitive desire for movement, for action, was sound and it corresponded to the common sense of the nation. His supreme blunder came when Japan entered the war and he sent warships to Singapore, which they could not defend, and continued sending to Russia fighter aircraft, which might have saved Singapore. After Singapore it was no longer possible for Britain to maintain the Eastern Empire, which was, therefore, lost by the man who, more than any other, believed in it. But the blunder belonged to the man's fighting spirit, which had kept Britain in the war at an hour when everything had seemed to be lost.

When at last peace came, it brought political defeat for Churchill, which was a heavy blow to him, scarcely lightened when the Queen conferred on him the Order of Merit and the Garter. He had been too absorbed in the great struggle to realize that vast changes were impending and that other politicians were determined to bring them about. He spent the years in Opposition in writing his history of the Second World War which matches in sweep and grandeur his account of the first conflict. In October, 1951, he came back to power, concentrating his interest on foreign affairs and, above all, on the attempt to build up a European association of nations capable of sustaining itself against the Russian empire, the western border of which was by this time on the Elbe. He resigned the premiership in 1955 and died ten years later, on 24 January, 1965, after a long, melancholy decline. His funeral, which he had planned with some care ("above all, plenty of bands"), was a profoundly moving occasion and was recognized as such by the vast crowds that witnessed it. It was not the passing of an age of greatness, the greatness was already in the grave; it was the memorial of an empire which, on its very deathbed, had saved civilization, and of the man who had made that achievement possible.

XLII

❧ CLEMENT RICHARD ATTLEE ❧

1945–51

Nothing in the world was easier than to underrate Clement Attlee. He looked and talked exactly as was to be expected of one who was the son of a successful London solicitor and who had been a major in a battalion which had fought at Gallipoli. There he sat, doodling at the Cabinet table or smoking his pipe on a Labour Party platform, a caricaturist's dream of "the little man", who would utter a few unmemorable sentences in a high, clipped manner before hurrying, by public transport, to put on his slippers in his home in the suburbs. It was easy to be scornful of him; when a companion said to Churchill, "Looks a modest little chap," the great man is said to have replied: "Yes, he has a lot to be modest about." Churchill lived to know better.

There are two styles in Prime Minister—prose and poetry. Attlee was prose; and, it seemed, colourless prose at that. He was unsentimental, business-like, economical of words and wit, distrustful of eloquence. When he dismissed a minister, he said, "Sorry to have to ask for your resignation."

"Why, Prime Minister?" the victim asked.

"Simply not up to it, I'm afraid." And that was that.

He was a good, if secretive, judge of character, e.g. his distrust of Crossman, "plenty of ability, no judgment"; an excellent chairman of committees, one born, as it seemed, to be overlooked—"a sheep in sheep's clothing", as Churchill was reported to have said. He took two newspapers, *The Times* for the cricket scores and the *Daily Herald* for the sake of form. It was the party paper; he did not read it.

Yet he was leader of his party for twenty years and Prime Minister for six. And not only so, but head of a government which, in the stormy years after the Second World War, pushed through an ambitious programme of social legislation. Having accomplished what he set out to do, he resigned and contentedly lost the election. The man might not appear remarkable; the achievement was.

Born in Putney in 1883, educated at Haileybury and University College, Oxford, Clement Attlee was a conservative, Church of England young man and, to begin with, not much interested in politics. But there was a strong pull in him to social work, which, having private means, he could indulge; in 1907, a year after he was called to the Bar, he became manager of a boys' club in the East End, where he lived for fourteen years. There was a moral urge working in the young man which took him into the Independent Labour Party. He was at work in Socialist propaganda and a

90 Clement Attlee, by G. Harcourt.

lecturer at the London School of Economics when the war came in 1914 and he was commissioned in the South Lancashire Regiment.

When peace came he returned to Socialist politics and became Mayor of Stepney. In 1922, he married Violet Millar, by whom he had a son and three daughters. In the same year, he was elected MP for Limehouse and became Parliamentary Private Secretary to the party leader, Ramsay MacDonald, after which he was Under-Secretary at the War Office in the first Labour government and, in the second, Chancellor of the Duchy of Lancaster. When MacDonald left the party and formed the coalition government, in 1931, Attlee had a stroke of luck. He held his Limehouse seat at a time when experienced Labour politicians were almost annihilated at the polls. He became deputy leader of the party, which was led by George Lansbury, who lacked many of the qualifications needed in an effective Parliamentary debater and was also an ailing man. After the election of 1935, the Parliamentary Labour Party chose Attlee as its leader rather than Arthur Greenwood or Herbert Morrison. He was the spokesman of a middle-of-the-road democratic Socialism.

When war came and, a year later, Neville Chamberlain's government fell, Attlee entered Churchill's government as Lord Privy Seal. He was, in fact, Deputy Prime Minister, which he formally became in 1942. His two Labour colleagues in the government, Ernest Bevin (Minister of Labour), and Herbert Morrison (Home Secretary), were in key executive posts and were, necessarily, more in the public eye than he was.

But Attlee's role of loyal subordination to Churchill was vital to the successful conduct of the war during a period of intense social stresses and military ordeals. At the end of the war, he won the ensuing general election by a landslide majority. Somewhat surprised, but completely confident in his abilities after the war years as Churchill's deputy, Attlee was now Prime Minister.

He had inherited the centralized machinery with which Churchill had conducted the war. He did not reduce it. "Under him, the enlarged Cabinet Secretariat and the elaborate system of Cabinet committees was maintained and reorganized for peace-time purposes. In this way," argues R. H. S. Crossman,* "the point of decision, which in the 1930s still rested inside the Cabinet, was now permanently transferred either downwards to these powerful Cabinet committees, or upwards to the Prime Minister." So Crossman sees the system which Churchill created and Attlee perpetuated. But his view should be regarded with caution.

Atlee led a powerful, experienced and difficult team of ministers. Ernest Bevin, with whom Attlee formed a close friendship and alliance, Morrison, Cripps and—a brilliant younger man who had spent the war in Opposition—Aneurin Bevan.

It was, in fact, Bevan's National Health Service that proved to be the most important piece of social legislation of the new government, although, faithful to their creed, they nationalized coal, gas, electricity, the railways and steel. Britain was now a half-Socialist country, even if the consequences of transformation fell somewhat short of the hopes raised by Socialist propaganda. With two acts of government, Attlee was particularly identified: the decision to make a British atom

---

*Bagehot. *The English Constitution*. Introduction by Crossman, p. 49.

91 Aneurin Bevan, by Low. As Minister of Health in Attlee's ministry, Bevan introduced the National Health Service.

bomb, and the conversion of India and Pakistan into independent states. It is alleged that he carried out the first without consulting the Cabinet. This is not quite the case. The intention to make the bomb was plainly, if unobviously, made clear in a Cabinet paper. All ministers needed to do was to read and use their intelligence.

It was ironic that, after all the years during which Indian politicians demanded their national rights, the main obstacle in carrying out the policy came from the Indians. But so it was.

When, during his last illness, a visitor said to him, "Clem, you will always be remembered for two things: the independence of India and the National Health Service", the old man thought for a moment. Then he said, "The first, yes, I suppose so. The second? It seemed all right at the time but I had underrated the selfishness of the public."

In fact, the independence and partition of India was one of the most blood-stained episodes in the history of that sub-continent. But that was something which was not on Attlee's conscience. India had to be "freed"; the price had to be paid. Lord Randolph Churchill had said, sixty years earlier, "Our rule in India is, as it were, a sheet of oil, spread out and keeping calm and quiet and unaffected by storms, an immense and profound ocean of humanity."* Now, almost casually, and with the least possible fuss, this protecting sheet was removed and the ocean was open to the full force of the winds. It was a great and daring act of state; its consequences must be immeasurable. It was carried out by the most matter-of-fact of men.

By 1950, it was clear that the Labour government was losing its original impetus. As Anthony Eden said, it "was but a shadow of its former self. Its message also was exhausted." An election in that year reduced the Labour majority to five; next year the Conservatives were back in power. In 1955, Attlee, who by this time had been given the Order of Merit, retired from politics; typical of his sensible refusal to be affected by any fashionable party sentimentality, he accepted an earldom and, later, the Garter. He died on 8 October, 1967.

Eden's summing up was crisp: "Attlee's modesty in expression conceals a firmness of purpose, though not imagination. He sees more clearly than most the limits of his action and never strays beyond them. He is infinitely patient . . . It was not in his nature to do so, but if he had to, he could snap and bite with the best. I trusted him completely as a colleague and respected him as an opponent." In that last sentence, maybe, is the secret of the success achieved in public life by this quiet, remarkable Englishman.

When Earl Attlee had written a volume of memoirs, he was interviewed for the BBC. The interviewer had, as is customary, brought to the studio a copy of the book and asked, "Would you be kind enough, Lord Attlee, to inscribe this for me?" Attlee took out his fountain pen and went over with the book to a desk where, for two or three minutes, he remained deep in thought or composition. The interviewer, although naturally interested in the inscription, which must surely be eloquent and, even, effusive, was too polite to look at it. Later on, he opened the book and read on the flyleaf what was written there:

"Attlee".

---

* *Speeches*, I, p. 212.

XLIII

❧ SIR ANTHONY EDEN ❧

1955–57

To have reached the Foreign Secretaryship at the age of thirty-eight implies unusual qualities of mind and character. Above all, it implies industry and tact. Anthony Eden, born 12 June, 1897, second son of Sir William Eden, Bart, in the army at eighteen, had what is called a "good war", in other words, he had displayed courage and ability . . . By the time of the Armistice in 1918, he was a brigade-major and had won the MC. He was educated at Eton and Oxford, where he was a scholar of distinction in Persian and an enthusiast for post-impressionist art. In politics, he showed skill in debate and in negotiation. It seemed that the young Conservative MP for Leamington (which he became in 1923) was a born diplomat. It was not his only claim to international fame. It was said, "He and the Duke of Windsor are the only two Englishmen since Beau Brummell to be accorded respect on the Continent by sartorial experts."* In the same year he married Beatrice Helen Beckett. They had two sons. Eden's convictions were aligned with the idealism which was fashionable in Britain then and was focused on the League of Nations. For this reason, Eden was more popular in the country than most other spokesmen of his party. He established something like a power-base of his own. He became accordingly a semi-independent political force with a following in the country. When Sir Samuel Hoare made a bargain with Laval which involved giving a great area of Abyssinia to Mussolini, British public opinion was outraged. Too many carefully nurtured illusions about sanctions and "Collective Security" had been destroyed too suddenly. Hoare resigned. Eden, untainted by what had gone before, succeeded him as Foreign Secretary.

Almost at once, however, it was plain that Britain was faced with a peril to European peace far more formidable than Mussolini's African adventure. In the spring of 1936, Hitler sent troops into the Rhineland, which Germany, by the Treaty of Locarno, had agreed should be demilitarized. If this act was not—or could not be—resisted, then there was no hope of preventing Hitler's further plans for re-shaping Europe according to his ideas. So much seems obvious to us now, with the wisdom of hindsight. But it was not obvious then to the British public or its statesmen. It was not obvious to Eden. Later on, he came to think otherwise: Britain

* Lord Chandos.

92 Sir Anthony Eden.

had made a catastrophic blunder in failing to fall in with France's wish to oppose the Germans—which the French could have done without the slightest difficulty. But that is to overlook the plain truth about British opinion at that time: the public would not have understood an Anglo-French move of the kind required, a pre-emptive strike, as it would have seemed to be. The parties of the Left, Labour and Liberal, would have united with the pro-German faction on the government side. It is possible that the government would have been brought down; it is likely that Hitler would have been driven from power. But this was something that no reasonably cautious British Cabinet could be sure of.

After the Rhineland, Hitler's policy was developed in a succession of hammer blows. Diplomacy could do nothing to influence events. Appeasement began to look more and more like a surrender to force. A new Prime Minister, Chamberlain, increasingly influenced foreign policy. Eden, smarting under his interference waited until Chamberlain made the extraordinary blunder of brushing off an offer by Roosevelt to call a conference of the powers to discuss outstanding problems. Then Eden resigned (1938). Churchill looked on the situation with melodramatic gloom: "From midnight till dawn I lay in my bed consumed by emotions of sorrow and fear. There seemed one strong young figure standing up against long, dismal, drawling tides of drift and surrender. Now he was gone." Thus, Eden had the good fortune to have no part in the final disastrous phases of the appeasement policy.

When war came, Chamberlain overcame his antipathy and brought Eden back as Dominions Secretary (1939), a position of second-rank importance in the conditions of war. When Churchill took over the government, he made Eden Secretary of State for War until Lord Halifax gave up the Foreign Office for the Washington Embassy, upon which Eden was once more Foreign Secretary, the role for which both his aptitude and his training fitted him. He worked closely and for the most part in harmony with Churchill, who made him Leader of the House in 1942. This was a clear indication that he was marked out as a future Prime Minister. He was "Crown Prince" and did not find the position wholly enviable. Moreover, the double burden of work took a toll of his health and of his equanimity. In "the Office" he was observed to be more irritable; his colleagues in the government noted an increasing tendency to petulance. He was, however, a most successful Leader of the House. But the hours he worked told on his health. He returned from the San Francisco conference which set up the United Nations in time to take part in the British general election of 1945 which ended the Churchill government.

It was already clear to him that, if anyone had ever hoped that Russia would work in amity with her allies to set up a workable international system, this was already revealed as an illusion. Fortunately, British foreign policy was now in the hands of that stalwart realist, Ernest Bevin, and, in the United States, President Truman and General Marshall had the imagination which the situation demanded. The outcome was the Marshall Plan and, when the Russians blockaded Berlin, the Berlin airlift. Unhappily, Bevin's health collapsed and Eden, still in Opposition, had an ominous attack of virulent jaundice.

When, in 1951, Attlee's government was plainly exhausted, the Conservatives came back to power again under Churchill and Eden was, once more, Foreign Secretary. Tension in Europe was rising. Britain had been driven out of the oilfield at

Abadan. It was the most severe phase of the Cold War. And there was still no organization in Western Europe to compete with Russian imperialism. There were other complications. Early in 1953, Eden had an operation for the removal of his gall bladder. This was followed by trouble with his bile-duct and, at length, by a third operation, carried out in Boston. He returned to England to find that Winston Churchill had suffered a stroke. These events were, of course, known to the Russians, who did not fail to take advantage of them. In a series of conferences, in which Eden's resourcefulness and experience as a negotiator were revealed at their most useful, the situation was gradually improved. Eden's task was not made any easier by John Foster Dulles, the American Secretary of State, who was apt to use international conferences as occasions for blasting off against British "colonialism". This did not help the building of defences against the vigorous new colonialism which was being created in Europe, as was shown by Molotov's opposition to free elections in Germany. These years are thought by many to constitute Eden's claim to greatness as a diplomat. He committed British forces to the Continent and, by doing so, saved European defences, after France had refused to be part of the European Defence Community. He brought Germany into the North Atlantic Alliance. But outside Europe the scene was troubled. Shifts of power were going on in the Near and Far East. A few months before Eden succeeded Churchill as Prime Minister, in April, 1955, Nasser had become Dictator of Egypt. The stage was being set for a drama. Eden's first act, which upset some Conservatives, was to withdraw British troops from Suez. He thought that this would strengthen peace in the area. He soon found that he was wrong.

In its earlier stages, however, the action was centred on the Far East, where the French were involved in a colonial war which, it seemed, they could neither win nor end. Thus, Eden and the French Prime Minister, Mendès-France, produced a face-saving formula for French evacuation which seemed to annoy Dulles, who regarded it as a needless victory for the Communists.

After the success of the Iranian Mossadiq in driving the British out of Abadan, it seemed to Nasser that the time had come to inflict a new humiliation on the failing British power. He used his influence and money to force the Jordanian King to expel Glubb Pasha, the British soldier who was commander of the Arab Legion, the most formidable military unit in the Arab world. This was certainly a cause for resentment for Eden, but it was also a military advantage for Israel, as events were soon to show.

On 26 July, 1956, Nasser, annoyed because Dulles had called off a loan of 200 million dollars to help him to build a dam at Aswan, seized the Suez Canal. His timing was good. He could count on a Russian veto in the United Nations if any attempt was made to condemn the seizure; there was a weak President in the United States anxious to be re-elected and a Secretary of State whose antipathy to Eden was manifest. Eden's judgment was affected by attacks on him in the press. It had been alleged that he was a feeble Prime Minister: he was determined to show that he was a strong one.

Morally, he was in the right. He had the support of the great majority of the British people, of all parties. Aneurin Bevan was with him and so, until he changed his mind, was Hugh Gaitskell. Gaitskell was at a dinner party at 10 Downing Street when the news came of Nasser's coup. He compared Nasser with Hitler, a comparison he repeated in the House of Commons.

93 Sir Anthony Eden, by Low.

Against Eden were Krishna Menon, India's Foreign Minister and a malignant enemy of Britain; the United Nations, which had not yet lost its standing in the world; and, vastly more important, the United States. Failure to be sure of American support was Eden's crucial error; it proved to be fatal. In collaboration with the French, he delivered a sea-and-air attack on the Suez Canal zone. It was a slow and clumsy stroke. It was defended afterwards on the ground that it put the Franco-British force between the Egyptians and the Israelis. But what was the point of that since the Israelis were attacking—successfully, it may be said—with Britain's connivance? In the end, a drive against sterling frightened Britain into abandoning the whole misconceived and muddled enterprise. After Christmas, 1956, less than two months after the Suez failure, Eden had a return of his bile duct complaint, accompanied by a high fever. He resigned and took ship to New Zealand. It was the end of his political career. He had become a Knight of the Garter in 1954 and was created Earl of Avon in 1961. He died on 14 January, 1977, at his Wiltshire home, survived by his second wife Clarissa Churchill, whom he had married in 1952.

Since then, a re-appraisal of his later policy has become possible. One of its subsidiary effects was that it diverted notice from the Soviet rape of Hungary and, it was alleged in Britain, had it not been for Eden's Suez venture, the Russians would not have dared to flout Western opinion in this way. Nobody can believe such nonsense today. The chief and most damaging result of Suez was on the nation's self-confidence. Having over-estimated its strength, it proceeded to exaggerate its weakness, even to wallow in it. By the time of Suez, Britain had become a second-class power; after it, she was for a time in the third class.

XLIV

❧ MAURICE HAROLD MACMILLAN ❧

1957–63

It seemed that Fortune had picked Harold Macmillan (born 10 February, 1894) as one of her favourites: Scholar of Eton and Exhibitioner of Balliol; one of the heirs of a rich and important publishing house and—to give that final spice of the romantic—the grandson of a poor boy born on a Highland croft. For such a youth one could predict a smooth passage through a gilded and affluent world. But matters turned out differently: the war, the Guards, a wound at Loos and another wound, gravely serious, on the Somme. Harold Macmillan came out of hospital, at last, a serious young man in a serious and troubled world. During a spell as ADC to the Governor-General of Canada, the Duke of Devonshire, he met the Duke's daughter, Lady Dorothy Cavendish, and married her in 1920. He went into the family publishing business and, in 1923, fought Stockton-on-Tees as a Conservative, failed to take the seat but won it a year later. In Parliament, he became one of a group of idealistic young Conservatives known as "The YMCA". As the Depression closed in on industrial Britain—and Stockton was one of the areas most cruelly affected—Macmillan's radicalism became more pronounced.

"It had become evident," he discovered, "that the structure of capitalist society in its old form had broken down, not only in Britain but all over Europe and even in the United States. The whole system had to be reassessed." However, when he broke with his party it was on an issue of foreign policy. He voted against the government on the decision to abandon sanctions against Italy during the Abyssinian war.

Although he came back into the party fold in 1937, a year later he supported the Socialist against the Conservative candidate in the Oxford City by-election, fought on the issue of Chamberlain's Munich policy. When war came, and Churchill took over the premiership, Macmillan, at last, was given office, as Parliamentary Secretary to the Ministry of Supply. His first real opportunity came when Churchill made him Minister Resident at Allied HQ in North West Africa; he was now a member of the Cabinet; more important, he enjoyed a great amount of freedom to exercise his diplomatic and political gifts. A man of imagination could hardly have asked for more. During the period of his service in the Mediterranean, Macmillan became the close friend of General Eisenhower and General de Gaulle, for both of whom he had an intense admiration, although to the end he found something baffling about the Frenchman's character. Years later, the two were to meet again.

When the war ended, Macmillan's proconsular role was finished. He returned to

94 Maurice Harold Macmillan (photo by Patrick Lichfield).

Britain, to a general election in which he lost his seat and, although he was soon in the House of Commons again (as MP for Bromley), to a spell of the opposition and frustration which is part of the price paid by a man who enters politics. In 1951, frustration ended with Churchill's victory; Macmillan became Minister of Housing. No government post was, at that time, more important. None was less superficially attractive. However, Macmillan undertook the task and built the total of houses which he had promised to build—and which others said could not be built. After a short spell at the Ministry of Defence, he became Foreign Secretary (April, 1955) in Eden's government. However, he was only there for a few months and, in December, 1955, became Chancellor of the Exchequer. His Budget included a provision introducing Premium Bonds, a novelty which was, at that time, regarded with disapproval—as if it were a form of lottery.

Then came a dramatic turn in events. The Suez crisis—during which it was Macmillan's duty as Chancellor of the Exchequer to report to the Prime Minister that there was a run on the pound—was followed by the illness and resignation of Eden. After consultation, the Tory "establishment" decided that it preferred Macmillan to R. A. Butler as the new Prime Minister. He thought that his stay in Number 10 would be a brief one. He told the Queen his government would probably last about six weeks. (It lasted six years, nine months.) In fact, his pessimism about the longevity of the new administration was quite reasonable in the uneasy conditions that followed Suez, when American opinion was inflamed against Britain and, apart from the old Commonwealth, there seemed to be no good friends visible anywhere. The nation itself was divided, although the vast majority believed that Britain had been morally justified in her opposition to the Egyptian dictator, Nasser. However, there is no answer to failure.

Macmillan was left to pick up the pieces. The recovery of national self-confidence was quicker than might have been thought. The loss of the Suez Canal, which had been thought a disaster, turned out to be much less serious than expected. In the new age of the super-tanker, the Canal was almost irrelevant. The alliance with the United States was restored. At a conference in Bermuda, Macmillan spoke bluntly to his old friend, Eisenhower, about Dulles's treachery at the time of Suez, and this meeting was followed by the opening of a system of frank, informal talks across the Atlantic between Prime Minister and President. The United States was to supply Britain with guided missiles and Britain was to continue with nuclear tests. The first British H-bomb was exploded in May, 1957.

Early in 1959, Macmillan paid a visit to Russia which was marked by extraordinary ill-mannered behaviour by Krushchev, who did not, for a time, so much as meet Russia's guest. However, it led to the Summit meeting in Paris in the following year. This ended in failure. It coincided, probably not by accident, with the shooting down of an American U2 aircraft (a "spy plane") over Russia, which gave the Russians a good pretext to call the meeting off. De Gaulle, very sensibly, pointed out that as Russian spy satellites passed over the sky of France every day, there was no real difference between that and a plane, except that the satellite was higher up. But the Summit was broken off, to Macmillan's grief.

Macmillan's next meeting with Krushchev was at the United Nations Assembly in New York when the Russian, who had harangued the Assembly for three hours,

95 Vicky in the *Evening Standard*, 6 November, 1958.

interrupted Macmillan's speech by banging on the desk with his shoe, which, in preparation, he had unfastened some time before. At one point, Macmillan paused and asked, "Mr President, perhaps we could have a translation? I could not quite follow." The incident was widely reported, much to Krushchev's disadvantage. "His style of debate, which I enjoy and find amusing," Macmillan reported, "shocked the members, especially the new members, who are very dignified." An experienced politician like Macmillan, used to the rough and tumble of the House of Commons, had no difficulty in making Krushchev appear like a public house brawler.

Equally momentous was Macmillan's visit to Africa in January-February, 1960. In a speech at Cape Town he said, "The wind of change is blowing through the continent. Whether we like it or not, this growth of national consciousness is a political fact. We must all accept it." The time, the place, the wording—all combined to make it an historic utterance. It goes without saying that some social courage, as well as political boldness, was needed for Macmillan to make this declaration at a moment when he was the guest of the South African government.

With the advent of a new American President, John F. Kennedy, Macmillan found himself with an opportunity and in a good position to take advantage of it. "The policies and personality of a President of the United States today," as he wrote later, "are of deep importance to every government . . . With equal responsibilities and diminishing power, a British Prime Minister in a still divided Europe must inevitably look to Washington for support. Equally it may be of value to an American President to draw upon the long British experience of great affairs throughout the centuries."* Obviously, the building of a relationship of confidence between the two men was a matter which required enormous tact and goodwill. "With President Eisenhower . . . we could appeal to memories. With this new and comparatively young President we have nothing of the kind to draw on" (Macmillan to the Foreign Secretary). At that moment, Macmillan was engaged on an ambitious plan to tackle the political and economic problems of the free world: he called it "The Grand Design". The central idea of this conception was to strengthen European unity, economic and political.

Macmillan found it easier to get on terms of mutual trust with Kennedy after the latter had a taste, during an interview with Krushchev in Vienna, of Russsian diplomacy at its roughest. Relations between Britain and the United States were soon better than they had been at any time since Suez. This happened although Macmillan would take no part in the American adventure in Vietnam. Economically, Macmillan's term of office coincided with "boom" conditions in Britain. He said in 1957, "Let's be frank about it; most of our people have never had it so good." The phrase was widely quoted, but not the words he added: "What is beginning to worry some of us is, Is it too good to last? Can we control inflation? This is the problem of our time."

As the nineteen-sixties went on, it was apparent that Macmillan's doubts about the permanence of Britain's economic recovery were justified. A "pay pause" was introduced in 1961 in an attempt to stop the soaring wage spiral. Britain's competitive power in foreign markets was declining. In 1962, the Prime Minister tried to check public dissatisfaction with his government by making drastic changes in the Cabinet, the so-called "Night of the Long Knives". This was seen by Colin Coote† as betraying a failure of nerve on Macmillan's part and as doing great damage to Conservative voting strength in the country. Then the government's prestige was harmed by the Profumo debate which followed the disclosure that a minister had associated with a woman who was also friendly with a Russian diplomat. When, in October, 1963, Macmillan's term of office ended, the reason was different, however: he went into hospital for a prostate operation.

With style and an unfaltering display of coolness which his political opponents found vastly irritating, he had guided Britain, then in decline, through a difficult phase. He did not accept an earldom or the Garter; these distinctions were not suitable for the great-grandson of a Highland crofter. In 1976 he accepted the Order of Merit, to which no snobbish stigma attaches.

---

* Harold Macmillan. *Pointing the Way*, p. 306.
† Editor of the *Daily Telegraph*.

XLV

❧ SIR ALEC DOUGLAS-HOME ❧

1963–64

The Earl of Home (thirteenth) said to Lord Dunglass, "No Home can drink champagne. Also, I advise you against politics as a career." Lord Dunglass disagreed with his father on both points and proved that he was right. He became, in the course of an eventful political career, Earl of Home (fourteenth); Sir Alec Douglas-Home and, finally, Lord Home of the Hirsel. He was also Foreign Secretary and Prime Minister.

The Homes are an ancient family of the Scottish Borders, famous in the old days as keepers, or breakers, of the peace and, later, as farmers, sportsmen and fishermen. One of the clan's offshoots produced the greatest Scottish philosopher. In politics they were less distinguished but Lord Home, through his mother, is connected with the Lambtons and the Greys and, therefore, with what might be called the left wing of the Whig aristocracy—with Lord Grey of the Reform Bill and Lord Durham of the Constitution of Canada.

Lord Home (born 1903) trod the customary road of the well-to-do young man with political leanings—Eton and Christ Church, Oxford. At both, he was a fine cricketer, although he missed his Blue. He married (1936) Elizabeth Alington, daughter of the Head Master at Eton. Undeterred by his father's mistaken insistence that politics was "bunk", he stood for Parliament in 1929 for Coatbridge and was rejected. Two years later he was elected for South Lanark. He was picked out to be Parliamentary Private Secretary to Neville Chamberlain in 1937 which, at first, seemed a fine stroke of luck but which, later, meant that some of Chamberlain's unpopularity most unfairly rubbed off on him. He accompanied Chamberlain on the fatal trip to Munich. At the time that Chamberlain fell in 1940, Home (who was at that time still Lord Dunglass) was declared unfit for military service and was found to be suffering from tuberculosis of the spine. After an operation, he was ordered two years of absolute immobility. He could do nothing except talk and read. His first speech, when he returned to Parliament in 1944, was a protest against the over-hasty surrender to the Russians at Yalta. In the general election of 1945 he lost his seat to a Socialist, who had the folly to send the Communists a letter of thanks for their support. In 1950, in a later election, Home used that letter effectively against him.

By this time Home was learning the art of politics in the hard school of Lanarkshire elections. At one meeting, a woman, well-known in the town, rose to ask him a question about family allowances, which were then not paid until there were two

96 Sir Alec Douglas-Home.

children or more. The question was, "Why do I not get family allowance on my illegitimate child?" Home answered, "Madam, you will when your next one arrives."

The death of his father in the following year ended (as it seemed), or interrupted (as it turned out), his career in the House of Commons. When the Suez crisis broke, Home presented the Eden government's case in the House of Lords. He was shocked by the ineptness of Dulles's policy and remained afterwards of the belief that peaceful persuasion might have carried the day, had it not been for a lapse of American diplomacy. When Macmillan took over the premiership he made Home Foreign Secretary, to the astonishment of the press. The *Daily Mail* said, "The Prime Minister still has time to stop making a fool of himself." The *Daily Herald* asked, "What have we done to deserve this?"

He was accused of being a jingo but, in general, opinion moved his way. In the autumn of 1963, Macmillan was compelled by a breakdown in health to give up the leadership of the Tory Party. There was an intense crisis, which coincided with the party conference at Blackpool. Home was approached to be the successor and with many misgivings agreed to surrender his peerage and fight a by-election so that he

**97 "He thinks like a Tory, and talks like a Radical, and that's so important nowadays."
Oscar Wilde, *Lady Windermere's Fan*, Act II. Vicky in the *Evening Standard*,
28 October, 1963.**

could sit in the Commons. He became MP for Kinross and West Perthshire and, as Sir Alec Douglas-Home, was Prime Minister. Iain Macleod and Enoch Powell would not serve in his government. Now he found himself pitted against Harold Wilson, a master of slick political cross-talk: Wilson called him "the fourteenth Earl" until Home retorted, "I suppose *he* is the fourteenth Mr Wilson." That was the end of that particular gibe.

When Home lost the general election in the following year by a small margin, he resigned with all the cheerfulness in the world. Heath became leader of the Opposition and Home returned to foreign affairs, in which his main interest lay. And when Heath won the general election of 1970, Home was Foreign Secretary.

On this occasion, one of his first and, certainly, his most dramatic, actions was to clamp down on the Russian spy network which had been built up in their London Trade Mission on a large scale, relying on the weakness or cowardice of the British government. After warning the Russian Foreign Minister, Mr Gromyko, that he knew what was going on, and giving him ample opportunity, during a year, to recall the agents, Home acted. He expelled 105 named undesirables out of the 550 Russians in Britain with diplomatic privileges. Comparable figure for Britons in Moscow, 83. The result was as could have been predicted. The Russians blustered; for two years their relations with Britain were of the chilliest. But, from that day on, they behaved with more respect to Britain. "Are there any diplomats in Russia who have not been trained in the KGB?" Home asked Gromyko. It is quite possible that the embarrassment among Russian diplomats was due to the fact that they are not masters in their own house: the KGB rules the roost.

It is not surprising that Home was an enthusiastic supporter of the conception that Britain must have an independent deterrent in the form of her own nuclear weapon. It was hard to persuade the public of the need for this.

Having already in 1964 laid down "guide lines" for a Rhodesian settlement, Home went on to open fresh negotiations with Ian Smith and African leaders, out of which new proposals emerged. They were, however, rejected by the Africans, mainly because they distrusted Smith. Once more, the Rhodesian problem was held over for another year. Home was Foreign Secretary until 1974, in which year he was created a life peer. In 1962 he was given the Order of the Thistle.

XLVI

❧ JAMES HAROLD WILSON ❧

1964–70; 1974–76

When Harold Wilson was elected leader of the Labour Party after the death of Hugh Gaitskell in 1963, it was regarded by the left wing of the party as a victory for them. Just why, was not easy to see. For Wilson, with an impeccably middle-class Yorkshire background, Congregationalist by creed, academic by training, seemed to be another "desiccated calculating machine" such as Aneurin Bevan, spokesman of the soul of the Labour Party, had denounced. But the instinct of the Left, which had welcomed Wilson, turned out to be justified: his great purpose was to hold his party together and that, inevitably, meant making concessions to the Left.

His route into politics was unusual but direct. A brilliant boy at school, he became a brilliant student at Oxford, a statistician and economist, a don at twenty-one; very soon, he caught the eye of Sir William Beveridge, then about to take wing from Oxford to Whitehall, where he laid the foundations of the Welfare State. As a civil servant of exceptional ability, Wilson was selected as the Director of Economics and Statistics in the newly formed Ministry of Fuel and Power. By the time the war ended, he had already returned to his academic duties at University College, Oxford. By this time he was a convinced Socialist and at the general election of 1945 became MP for Ormskirk. The Prime Minister, Attlee, made him Parliamentary Secretary at the Ministry of Works. Aged twenty-nine, Wilson was the youngest member of the government. He was a rather prosy speaker at that time, but obviously well-informed and endowed with an impressive memory.

He had by this time married a minister's daughter and set up house in that favourite dwelling-place of Labour politicians, Hampstead Garden Suburb. He had a natural gift for publicity, which, in due course, he improved. As his Parliamentary performance became more effective, so, too, did his reputation for being too clever by half, a serious handicap in politics. As Secretary for Overseas Trade (1947), he went on a trade mission to Moscow which was spread over several months and, although it did not end in agreement, bolstered Wilson's self-confidence. Before the year was out, he was President of the Board of Trade and a member of the Cabinet. Immediately he went again to Moscow and concluded a trade agreement with Russia. About the same time, he struck up an alliance with Aneurin Bevan, many of whose views on policy he shared. Wilson needed all the political support he could get because he was being harshly criticized over his Russian deal, which was considered by many people as too favourable to the Soviet government.

98 Harold Wilson as a boy outside
10, Downing Street.

The general election of 1951, in which Wilson held the new-formed seat of Huyton, brought Labour back to power with a tiny majority after losing eighty-five seats. Now a crisis arose in the Cabinet, as a result of which Aneurin Bevan and Wilson resigned. Wilson found a post as consultant to Montague Meyer, a timber merchant. This provided him with a salary, a car and a secretary. Gaitskell produced a Budget in which he proposed to impose a fee of one shilling on prescriptions under the National Health Service. This was regarded as nothing short of betrayal by Bevan, who had come to regard the Health Service as the Socialist Ark of the Covenant. Wilson's speech of resignation concentrated on the fact that Gaitskell was providing for a massive rearmament programme, which Wilson believed to be unattainable and which was, in fact, reduced by a future Conservative government.

His second break with Gaitskell occurred in 1960 when Gaitskell was defeated in the Labour party conference over Clause Four, another of these sacred cows which cause so much excitement to Socialists. (It commits the party to common ownership of the means of production, distribution and exchange and is, therefore, sound Marxist orthodoxy.) Gaitskell thought it was high time to be rid of this incubus; Wilson thought that it was wrong to discard a basic dogma, and there is no doubt that, tactically, he was right. With Gaitskell's death, he became party leader, and, in 1964, Prime Minister of a Labour government with a tiny majority of five over Conservatives and Liberals together. He stayed in office for six years which, given the narrow margin between the parties in the early years, was a tribute to the discipline exerted by the Whips. Even more remarkable was the brisk legislative pace which, under Wilson's leadership, the government sustained. Labour found itself faced with a deficit of £600 million in the balance of payments and made the most of that in its propaganda. A surcharge of fifteen per cent on imports was the chief instrument employed to improve the nation's financial situation. A serious seamen's strike in 1966 was followed next year by devaluation of the pound. Then, in June, 1970, Wilson's government was defeated at the polls. He said, proudly, of his successor, "No Prime Minister in living memory has taken over a stronger economic situation."

The manner of his premiership had been highly individual. As he said, "Every Prime Minister's style of government must be different, but I find it hard to resist the view that a modern head of government must be the managing director as well as the chairman of his team." In other words, he must be *au fait* with the work of all the main departments. It is an entirely defensible outlook but it implies some willingness on the part of other ministers to be subordinate, as well as exceptional powers of application and memory on the part of the Prime Minister. These powers Wilson possessed. Did it not also mean a further advance towards presidential government? Mr Crossman certainly thought so. It is too early, however, to find evidence of a

99 James Harold Wilson.

"trend" in the style of one Prime Minister—or two, for Heath favoured the same managerial tendency as Wilson.

In 1974 Wilson became Prime Minister for the second time. In one respect, he had been fortunate. His wife had refused to allow politicians to visit the family home in Hampstead Garden Suburb; she met them as little as possible at Number 10. "All I have ever wanted," she said, "is a nice little house in North Oxford and a don for a husband."

Thus, Wilson was shielded from that airless little world of self-important intriguers which too many politicians inhabit. And thus opportunity was given to a clever, intensely political woman to act as Wilson's political assistant. She was Mrs Marcia Williams, a good-looking woman, who had been on the staff of Morgan Phillips, the general secretary of the Labour Party. She had been an anonymous source of information to Wilson about the internal affairs at Transport House. Before long, Wilson's colleagues were complaining about the amount of authority which he delegated to Mrs Williams: "Fix it up with Marcia." Mrs Williams was made Lady Falkender in 1974.

An important and, in a way, most revealing event of Wilson's career in office was

100 Chequers, the official country residence of British Prime Ministers since 1917.

his prolonged and serious attempt to solve the Rhodesian problem. On two occasions he met the Rhodesian leader, Ian Smith, and when the latter met the five conditions which Wilson had laid down for agreement it seemed that Wilson's diplomacy had succeeded. If the decision had rested solely with him it might, indeed, have done so. But he had to carry the assent of his Cabinet and there the resistance to him was too strong. In consequence, Wilson's spectacular meetings with the Rhodesian leader led to nothing.

On entry into the European Economic Community—the Common Market—his tactics were more successful. He was cool enough to the idea not to frighten off the members of his own party who were opposed to it; his attitude remained unchanged throughout—Britain should go in if the terms were right; a characteristically vague condition; those of his ministers who wished to, could campaign in favour of rejection; the issue would be decided by a referendum. Thus, almost unaware where it was going, Wilson—or his government—took Britain into the Common Market. As an exercise in political cunning it could hardly have been improved. At a dinner party in 1957 Wilson told a journalist, "Macmillan is a genius. He is holding up the banner of Suez for the party to follow and is leading the party away from Suez. That's what I'd like to do with the Labour Party." On one important issue, he did just that.

The closing days of his government were clouded by the honours which he gave to people, some of whom were thought to be unworthy. There was also talk about a "Kitchen Cabinet". About such matters the Labour Party is apt to be intensely—and rightly—puritanical. This Wilson should have recognized, as one who had been critical when there seemed to be lapses during the Conservative government. "This," he had said, "could never have happened in Attlee's time."

He resigned in March, 1976. It was felt that he had managed his resignation with style. Mr James Callaghan paid him a handsome tribute at his final Cabinet which impressed, as an impromptu effort, all who heard it. All but one. Denis Healey said, "Spur of the moment! The b—— was given six months to practise!" That was before the impact of Wilson's Resignation Honours List, on which Roy Jenkins remarked, "How typical of Harold that after making such a graceful exit, he had to do this on the doorstep." Callaghan said, "Harold, I believe history will treat you more kindly than your contemporaries." Joe Haines, Wilson's press secretary, comments, "But the judgment of history must be founded upon all the facts . . . For too long, Lady Falkender had counted for too much."*

Wilson became a Knight of the Garter. He had been Prime Minister for eight years and had accomplished his main ambition: he had made the Labour Party accepted as a normal governing party in Britain—that is to say, as an integral part of the Establishment.

---

* Haines. *The Politics of Power*, p. 222.

XLVII

❧ EDWARD RICHARD GEORGE HEATH ❧

1970–74

It is strange to think that Edward Heath is one of the most puzzling of politicians, for he is one of the most straightforward of men. He is what he looks, English of the English, born and brought up on the Kentish coast with a family background that included a coastguard, a boatman and a merchant seaman. Heath's own father, William Heath, was first a carpenter and then a master-builder; his mother dreamed great dreams for her son. About their son, Edward Richard George Heath, born in 1916, there is something of the independence and down-to-earthness of the good craftsman, one who would want to "get on" and even have a touch of ruthlessness as he pushed forward, but who would be unlikely to have excessive ambition. However, this is to overlook the complexity of the man's character. There is something cool and withdrawn about him, a driving power and also a sense of direction. "Stiff and awkard socially, he has none of the amiable, lubricant small-talk of other politicians which, however artificial, eases the way." (John Boyd-Carpenter in his memoirs, *Way of Life*.)

When Heath went to Balliol after education at the local grammar school at Ramsgate, the admissions tutor, Charles (now Lord) Morris, asked him what he wanted to be. Heath answered, "a professional politician". It was the only time Morris ever had that answer to that question. Heath was—and is—a loner, one who was withdrawn, who could even keep his closest friends at a distance, who had girls, especially one girl, he was fond of, but did not seem to think of marrying. "He was always upset when they got married," says a friend. But before he is classed as a "cold fish", his passionate love of music must be mentioned. It is here, it seems, that the emotional side of Heath's nature has found its outlet.

He went to Oxford on a £90-a-year loan from Kent Education Committee and, at the end of his first term, won an organ scholarship worth £100 a year. His talk at that time was all concerned with politics; as a convinced Conservative he was bitterly opposed to Chamberlain's policy of appeasement. He left Oxford with a second-class degree. On holiday to Germany, he came home two days before war broke out. He was called up in the Royal Artillery in July, 1940. When he was demobilized as a lieutenant-colonel six years later, he was uncertain about his future career: music? politics? But he was without money. He went into the Civil Service, passing out joint-first in the examination for the administrative grade. And he began to look for a constituency, finding one at Bexley.

101 Edward Heath.

After a spell as news editor of the *Church Times*, "a political fish in holy water", as he said, he got a job with Brown, Shipley and Company, a merchant bank (salary £200). He won Bexley by 133 votes in 1950. In the House of Commons he was one of the nine founder-members of the One Nation Group, dedicated to making the "new Toryism" effective. In his maiden speech, the new member for Bexley came out unequivocally for the European idea. He was still employed by Brown, Shipley, whom he persuaded to send him on a trip to South America. In October, 1951, he was returned for Bexley with an increased majority in a general election which brought the Tories back to office with a majority of seventeen. Heath was made an Assistant Whip, at the same time ending his career with Brown, Shipley.

He was an efficient and unpopular Whip at a time when firm discipline was needed in the Tory party. Lord Hailes, the Chief Whip, slightly puzzled by his assistant, said, "He enjoys people but I don't know that he needs them; he is extraordinarily self-sufficient." At the end of 1955, Eden was Prime Minister and Heath his Chief Whip, "a bloody bad-tempered man", as one member recalls. When Suez brought about the downfall of Eden, Macmillan, the new Prime Minister, kept Heath on in his post and gave him a champagne dinner in the Turf Club. Heath was now one of the Inner Cabinet.

He was Minister of Labour in 1960 and, after that, was second man in the Foreign Office with the special task of engineering Britain's entry into the Common Market, a project which de Gaulle frustrated in 1963. This was a blow to Heath but one from which he made a speedy recovery. When Macmillan retired, Heath supported Lord Home (later Sir Alec Douglas-Home) for the succession and was given the Board of Trade. He used his office to attack Resale Price Maintenance and carried the necessary legislation in spite of the fact that the Cabinet was divided on the issue. It was an indication of his strength of character and conviction. However, Labour won the general election of 1964 and Douglas-Home retreated before a strong movement against him in the party. Heath became party leader as a result of a vigorous campaign waged on his behalf by Peter Walker.* However, the Tories lost the election of March 1966 by a hundred seats.

In the months following, Heath, conducting a dogged fight on two fronts, made some headway against Harold Wilson while at the same time beating off Enoch Powell's attack on the main philosophical position of the Tory party. Finally, he drove Powell out of the Shadow Cabinet after what he regarded as a "racialist" speech in Birmingham. By 1970, public opinion polls showing Labour in the ascendancy encouraged Harold Wilson to hold a general election, which he lost.

In June of that year, then, Edward Heath was Prime Minister. He owed the victory to his own determination. As the results of the election came through, the television commentaries altered. Heath said, "They've been telling me all week I was going to lose and now they are picking my bloody Cabinet for me."

Years before, he had meant to be a professional politician. Now he was at the top of the profession, which is where a professional must want to be. As 1971 went on, with 600,000 unemployed growing to 750,000, he pumped hundreds of millions of pounds into the economy—and by the last months of 1972 was faced with the threat

---

*Minister of Agriculture in Mrs Thatcher's government, 1979–.

of inflation, which he tried to meet with a statutory control of wages and prices. All was going smoothly forward when the miners went on strike over wages and brought his government down. Labour's majority after the election was only five, but it was enough.

In 1974, Heath lost the third of the four general elections in which he had led his troops into battle. Now it was a question not of whether he was to lose the leadership of the party but when this would happen. What was remarkable about the situation was that he seemed to be unable to accept the fact that his removal was, in the circumstances, inevitable. No party leader could have survived such a record of defeats. It might be unjust, but it was something that could not be averted. There was no need at all to make it an occasion for a display of pique or resentment. Yet that was exactly what Heath did.

That he was beaten by a woman, Margaret Thatcher—a fact which might have made it easier for another man to bear—seems to have been regarded by him as another humiliation. So, at least, it appeared to the public outside. In the absence of any personal reasons for resentment, Heath's behaviour at that time was mystifying. Heath was thought to have shown "poor sportsmanship"; a serious fault in English eyes. But there is this to be said: politics is not a game and its misfortunes should not be regarded as if they were tumbles in the hunting field. It is a serious business, especially to the professionals, of whom Heath is emphatically one. Another thing: the "loner" is more susceptible to setbacks than one who has close companions on his way through life.

XLVIII

❧ LEONARD JAMES CALLAGHAN ❧

1976–79

The family name of Caraghan was changed some time after James Callaghan's great-grandfather, a weaver, came over from Ireland in the "Hungry Forties". After that, the Callaghans were a naval family and James Callaghan's father was a chief petty officer in the Royal Navy who was wounded at Jutland and died in 1921, when the boy was nine. After that, Callaghan, his mother and his sister had a hard time of it. There was no pension.

Leonard James Callaghan was born in Portsmouth in 1912. He went to school at the local council school and, later, to Portsmouth Grammar School. By that time his mother had an allowance of thirty-six shillings a week, thanks to the endeavours of a Labour MP. There could be no question, however, of the boy going to a university. The family budget did not run to that.

Leonard's education stopped when he was seventeen and he went to work as a clerk in an Income Tax Inspector's office. What was more important, as it turned out, was that he was a member of the Inland Revenue Staff Federation, the trade union of the revenue service, in which he was successively branch secretary, member of the union's executive and, in 1936, full-time National Assistant Secretary. He joined the Labour Party and was a lecturer for the Workers' Educational Association.

In 1938, he married Audrey Moulton, whom he had met at the Baptist Church at Maidstone which he attended regularly. She was an energetic, socially-minded young woman. The Callaghans have a son and two daughters.

In 1942, Callaghan enlisted in the Royal Navy as an ordinary seaman and served in Far Eastern waters, rising to the rank of lieutenant. He was still wearing uniform when he was chosen as Labour candidate for Cardiff South. He won the seat in 1945 and held it from that time on. His first government post was as Parliamentary Private Secretary to the Under-Secretary of State for the Dominions. He was appointed adviser (i.e. lobbyist) to the Police Federation.

In the Shadow Cabinet, following Labour's defeat in 1951, he was spokesman for the Colonies. In 1960 he supported Gaitskell in the bitter controversy over unilateral nuclear disarmament and followed Harold Wilson as Shadow Chancellor. On Gaitskell's death in 1963, he stood in the election for the party leadership but was beaten by Wilson and George Brown.

But when Labour was returned to power in the general election of 1964, Callaghan was appointed Chancellor of the Exchequer by Wilson. In this post, his ignorance of

102 Leonard James Callaghan.

economics might have been a handicap and he took advice from two Hungarian experts, Kaldor and Balogh, whose advice was at that time believed to be essential for a sound management of the national finances.

He imposed novel forms of taxation, such as the Selective Employment Tax, aimed at diverting investment from unproductive services; he instituted a short-lived system of investment grants for manufacturers and mining, and eventually was forced to devalue the pound—all of which he did without losing his popularity in the

Labour Party, where in fact his agreeable manner, friendly ways and ability to make convincing speeches brought him a growing number of supporters.

As Home Secretary, he was responsible for the decision to disband the "B" special constables in Ulster, a well-intentioned stroke of policy which, as it turned out, did something to unleash on the province a decade of bloodshed. But by the time the death roll had become significant, Callaghan was no longer at the Home Office. He always regarded his chief achievements as the introduction of cat's eyes and zebra crossings on the roads.

His reputation as an astute party man was enhanced when Barbara Castle produced her policy document, *In Place of Strife*. This was held to attack the special position of the trade unions, and Callaghan made it clear that he could not support it. When somebody said that some changes of the kind were inevitable, he retorted, "If it is inevitable, let the Tories pass it." As a realistic politician he always regarded the alliance with the trade unions, the party's paymasters, as one in which the unions were the dominant partner.

After the general election of 1970, he continued to rise in the party hierarchy—vice-chairman, 1973, chairman 1974. By then he was Foreign Secretary and was under-going an evolution of opinion from opposition to the Common Market to a cautious acceptance of it. When the time came to hold a referendum on the subject, it was held on the terms of entry which he had negotiated. When Wilson resigned in 1976, Callaghan was elected Parliamentary party leader and, therefore, Prime Minister, receiving 176 votes against 137 for Michael Foot.

He became First Minister of the Crown at a time when the early pioneering enthusiasm of the Labour Party was being dented by powerful economic and financial forces which compelled the Chancellor of the Exchequer, Denis Healey, to seek aid from the International Monetary Fund and to accept it on their terms. The alternative would have been a siege economy.

From 1978 onwards, the life of the government was precarious, dependent on Liberal support. In May, 1978, the government was defeated on an Opposition amendment to the Finance Bill reducing income tax by 1p in the £. It was a strange situation, the Opposition fixing the level of revenue but without any responsibility for administering expenditure. Callaghan, however, would not resign.

While this highly unpalatable situation was developing, there was a change in the power structure, both in the Labour Party and the trade unions. The Left, i.e. the Marxists, became dominant in each. In the unions, the power of the shop stewards was used to embarrass the government by means of a series of anti-social strikes. The result was bitterly ironical for Callaghan. He, the champion of the trade union arm of the Labour movement, was defeated in a general election in May, 1979, as a direct consequence of public disgust with the reckless and inconsiderate conduct of unions under the influence of extremists.

It is true that issues of lesser importance had their effect. For instance, Scotland, in a referendum, showed no enthusiasm for the government's proposals on devolution. But the main factor in the Callaghan defeat was the alarm caused by the unions. Needless to say, the blame for the setback was put on him. He had much to think about on the 138-acre Hampshire farm he and a partner had bought for £22,000 in 1968 and which, by that time, was believed to be worth £100,000.

XLIX

❧ MARGARET HILDA THATCHER ❧

1979–?

"She is a fierce and ardent champion of the land-owning classes. She flutters like an iron butterfly and is unpopular, cool and hard"—Warsaw radio. The "iron butterfly", now Margaret Thatcher, was born on 13 October, 1925, to Mrs Roberts, in a flat above a grocer's shop in North Parade, Grantham. The shop belonged to Alfred Roberts, who, twice a week, went the rounds of his customers, took their orders and delivered the goods. The flat had no bath or running hot water; it had an outside toilet. Sometimes, as a girl, Margaret Hilda Roberts accompanied her father on his rounds; sometimes she helped in the shop. Every Sunday she accompanied her parents to the local Methodist church. Aged eleven, the girl won a scholarship to the Kesteven and Grantham Girls' High School, later, a bursary enabled her to go to Somerville College, Oxford, where she read Chemistry, sang in the Bach Choir and, in her third year, became chairman of the Conservative Association. Later she became a Fellow of the College. In 1948 she canvassed for the Conservative candidate in Oxford and began to think about a career in politics for herself. However, the first priority after leaving the University was to get a job. With a second class honours in Chemistry, she found employment in a plastics factory at Manningtree, Essex. She lodged in Colchester and joined the local Conservative Association.

In 1948, she was adopted as Conservative candidate for Dartford, from the Tory point of view, a hopeless seat, and on the same evening met Major Denis Thatcher, manager of a paint firm in Erith. As part of her agreement with the Dartford Tories, she gave up her job in Manningtree and went to live in Dartford, taking a research job with J. Lyons & Company at Cadby Hall. In the 1950 election she increased the Conservative vote at Dartford by fifty per cent; it was not enough to win Dartford, which, in fact, was held by Labour in 1957. In that year she married Denis Thatcher at Wesley's Chapel in the City. She started reading for the Bar, first in a chambers in the Temple with a criminal law practice, then in tax law.

In 1953, she became a qualified barrister. She had two children, a boy and a girl.

Politics were for a time in abeyance but they were on the way back, although Mrs Thatcher encountered some opposition from local Conservative Associations on account of her sex. "Go home and look after your children," she was told more than once. However, she was selected for Barnet and won the seat in 1954.

She had not been long in the House of Commons before it was plain that she had a thorough grasp of public finance and taxation policies. Her years at the Chancery Bar were of use to her. She had become one of the best-informed persons in Britain on taxation questions. But she made her first mark on Parliament when, in her first session, she won the ballot for the right to introduce a private members' bill and brought in a bill giving the press and the public a statutory right of admission to meetings of public bodies, local and regional. This bill became an Act of Parliament in 1960. She was very soon a well-known figure in the House of Commons, which has a male interest in good-looking women members and a tendency to male jealousy if they succeed. "The ladies have an advantage," said Lord Shinwell. "I should know. I've had three wives."

Her first ministerial appointment came in 1961 when she was appointed Parliamentary Secretary to the Ministry of Pensions and National Insurance, a post she held until Labour came back to power.

When Heath formed his Cabinet in June 1970, Mrs Thatcher was made Secretary of State for Education and Science. She produced an Education White Paper which contemplated an increased expenditure of £1,000 million a year in State spending on education, including a substantial increase in the number of teachers in secondary schools and an increase in funds for universities. She was recognized as the outstanding woman in the government, so that when the Tories were thrown out in 1974, nobody was surprised when she became responsible for the Environment in the Shadow Cabinet. In that capacity she announced that the Opposition planned to help occupiers to buy their homes by pegging mortgage rates to $9\frac{1}{2}$ per cent. This promise Anthony Crosland regarded as fraudulent. Already Mrs Thatcher was seen as a formidable personality and a possible successor to Edward Heath. In November, 1974, Heath promoted her Number Two to Robert Carr, the Shadow Chancellor. The battle for the leadership of the party was now about to break out.

Heath said that he would seek re-election and Mrs Thatcher told Heath and the Chief Whip that she was prepared to be the party leader if voted into that office. A new procedure for the party vote was laid down and the scene was set for an election in February, 1975. The case against Heath was that he had lost three general elections in succession. In addition, some party members disliked his personal style. Mrs Thatcher had won a glowing reputation for her determined and skilful opposition in Parliament. She was opposed for the leadership by Hugh Fraser, on the grounds that the time was not yet ripe for a woman leader of the party. In the first ballot, the voting was: Mrs Thatcher 130; Heath 119; Fraser 16. Heath withdrew and made it known that he would not accept a place in Mrs Thatcher's Shadow Cabinet. In the second ballot, Mrs Thatcher had 146 out of a total vote of 271. She, therefore, had an overall majority (June, 1975).

During the months that followed, Mrs Thatcher proved to be a resourceful party leader, in and out of Parliament. The pact made between the Liberals and the minority Labour government she denounced as a "shabby manipulation". At the party conference, she roused the gathering with a speech warning the delegates of the direction of the Labour policy: "Britain beware! This way to the total Socialist State!" Her own views were crystal-clear: "A man's right to work as he will, to spend what he earns, to own property and to have the State as servant, not as master—these are the British inheritance." Callaghan struck back at her "one-sentence solutions"

103 Margaret Thatcher.

to the country's problems. She retorted by scathing references to "a broken-backed government that has no longer any authority". These are routine courtesies in any run-up to a general election. What made the situation different was that, for the first time since the war, there was a real ideological clash between the two parties.

This was the outcome of Margaret Thatcher's appointment as party leader: she was committing her party, not to a modified Socialism but to a diametrically opposed philosophy; a return to the market economy, a heavy reduction in government power and bureaucratic influence, a greater scope for individual initiative and—which was of immense relevance at the time—an attack on inflation by control of the money supply.

The general election of May, 1979, was held at a moment when the breakdown of discipline in the trade unions put a heavy handicap on the Labour Party, which was financed by the unions. The party itself was split from top to bottom on the issue of how to deal with inflation and unemployment. The left wing had a skilful new leader, Mr Anthony Wedgwood Benn. In consequence, the party could not mobilize its full fighting strength against the Conservatives and it was Mrs Thatcher who became the first woman to be Prime Minister of Britain, in May, 1979. She had a working majority and a complete conviction that her strategy for recovery was best. And she did not need to be told that the risks she was incurring were considerable. It remained to be seen whether she and her government would be able to translate her philosophy into action.

FURTHER READING

GENERAL
Walter Bagehot. *The English Constitution*. Edition of 1963, with introduction by R. H. S. Crossman
The Prime Ministers, introductions by G. W. Jones and Robert Blake. Two Vols, 1974 and 1975
J. P. Mackintosh. *The Government and Politics of Britain*. 1970
R. H. S. Crossman. *Inside View. Three lectures on Prime Ministerial Government*. 1972
British Prime Ministers. Essays on seventeen of them, with introduction by Duff Cooper. 1953

SIR ROBERT WALPOLE
Lord Hervey. *Memoirs*. 1952
J. H. Plumb. *Sir Robert Walpole*. 1956
Basil Williams. *The Whig Supremacy, 1714–16*. 1939

SPENCER COMPTON, EARL OF WILMINGTON
Pembarton Baring. *Carteret*. 1936

HENRY PELHAM AND THOMAS PELHAM-HOLLES, DUKE OF NEWCASTLE
John B. Owen. *The Rise of the Pelhams*. 1959
Horace Walpole. *Memoirs of the Last Ten Years of the Reign of George III*. 1847
J. W. Wilkes. *A Whig in Power (Henry Pelham)*. 1964
Basil Williams. *Carteret and Newcastle*. 1966

WILLIAM CAVENDISH, 4TH DUKE OF DEVONSHIRE
O. A. Sherrard. *Pitt and the Seven Years War*. 1958
Brian Tunstall, *William Pitt, Earl of Chatham*. 1938
Basil Williams. *William Pitt*. 1913

JOHN STUART, 3RD EARL OF BUTE
J. Lovat Fraser. *John Stuart, Earl of Bute*. 1912
Sir Lewis Namier. *England in the Age of the American Revolution*. 1901
Sir Lewis Namier. *The Structure of Politics at the Accession of George III*. 1929

Romney Sedgwick. *Letters From George III to Lord Bute*. 1939

GEORGE GRENVILLE
R. J. White. *The Age of George III*. 1968
Lewis M. Wiggins. *The Faction of Cousins*. 1958

CHARLES WENTWORTH, 2ND MARQUIS OF ROCKINGHAM
J. A. Cannon. *The Fox-North Coalition*. 1969
P. Langford. *The First Rockingham Administration*. 1973

WILLIAM PITT, EARL OF CHATHAM
J. H. Plumb. *Chatham*. 1953
Lord Rosebery. *Chatham—His Early Life*. 1910
Basil Williams. *William Pitt*. 1913

AUGUSTUS FITZROY, 3RD DUKE OF GRAFTON
Sir W. R. Anson (ed), *The Autobiography and Political Correspondence of the Third Duke of Grafton*. 1898

FREDERICK, LORD NORTH
J. A. Cannon. *The Fox-North Coalition*. 1969
R. Lucas. *Lord North*. 1913

WILLIAM FITZMAURICE, 2ND EARL OF SHELBURNE
Lord E. Fitzmaurice. *Life of William, Earl of Shelburne*. 1875–76
John Norris. *Shelburne and Reform*. 1963

WILLIAM PITT (the younger)
John Ehrman. *The Younger Pitt*. 1969
Sir Philip Magnus. *Edmund Burke*. 1939
G. Holland Rose. *William Pitt and the Great War*. 1911

HENRY ADDINGTON
Philip Ziegler. *Life of Henry Addington*. 1965

WILLIAM WYNDHAM, LORD GRENVILLE
M. Roberts. *The Whig Party 1807–12*. 1939

SPENCER PERCEVAL
Denis Gray. *Spencer Perceval*. 1963

ROBERT JENKINSON, 2ND EARL OF LIVERPOOL
C. Petrie. *Lord Liverpool*. 1956

GEORGE CANNING
Peter Dixon. *Politician and Statesman*. 1976
Wendy Hindle. *George Canning*. 1973
P. G. V. Rolo. *George Canning*. 1965

FREDERICK ROBINSON, VISCOUNT GODERICH
W. D. Jones. *Prosperity Robinson*. 1967

ARTHUR WELLESLEY, DUKE OF WELLINGTON
Elizabeth Longford. *Pillar of State*. 1972

CHARLES, 2ND EARL GREY
J. R. M. Butler. *The Passing of the Great Reform
Bill*. 1914
G. M. Trevelyan. *Earl Grey of the Reform Bill*.
1920

WILLIAM LAMB, 2ND VISCOUNT MELBOURNE
David Cecil. *The Young Melbourne*. 1939
Lord M. 1954

SIR ROBERT PEEL
Norman Gash. *Sir Robert Peel*. 1971
Norman Gash. *Politics in the Age of Peel*. 1953

LORD JOHN RUSSELL
John Prest. *Lord John Russell*. 1972
A. W. Tilby. *Lord John Russell*. 1930

EDWARD STANLEY, 14TH EARL OF DERBY
Charles Greville. *Diary*.
George Saintsbury. *The Earl of Derby*. 1892

GEORGE GORDON, 4TH EARL OF ABERDEEN
Lucille Iremonger. *Lord Aberdeen*. 1978

HENRY TEMPLE, 3RD VISCOUNT PALMERSTON
Denis Judd. *Palmerston*. 1975
W. B. Pemberton. *Lord Palmerston*. 1934
Jasper Ridley. *Lord Palmerston*. 1970

BENJAMIN DISRAELI, EARL OF BEACONSFIELD
Robert Blake. *Disraeli*. 1966

WILLIAM EWART GLADSTONE
Philip Magnus. *Gladstone*. 1954

ROBERT GASCOYNE-CECIL, 3RD MARQUIS OF
SALISBURY
David Cecil. *The Cecils of Hatfield*. 1973
Lady Gwendolyn Cecil. *Life of Robert, Marquis of
Salisbury*. 1921–32
A. L. Kennedy. *Salisbury 1830–1907*. 1953

ARCHIBALD PRIMROSE, 5TH EARL OF ROSEBERY
Lord Crewe. *Lord Rosebery*. 1931
R. Rhodes James. *Rosebery*. 1963

ARTHUR JAMES BALFOUR
Blanche Dugdale. *A. J. Balfour*. 1936
Kenneth Young. *A. J. Balfour*. 1963

SIR HENRY CAMPBELL-BANNERMAN
John Wilson. *C.B.* 1973

HERBERT HENRY ASQUITH
Roy Jenkins. *Asquith*. 1964

DAVID LLOYD GEORGE
J. Grigg. *The Young Lloyd George*. 1972
Frank Owen. *Tempestuous Journey: Lloyd George,
His Life and Time*. 1954

ANDREW BONAR LAW
Robert Blake. *The Unknown Prime Minister*. 1955
A. J. P. Taylor. *Beaverbrook*. 1972

STANLEY BALDWIN
Keith Middlemas and John Barnes. *Baldwin*.
1969
G. M. Young. *Stanley Baldwin*. 1952

JAMES RAMSAY MACDONALD
Lord Elton. *Life of James Ramsay MacDonald*.
1939

ARTHUR NEVILLE CHAMBERLAIN
Keith Feiling. *The Life of Neville Chamberlain*.
1946

SIR WINSTON CHURCHILL
Beaverbrook. *Men and Power*. 1956
Life, by Randolph Churchill and Martin Gilbert.
(Five volumes, and eight volumes of notes;
incomplete.) Several volumes of autobiography.

CLEMENT ATTLEE
Roy Jenkins. *Mr Attlee: An Interim Biography*.
1948

SIR ANTHONY EDEN
Memoirs. 1960, etc.

MAURICE HAROLD MACMILLAN
Memoirs. (Six volumes.) 1966–73

SIR ALEC DOUGLAS-HOME
The Way the Wind Blows. 1976

JAMES HAROLD WILSON
His governments have been recorded with
unusual promptness and amplitude in the diaries
of Richard Crossman and Barbara Castle. There
is also the account of 10 Downing Street in his
time, written by his press secretary, Joe Haines.

EDWARD HEATH
Margaret Laing. *Edward Heath*. 1972